I0831650

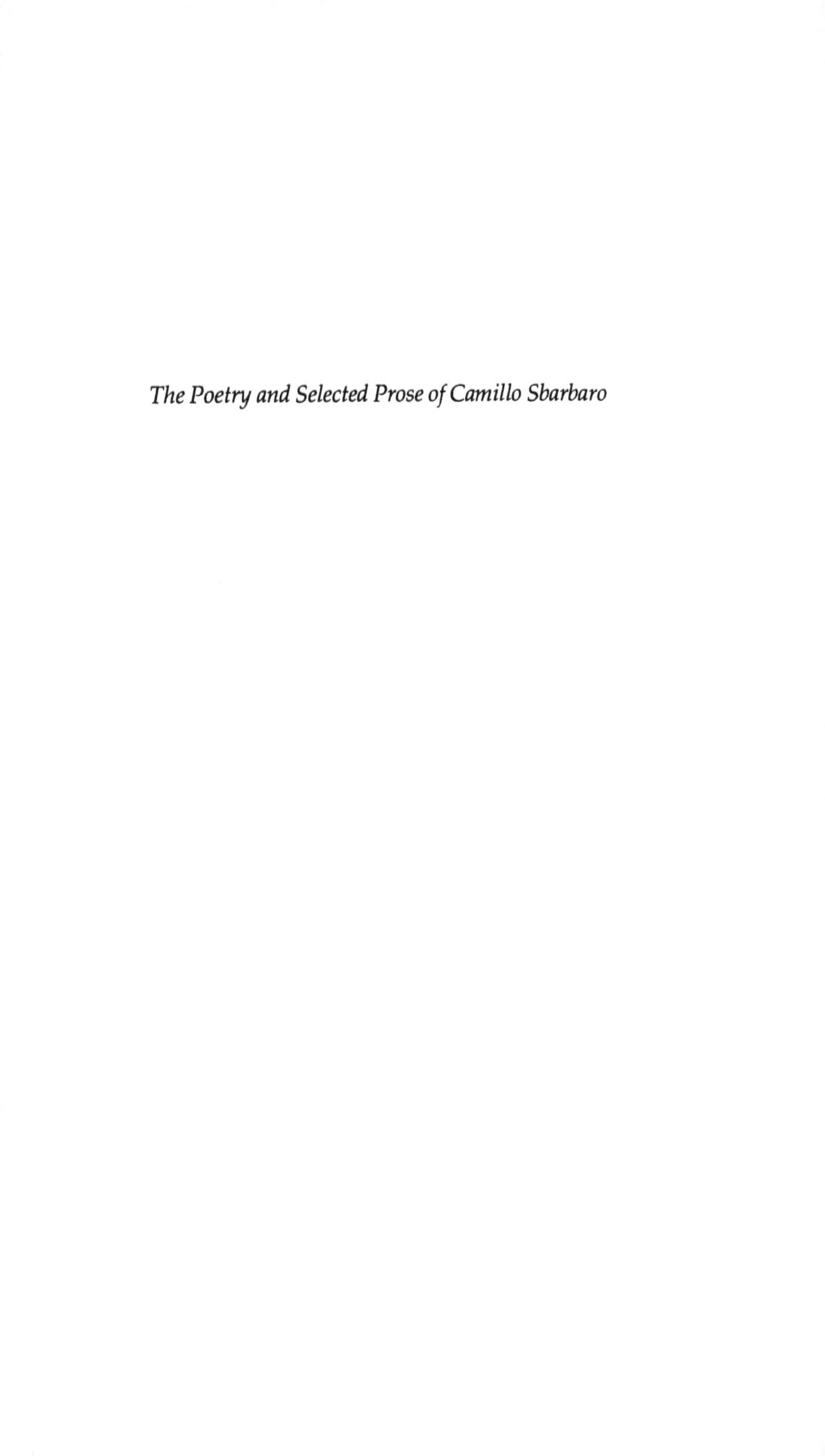

The Poetry and Selected Prose of Camillo Sbarbaro

Scripta humanistica

The Poetry and Selected Prose of Camillo Sbarbaro

Edited and Translated by
Vittorio Felaco

Preface by
Franco Fido

Scripta humanistica

12

Library of Congress Cataloging in Publication Data

Sbarbaro, Camillo, 1888–1967.
The poetry and selected prose of Camillo Sbarbaro.

(Scripta humanistica)
Bibliography: p. 23.
Includes index.
I. Felaco, Vittorio, 1940– . II. Title. III. Series.
PQ 4841.B3A6 1985 851'.912 84–51570
ISBN 0–9163–79–19–1

Publisher and Distributor:
SCRIPTA HUMANISTICA
1383 Kersey Lane
Potomac, Maryland 20854 U.S.A.

Library of Congress Catalog Card Number 84–051570
International Standard Book Number 0–9163–79–19–1
L. C. Classification Number PQ 4841.B3A6 1985

to Maja

Contents

Acknowledgements

I wish to express my gratitude to my former professors at Brown University, Franco Fido and Tony Oldcorn. In addition to honoring this volume with his elegant preface, Franco has supplied a number of important textual clarifications. Tony, who first introduced me to the poetry and prose of Camillo Sbarbaro, has been constant in his friendship and encouragement.

Charles and Camilla Russel, my colleagues at the University of Maryland, have been generous with their guidance and support, as have been my special reader Maurice Bennett and my wife Maja who have both made innumerable editorial comments.

I wish to acknowledge also my sincere gratitude to Signor Vanni Scheiwiller for his gracious consent to the reprinting of Sbarbaro's poetry and selections from *Trucioli* and *Fuochi Fatui*, and to Signora Gina Lagorio for her great contribution to the study of Camillo Sbarbaro.

This project has been funded with a Summer Grant and a Book Subsidy Award from the Research Board of the University of Maryland. I am proud to acknowledge here the generosity of the Board.

Vittorio Felaco
New Carrollton, April, 1985

Preface
by Franco Fido

For centuries Genoa—a place of sailors and merchants—was virtually absent from the development of Italian literary civilization: but the city emerged from this long silence suddenly, between the end of the XIX and the beginning of the XX century, as Italy entered the modern world of capitalist, industrial society with its technologies and its speculations.

When the models of an older classical tradition seemed inadequate, what had kept businesslike, tough Genoa away from art and poetry became a favorable condition for coping with the present. If, in the Genoese past, private enjoyment and profitable investment of wealth had inhibited the kind of public magnificence in civic buildings and patronage of the arts that we find elsewhere, in Florence or in Venice, at the turn of the century it was a commercial publication, *La riviera ligure*, founded in 1899 by Mario Novaro to advertise the excellent olive oil produced by his family, that opened its pages to several young talents who were to make Genoa a center of poetic activity: an instinctive and "maudit" bohemian like Ceccardo Roccatagliata Ceccardi, a religious and rigorous spirit like Giovanni Boine, a poet of sensations and landscapes like the editor-industrialist Novaro himself, and, the best of them all, Camillo Sbarbaro.

In those same years—between the beginning of the century and the first world war—the great Ligurian seaport surprisingly also becomes a poetic object, a kind of "country of the soul," for poets born elsewhere, like the Tuscan of the Apennines Dino Campana:

Come le cateratte del Niagara
Canta, ride svaria ferrea la sinfonia feconda urgente del mare:
Genova canta il tuo canto!

Like the Niagara Falls
Sings, laughs, steellike varies the fecund, urgent symphony of the sea:
Genoa sing your song!

(Canti orfici)

or a younger Tuscan of the Tirrenian seashore, Giorgio Caproni:

Genova mia città intera
Geranio, Polveriera
Genova di ferro e aria
Mia lavagna! arenaria.
Genova città pulita
Brezza, e luce in salita . . .

Genoa my integer city
Geranium, powder house.
Genoa of iron and air,
my slate, sandstone.
Genoa clean city
Breeze, uphill light . . .

(and so on and so forth, for more than 100 couplets: "Litania," in *Il passaggio di Enea*).

Another striking effect of this "Ligurian Renaissance" between the two wars is the flourishing of a Genoese dialect poetry far superior in quality to anything done before: in fact, for the first time, a poet in Genoese dialect, Edoardo Firpo, achieved a small national reputation:

e vedde Zena lontann-a
fra i monti scui e a marinn-a
tâgnâ de feugo ch'a a tremma
posa in sce l'aia do ma . . .

and to see Genoa far away
between the dark mountains and the shore,

cobweb of fire that trembles
suspended in the air of the sea.

("Zena de neutte da-i monti," in *'O grillo cantadò*).

What the writers of the *Riviera ligure* had in common was the feeling of belonging to a hard and unyielding land whose meager fruits had to be sparingly used; far from representing a privileged condition and a key to full possession of reality and self-assertion (as was the case with the period's "official" poets Carducci and D'Annunzio) poetry was for them a sobering mirror of weakness in which daily experience is reflected for what it is: precarious, fragmented, the realm of the ephemeral and the discontinuous par excellence. The titles of verse or prose collections produced in this climate speak for themselves, from the *Libro dei frammenti* of Roccatagliata Ceccardi (1894, followed posthumously by *Sillabe ed ombre, Syllables and Shades*, 1928), to the *Murmuri ed echi* of Mario Novaro (*Murmurs and Echoes*, 1912), and the first *Frantumi* of Boine (*Smithereens*, 1915).

The analogy between stony Liguria and the predicament of modern man, leads finally in 1925 to this century's greatest book of Italian poetry, Montale's *Ossi di seppia*, where the reductive or "negative" poetic of his predecessors is condensed in the objective correlative of the white cuttlefish bones, that, spit out by the sea, shine modest and perfect on the shore as well as in the title of his collection.

Halfway, as it were, between the cosmic relevance of *Ossi di seppia* and the authentic but provincial vein of the poets mentioned above, stands the case of Camillo Sbarbaro, closer to the latter if we attend to the exterior circumstances of his uneventful career, but worthy of being remembered with Montale for the quality of his work: he is in fact the only poet present in the *Ossi*, with two poems dedicated to him, "*storico di cupidige e di brividi*" ("historian of cupidities and thrills"), but also "*estroso fanciullo,*" a "fanciful child" who

piega versicolori
carte e ne trae navicelle che affida alla fanghiglia
mobile di un rigagno

folds colour-changing papers
and makes little boats which he trusts
to the mobile slush of a gutter . . .

("Epigramma," in *Ossi di seppia*)

The themes of Sbarbaro are not new: nightwalks through the city as a metaphorical descent into a mediocre *enfer* of drunkards and prostitutes; the memory of his dead father and the presence of his sister as the heavenly opposite of that hell; the arid and stony landscape of Liguria; a lucid contemplation of his own passivity culminating in the well-known simile of the mirror:

Io sono come uno specchio rassegnato
che riflette ogni cosa per la via.
In me stesso non guardo perché nulla
vi troverei . . .

I am resigned like a mirror
that reflects all things in the street.
Into myself I don't look because nothing
Would I find there . . .

("Taci anima mia," in *Pianissimo*)

But if we compare just these few lines with those of the "crepuscular" Sergio Corazzini that Sbarbaro had probably in mind:

sono, oramai,
rassegnato come uno specchio,
come un povero specchio melanconico

I am, by now,
resigned like a mirror
a poor melancholic mirror

("Desolazione del povero poeta sentimentale," in *Liriche*, 1909)

we begin to see where the originality of Sbarbaro lies. What is different and new in his poetry is that he shuns the literary language of his predecessors and contemporaries and tries to speak as simply and plainly as possible, defusing as it were the "decadent" or "*maudit*" potential of even the most baudelairian situations.

The reductive *parti pris* already noted in several titles of his Ligurian fellow poets becomes more systematic throughout Sbarbaro's scanty production, from his first verse collection *Pianissimo* (1914), and the prose of *Trucioli* (*Shavings*, 1920), to *Liquidazione (Clearance*, 1928), *Rimanenze (Remains*, 1955), *Fuochi fatui (Will-o'-the-wisp*, 1956), *Scampoli (Remnants*, 1960), *Gocce (Drops*, 1963), etc.

Among Sbarbaro's poems, the most original remain those of *Pianissimo*, especially in the early collection of 1914, which is the text used by Vittorio Felaco in the present volume. Against this judgment, it could be argued that some of the highest moments in his poetry are to be found—characteristically enough—in the "discarded and forgotten" compositions (published later thanks to the loving care of friends) of *Rimanenze (Remains)*, like the five poems "A Dina" (1931). But in Sbarbaro's second collection we also realize that his poetry is defined by (and bound to) its being uttered "a bassa voce": as the tone of poetic discourse rises, so grows the risk of falling into rhetoric or banality. Take a few lines from the longest poem of *Rimanenze*, which is a song to his region:

Liguria,
l'immagine di te sempre nel cuore,
mia terra, porterò, come chi parte
il rozzo scapolare che gli appese
lagrimando la madre . . .

("*Scarsa lingua di terra . . .*")

and compare their poor man's "*pascolismo*" with the simplicity and intensity of *Pianissimo*:

. . . a me par, vivendo questa mia
povera vita, un' altra rasentarne
come nel sonno, e che quel sonno sia
la mia vita presente.

. . . For I seem, in living this
poor life of mine, to skim another
as if in a dream, and that dream
is my present life.

("Talor, mentre cammino . . .," in *Pianissimo*)

The same "return to literature" (or "of literature," if you prefer) that one senses in *Rimanenze* as compared with *Pianissimo* distinguishes Sbarbaro's prose from his poetry. The two editions of *Trucioli* (Firenze, 1924 and Milano, 1948), and the many translations from classical Greek and French witness his cultured command of a wide stylistic register, from the pictorial annotation "à la De Pisis" ("Via ventisettembre al primo sole, rossiccio . . .") to the *poème en prose* ("Percorrendo una via deserta fra buie forme di monti . . ."); from the macaronic *divertissement* of *Delli ammaestramenti a Polidoro* to diaristic storytelling (*Gente all'osteria*).

As a document of assiduous experimentation, Sbarbaro's prose may be considered (and has been, by some critics) more interesting than his poetry. It is not by chance, that Montale's debt to *Trucioli* is greater than to *Pianissimo*. A "truciolo" such as *Quest'anno le agavi del litorale han messo il fiore* seems a kind of pattern book for *Ossi di seppia*, and sometimes formal analogies become (intentionally, perhaps) almost verbatim quotations:

> Gli abitanti *del mare*! ingombranti alcuni; *labili* altri *come schiuma* . . .
>
> (*Trucioli*, n. 46—first published in 1921)

vorrei prima di cedere segnarti
codesta via di fuga
labile come nei sommossi campi
del mare spuma o ruga

("Casa sul mare," in *Ossi*)

Felaco's decision to append selections from *Trucioli* to the complete translation of *Pianissimo* and *Rimanenze* is thus fully justified, because it will give Sbarbaro's new readers a far better idea of his poetic career.

Others—native speakers of English, or specialists in the difficult art of translating poetry—will assess more competently than I Felaco's work as translator. But even a non-specialist can appreciate his effort to remain faithful to the refined, elusive medietas of the original, and above all, his commitment to help readers of his "bilingual Sbarbaro" with introductions and commentary that, taken together, provide an ample cultural background against which to appraise the originality of the Ligurian poet and his position in XX century literary history.

In each country, the "discovery" of foreign authors happens somewhat at random. Not only the favor of the reading public, but the interest of the critic goes—with the frequent complicity of literary prizes, the Nobel first of all—not to the best, but to the most facile, or at least to those who seem to confirm the ideas and clichés currently applied to their nation. So in many parts of the world Bourget and Rolland were widely known and admired before Proust, Werfel before Musil, Galsworthy or Maugham before Ford Madox Ford or Forster, Edgar Lee Masters before William Carlos Williams. The same can be said of the "exportation" of Italian writers: think of the popularity of Ugo Betti (or even Carlo Coccioli!) in France, of Silone and Quasimodo in the United States, and by contrast, the delay with which far greater authors like Saba or Gadda were recognized in the same countries: not to mention other authors, like Landolfi and Sereni, still to be "discovered" by cultivated Americans. In spite of the enlightened initiatives of a publishing house like New Directions, and a few outstanding translators like Allen Mandelbaum and William Weaver, there is still much to be done to adjust our knowledge of Italian contemporary writers to a more plausible set of values. This book provides an opportunity to become better acquainted with Sbarbaro, and therefore represents a step in the right direction.

Introduction

The historical background

When Sbarbaro first appeared on the literary scene, in the first decades of the 20th century, the literature of the Italian avantgarde was closely related to the social and political events that shaped European history from the middle of the 19th century to that mythical year of 1914. However the political, social and intellectual crisis experienced at the end of the 19th century in the rest of Europe failed to bring in Italy the kind of transformation of the political and social structures that had been experienced elsewhere. While many movements paralleled similar events in France and other countries (for example the formation of the Socialist Party in 1892, the *fasci dei lavoratori* of 1893 in Sicily, the labor movements in Milan and Turin and other major Italian cities, etc.), the overall intellectual and social direction of Italy remained somewhat repressive and backward. The State with its aristocratic and wealthy interests continued to oppose any populist movement that would grant even the smallest ackowledgement of the rights of workers or that would lead to universal electoral suffrage. The State countered any movement with additional doses of taxation, growing bureaucratization of its own structures, the expansion of police powers and an ill-timed imperialistic adventurism in Africa. The ruling class, evermore defensive in the presence of such transformations, continued to promulgate a government reserved for the elected officials in an attempt to silence the masses.[1]

All this represented a rather strong reaction to the hopes that had been expressed by "positivism," the major European current of thought which trusted in the liberating power of science and fostered ideals of progress. This movement had been responsible for the progressive and liberal attitudes of the ruling classes. With the decline of those ideals, the hopes and the attitudes of positivism with its parallel emphasis on art solidly grounded in the real also declined. Suddenly, the narrow and restrictive canons of *vraisemblance* appeared to deprive the artist and the intellectual of the broadest possible universe for the imagination. In reaction, decadent artists displayed an urgent desire to go beyond a narrowly defined reality, even if this meant a serious setback to the illuministic hopes of positivism and liberalism.

The decadents sought to create new modules of expression even at the risk of exploding the semantic limits of the word, to give free rein to the previously ill-expressed world of the fantastic, the allusive and the oneiric. However, these tendencies were part of a social revolution that had basically gone sour. Writing in 1947 on the *Politecnico*, precisely on the problem of literature of the "crisis," Elio Vittorini said:

> It is filled with individualism and decadentism. But it is also filled with the necessity to come out of it, and it is a search for a way

[1] For an exhaustive introduction to the late Ottocento and the relationship of literature to society see Francesco Flora, *Storia della letteratura italiana*, Vol. V, Secondo Ottocento e Primo Novecento, Mondadori, Milan, 1940, XIII Edition 1962; *Storia della letteratura italiana*, Vols. VIII-IX, Garzanti, Milan, 1968 and 1969.

> out . . . Its bourgeois motives are motives of shame to be bourgeois and of desperation to be bourgeois.[2]

This literature of the crisis, a crisis of intellectual, social and spiritual dimensions, produced a breakdown of the basic structures of the poetic language. Reacting to the positivist tenets of linguistic terms grounded in the "real," the modernist poet rejected all notions of art as a description or mimesis. Literary language was viewed as autotelic, and conventional language as "de-potentiated," "de-substantiated" and "hollowed-out." The task of the modern poet was:

> the creation of a redeemed visionary world of language in which, as André Breton put it in *The Disdainful Confession* (1924), 'something fundamental' is given back to form and in which the lost dimension of language and the human psyche is rediscovered or preserved.[3]

The traditional use and juxtaposition of lexical units and the traditional syntax that governed them were overturned in favor of their component parts even when their lack of structure and pre-established conventional order led to nonsense.

> The modernist crisis of language is thus located not in the impotence of the creative individual or a literary style within a language which is assumed to be living and potentiated, but in the 'de-potentiation' of an entire language as such. Hence the modernist poet ceases to be the manipulator of fixed *quanta* and attempts to liberate the repressed expressive energies of language; ceases to be the celebrant of a human order and becomes the experimenter who searches for a barely possible 'redeemed and redeeming image' amid a protean universe in apparently chaotic process.[4]

In Italy these trends came almost exclusively from France. Working on premises already implied and partially exemplified by Baudelaire, poets like Arthur Rimbaud, Paul Verlaine, and Stéphane Mallarmé established the basis for

---

[2] Elio Vittorini, *Diario in pubblico*, Bompiani, Milan, 1957, first paperback edition 1976, p. 305. All translations are my own unless otherwise indicated.

[3] Richard Sheppard, "The Crisis of Language" in *Modernism*, edited by Malcolm Bradbury and James McFarlane, Penguin Books, New York, 1976, p. 329.

[4] *Ibidem*.

future literary expression. Rimbaud saw poetry as the expression of the "seer," whose task is to express the "ineffable." Verlaine felt that the poet's task, more than to give an inventory of reality, and "to say," was to offer vague "suggestions" of the phenomenological world. To this end the true nature of poetry was music (*Art Poétique*). Mallarmé sought to give the world a truly sacral, enchanting connotation that would give an evolutionary and creative sense of reality rather than a mere representation of it. Developing further the *correspondances* of Baudelaire, he affirmed that analogies were the basic structural elements of a universe which escapes rationality. The poet's task is to capture these analogies in pregnant, perhaps obscure, but always "suggestive" groups of words.[5]

This flight from the real with its accompanying and intimately related taste for the different and the complex, the superhuman and the oneiric found its highest expression in France in Joris-Karl Huysmans' *A Rebours* (a work that Sbarbaro greatly loved and translated into Italian—see bibliography), in England in Wilde's *The Picture of Dorian Gray*, in Germany in E. T. A. Hoffman, Novalis, Wagner, and in Italy in Pascoli and D'Annunzio, as well as in Antonio Fogazzaro's religious mysticism. These same modernist, decadent trends continued also in Italy in writers like Pirandello and Svevo who became two of the most articulate spokesmen of that crisis and the *malaise* of modern man.

Toward the end of the 19th century decadentism (a term that has, of course, lost all the negative connotations on which critics had originally counted) was fully defined and, in a way completed. Thus Walter Binni could affirm:

> the poetics of decadence arrive at a positive antithesis of the classical one, and to an essential differentiation of the romantic one: while the classical wants the triumph of serenity over sentiment, and the romantic lives of outbursts, of intense affirmation of personality, the decadent constructs a purely musical atmosphere that

[5] For Verlaine and Mallarmé see *Les Poètes Maudits*, AMS, New York, 1972; *Correspondances*, Gallimard, Paris, 1959–1983.

carries the echo of a new and mysterious world unknown to the ancients.[6]

For some, this mysterious world became a world of *symbols*. For Mallarmé in fact, the poetics of the *correspondances* was no longer an end in itself, rather the basic presupposition that allowed the poet to arrive at a language of symbolic relationships. Baudelaire himself had suggested that in certain emotional states, when the individual poet feels himself closer to the supernatural, the depth of one's experience can be revealed through the reality, no matter how common, that is before the poet. The description of that spectacle becomes thus the symbol of the poet's own interiority.

In Italy D'Annunzio and Pascoli, more than others, succeeded in breaking away from the traditional patterns of Italian poetry, for they were able to conceive of poetry as pure intuition, to capture the poeticity of things and the refined musicality of human sensations as absolute values in themselves. They remain two of the greatest poets and perhaps, with Giosué Carducci (*Le Tre Corone*), the poets who are ultimately most responsible for the various trends and reactions of the *Novecento*. The poetic language and the new expressions they devised in their works permeate the poetry of subsequent poets much the way Dante and Petrarch determined the course of poetry for centuries.

Of the schools and movements to which symbolism and the other currents at the turn of the century gave rise in Italy, the most significant to an understanding of the poetry of Camillo Sbarbaro are the *crepuscolari* and the futurists.

The word *crepuscolari* was coined by the well known critic and novelist Giuseppe Borgese.[7] In a review of poems by

---

[6] Walter Binni, *La poetica del decadentismo*, Sansoni, Firenze, 1961, p. 30.

[7] Giuseppe Antonio Borgese (1881–1952), essayist, critic, poet, novelist, teacher and political activist, is best known for his 1921 novel *Rubè*, in which the protagonist, the typical inept antihero, dies in the end during a political demonstration, holding on to both the communist and the fascist flags, caught between two ideologies.

Martini, Moretti and Chiaves[8] in *La Stampa* (Sep. 10, 1910) Borgese defined the three poets as belonging to the "twilight" of the great literary period that had begun with Giuseppe Parini (1729–1799); that is to say they represented a shadowy period that marked the very end of the Italian classical tradition of poetry which in the earlier 19th century had been dominated by Alessandro Manzoni and Giacomo Leopardi.

The most distinctive element of the poetry of the *crepuscolari* was the refusal to deal with traditional themes and issues. This divergence encompassed as well the tendency of Parnassians and Symbolists to avoid a narrative style. The *crepuscolari* made narration of the most mundane daily events affecting their lives the explicit and deliberate form of their poetry. Thus Binazzi could say expressly:

Raccontiamo, raccontiamo
ma senza dolore
e senza nostalgia,
tanto per passar l'ore
e scacciar la malinconia.[9]

(We narrate and narrate / but without pain / and without nostalgia / just to pass the hours / and ban melancholy.)

In their narration they proceeded with an almost cinematographic technique brought to its slowest, deliberate speed to give a somber, lazy and inert representation of life void of any physical and emotional intensity, in an attempt to declare their fundamental aridity, their rejection of any sentimental enthusiasm, of any old-fashioned declamation. Yet, as Walter Binni has accurately noted, their poetics express a need

---

[8] Fausto Maria Martini (1886–1931), Roman journalist, novelist, and poet, was a close friend of Corazzini, and a leader of the Roman twilight poets. His poetry is collected in *Le piccole morte* (1906), *Pane nostrum* (1907) and *Poesie provinciali* of 1910. A complete edition of his poems *Poesie disperse e inedite* appeared in Milan edited by G. Farinelli. Marino Moretti (1885–), is the only living twilight poet. See *Tutte le novelle*, Mondadori, Milano, 1959, and *Tutte le poesie*, Mondadori, Milano, 1966. Carlo Chiaves (1883–1919), his poetry was collected in one volume *Sogno e ironia* (*Dream and Irony*) in 1910 and reprinted by Aldo Camerino in 1956.

[9] In Walter Binni, La poetica del decadentismo, *op. cit.*, p. 137.

for a defense against rhetoric and pretentiousness and represent a search for a special lyricism that through the usual and the commonplace can give us a sense of their passions.[10] For Guido Gozzano, the most important and authoritative figure of this movement (often referred to as *stile liberty*), this can be achieved by means of a sharp and biting irony most often aimed at himself, for the true son of our times is marked by much culture and taste for the written word, scarcity of brain, of morals, but a dreadful clairvoyance. That is how Gozzano describes Totò Merùmeni.[11]

Most often the *crepuscolari* aim at a total desecration of the literary mythologies of the past and look for a *verità non convenuta*, the achievement of a truth freed of all conventions.[12] Their invective becomes most pungent when directed particularly at Gabriele D'Annunzio, whose influence dominated the Italian literary scene, and at his epigones.

The style of the twilight poets, like that of generations that followed, remained essentially fragmentary. In the rapid and spontaneous fulgurations of the fragment they sought to define *il male di vivere*, which Gozzano outlined in his incomplete poem "Le farfalle: Epistole entomologiche".[13] *Il male di vivere* is man's basic incompatibility with nature, the Leopardian concept that Montale eventually immortalized in his *Ossi di seppia* (*Cuttlefish Bones*, 1925).[14]

---

[10] See "Crepuscolari e futuristi" in *La poetica del decadentismo*, pp. 127–148.

[11] Guido Gozzano, *The Man I Pretend to Be*, bilingual edition, edited and translated by Michael Palma, Princeton University Press, Princeton, 1981, p. 124. Most other references to Gozzano will come from this bilingual edition more accessible to the American reader, but some occasional translations are still my own unless otherwise noted.

[12] Guido Gozzano, "Pioggia d'agosto", in *The Colloquies*, in *The Man I Pretend to Be*, *op. cit.*, p. 162, v. 35.

[13] In Guido Gozzano, *Poesie*, Introduzione e note di Giorgio Bàrberi Squarotti, Rizzoli, Milan, 1977, pp. 243–299.

[14] Eugenio Montale, *Gli ossi di seppia*, in *Tutte le poesie*, Mondadori, Milano, 1977. For a list of notable English translations of Montale works see: Jonathan Galassi's, *The Second Life of Art, Selected Essays of Eugenio Montale*, The Ecco Press, New York, 1982, pp. 342–43.

In this same atmosphere of spiritual crisis developed also *il futurismo*, a movement as original and as pervasively revolutionary as any ever outlined by any avantgarde before or since, and a movement that has had broad and far-reaching repercussions throughout the world. Futurism's immediate artistic / literary heir is Visual Poetry which continues to be a vital and growing force and a viable formula capable of capturing the imagination of new generations dissatisfied with the verbal conventions and restraints of language, a tendency which is aided by the new technological developments of the computer age.[15]

The first Futurist Manifesto (*Fondazione e manifesto del Futurismo*) by Filippo Tommaso Marinetti (1875–1944) appeared in *Le Figaro* on February 20, 1909.[16] The main themes outlined in this and subsequent manifestoes were an anarchical vitalism, a rebellion against *passéisme* (love of the past) to which it countered an exaggerated trust and confidence in the future, in the achievements of the technological civilization, boldly embracing the machine and mechanical force, along with the beauty of speed, as its symbols of a new aesthetics. Instead of the timidity of the *crepuscolari* in the presence of change and of action, the *futuristi* displayed a bombastic and arrogant disregard for danger and fear. Expression and communication were not to be in any way restricted or limited by conventional logic and by the syntactical, grammatical and lexical confines of language. Transcendental values could and should be sacrificed in the expectation and determination of forging ahead toward a new world order in which "action" was always superior to "meditation" and "reflection." If reality is chaotic then chaos is the force that can control and shape it. So essentially argued proponents of futurism.

In Italy futurism was, at least in its immediate historical

---

[15] For a bibliography see *Italian Visual Poetry* edited by Luigi Ballerini, Istituto Italiano di Cultura, New York.

[16] On Marinetti see *Selected Writings*, edited by R.W. Flint, Noonday, New York, 1972, and Michael Kirby, *Futurist Performances*, Dutton, New York, 1971.

development, short lived. Besides the manifestoes and the various *serate futuriste,* truly frenetic and polemically wild happenings, it saw its hightest literary expression in Marinetti's *Distruzione,* in Aldo Pallazzeschi's *L'Incendiario,* Gian Pietro Lucini's *Revolverate,* in Luciano Folgore's *Canto dei motori,* in Corrado Govoni's *Poesie elettriche,* and in Ardengo Soffici's *Simultaneità e Chimismi lirici.*[17]

The linguistic and artistic revolution of the symbolists had come full tilt and been pushed to its highest potential or to its most absurd mockery. Speaking of the influence of the Symbolists on himself and other Italian artists in the early decades of the century, Eugenio Montale declared in his 1946 "Imaginary Interview":

> Of the french symbolists I knew as much as one could gather from the Anthology of Van Bever and Léautaud. Later I read a lot more. But the innovations of symbolism were already in the air and were known even by those who were not acquainted with the originals. Our Futurists and the writers of *La Voce* had learned their lesson, and often misunderstood it.[18]

Despite these signs of vitality and variety of artistic and ideological expression, in Italy a mood of provincialism, a closed and forbidden universe dominated the cultural scene. The "three crowns," Carducci, Pascoli and D'Annunzio, dominated publishing and literary honors. Around them a number of insignificant professor/poets imitated their style. As a result, even great literary figures like Giovanni Verga, Italo Svevo and Luigi Pirandello (who later achieved some success as a playwright during fascism in the 20's and 30's), were often unable to command any significant attention or readership. Verga's Sicilian masterpieces were essentially ignored, and he lived the last decades of his long life in virtual neglect. Svevo was essentially unknown, though *Una vita* and *Senilità* were published respectively in 1893 and 1898, and Pirandello's *Il fu*

---

[17] Now in *Opere,* Vallecchi, Florence, 1959–1968.

[18] *La Rassegna D'Italia,* Vol. I, no. 1, Milan, January 1946, now in *Sulla poesia* (*On Poetry*), edited by Giorgio Zampa, Mondadori, Milano, 1976. See also Jonathan Galassi's translation in *The Second Life in Art, op. cit.,* p. 300.

Mattia Pascal had come out in 1904. It took the double efforts of James Joyce and Eugenio Montale, as well as Cremieux and Larbaud in France to bring Svevo to the belated attention of European readers.

In other words, the Italian literary scene (more precisely *il costume letterario*) lagged terribly behind that of other European countries. The cultural environment of Italy was tightly controlled not only by truly reactionary forces, but also by frequently brilliant critics who over-emphasized the work of the "three crowns," while ignoring both some truly great men of letters, and others who were thus deprived of attention and relegated to the status of minors.

Even exceptionally astute critics like Benedetto Croce, Attilio Momigliano and Renato Serra were unable to accept the bold new ways of the avantgarde and, as a rule, denigrated the new poets on the grounds that their poetry lacked moral and spiritual values. Croce considered poetry after Pascoli and D'Annunzio not only bad and pseudopoetic but a

> literary manifestation of irrationalism, devoid of religious guidance, lacking faith in liberty, displaying the ability to shock, leaning toward animality and bestiality, thus embracing the inhumanity which troubles the entire world.[19]

Although Croce recognized that the theories of these poets originated in the poetry of Mallarmé and Valery, he still felt that if he were to read their little volumes and booklets of verses he would look only for those "things that speak to my sensibilities, to my fantasy and to my sense of beauty."[20]

Momigliano found the fragmentary quality of the new poets to be their biggest drawback. He observed that Manzoni's work contained and presupposed centuries of European thought, Carducci's centuries of erudition and the powerful temperament of a man and an Italian, D'Annunzio's the egocentric refinement of a true poet. By contrast, according to Momigliano, the new poets' vision was one of impoverish-

---

[19] Benedetto Croce, *Letture di poeti*, Laterza, Bari, 1950, pp. 271–272.
[20] *Ibidem*, pp. 270–271.

ment and restriction, a result of the cultural and moral crisis at the turn of the century. In addition, the critic felt that the new poets were excessively concerned with themselves.[21]

Renato Serra pointed out:

> Today the real poet is yet to come; it is useless to make a frame for a picture that's not there.[22]

He preferred therefore to speak of "verses" rather than of poetry. To him, the greatest fault of the younger poets was their writing verses in the manner of others, imitating the popular but hopelessly sentimental Guido da Verona, the classicists, the lyricists, the futurists, and even Pascoli, D'Annunzio and Carducci.

> You need only mention a poetic category, and everyone with absolute certainty knows what to expect: subject matter, phraseology, ambitions; everything is fixed and precise. To add the title of the poem and the name of the author is so needlessly superfluous.[23]

In a letter to Giuseppe De Robertis, the editor of *La Voce*, Renato Serra criticized some of the contributors to what is now considered one of the finest literary journals of the time.

> The piece by Bastianelli is good—but too specialized. And the rest counts little . . . Govoni has fine qualities; but he is not original, his lyricism is indirect. Sbarbaro, Onofri for now are inconclusive: they merely offer some experiments of a new sensibility of an altogether generic worth . . . In other words something is missing in this new *Voce*; it's not your fault, rather of the times. Even the best did not give you what they were capable of giving. Having added to the family of *La Voce* a Linati and a Baldini has been good; but they are only names; Baldini especially gave you only 'crumbs' and his signature. You need more.[24]

Although Serra concludes that something has been done, and

---

[21] Attilio Momigliano, "Le tendenze della lirica italiana dal Carducci ad oggi", 1934, quoted in Alberto Frattini, "Sul rinnovamento della poesia italiana nel primo Novecento" in *Nuova Antologia*, vol. 503, July, 1968, p. 399–400.

[22] In *Lettere*, La Voce, Roma, 1920, p. 91.

[23] *Ibidem*.

[24] *Epistolario*, a cura di Luigi Ambrosini, Giuseppe De Robertis and Alfredo Grilli, Le Monnier, Florence, 1934, p. 549.

something will remain of this attempt, the misunderstanding and the hostility of even the most intelligent critics and literary historians established such a strong negative prejudice that it took several decades to overcome it.

Later this damage was somewhat institutionalized by a different kind of incomprehension, the reading *à clef* of the hermetic critics who followed them. Great poets like Umberto Saba, minor ones like Delio Tessa, dialectal poets like the Venetians Biagio Marin and Giacomo Noventa, in part even Sbarbaro, were often ignored in favor of others more in tune with the current school of hermeticism, of the so-called "pure poets" like Dino Campana, and Salvatore Quasimodo.

Even today, while the importance of the early avantgarde and lyric poets is unanimously accepted, critics still differ essentially on the origins of contemporary Italian poetry. Some find those origins in Pascoli's novel use of language, characterized by an abundant use of rich and varied vocabulary, including dialectal and technical terms, and of poetic devices such as analogies, chromatic imagery, onomatopoeia, synesthesia, rhyme structures, even the rhythms with which the poet expressed ordinary and elementary themes thus making Italian poetry for the first time anti-literary. Others place the origins between the *crepuscolari* and the futurists, more specifically between Aldo Palazzeschi and Corrado Govoni, that is to say in an area that in part accepts and in part rejects the themes and the language of decadentism.

Some critics find the beginnings of contemporary Italian poetry in the work of Giuseppe Ungaretti who was born in Alexandria, Egypt, and schooled in the best French tradition. He even wrote his first poems in French and lived in Paris where he had ample opportunity to absorb the moods and the spirit of various avantgarde movements in the first few years of the *Novecento*. It is normally believed that his first collection of poems, *L'allegria* (1914), along with Sbarbaro's *Pianissimo* (1914) mark the first poetic works to "wring the neck of rhetoric" (Pier Vincenzo Mengaldo) and achieve a truly modern poetic expression completely free of any traditional and conventional forms.

The poet Franco Fortini, who has most recently summarized these three differing positions on the origins of contemporary Italian poetry, reminds us that the Ungaretti theory tries to establish a direct line from the *Vociani* to the *ermetici*. The hermetic critics, of course, favored this position. Proponents of the futurist theory, while contesting the Ungaretti one, proposed too radical a change and break from tradition.

Only with Pascoli, by recognizing the virtual annullment of high and low tones in his work and recognizing the prevailing of "a-semantic" and "phono-symbolic" values

> can we possibly recover all that there was of expressionistic, plurilinguistic and dialectal in the last sixty years.[25]

As we will see later, this position has been more accurately confirmed by the recent studies into contemporary poetic language conducted by the critic and literary historian Pier Vincenzo Mengaldo and a number of other scholars of the Circolo Filologico Linguistico Padovano directed by Gianfranco Folena.

Even the newest avantgarde poets, the Gruppo '63, the Novissimi (who revolved around Edoardo Sanguineti, Pier Paolo Pasolini, Antonio Porta, Elio Pagliarani, Nanni Balestrini and Alfredo Giuliani), as well as the poets of the Club Turati of Milan, have confirmed and embraced the Pascoli theory.

Although a detailed discussion of these new poets would go beyond the limits of this introduction, it should be pointed out that the most important way in which the *Novissimi* confirm the linguistic and stylistic novelty of the earlier avantgarde is in their profound understanding that

> language is, indeed, a rational elaboration of thought but its material is psychologically and ideologically indistinct, it deposits social sedimentations of any origin, is insufficient and discontinuous, inert or ebullient, putrified or crystalline; the poet cultivates this deceitful material (thing, sentiment, nexus, idea, notion, arche-

[25] Franco Fortini, *I poeti del Novecento*, Letteratura Italiana Laterza, Bari, 1977, p. 3.

type, joke / play), selects it, manipulates it without regard to any fore-truth it might contain.[26]

The reactions of the avantgarde movements of the sixties and seventies were directed to the excesses of Italian hermeticism.

Hermeticism, a term that the critic Francesco Flora popularized with his volume *La poesia ermetica* (1936) on the poetry of Ungaretti, Quasimodo, and Montale, became the Italian version of "pure" or "naked" poetry. The geographic center of *ermetismo* was Florence, its major publications were *Frontespizio* and *Campo di Marte*.[27]

Soon *ermetico* took on its nearest allusive meaning of "closed," thus of "occult" and incomprehensible to all but the initiated. It was suggested that the term appropriately derived from Hermes Trismegistus, the Greek denomination of the Egyptian divinity Thoth, the scribe of the gods, measurer of time and inventor of numbers, hence the god of wisdom and magic.

The poetry of the *ermetici* aimed to exploit the total allusive, suggestive and musical power of the word to go beyond its historical, popular and common sense, even as they wished to retain the personal and "incidental" occurrence of its use. The word thus recaptured in all its power of evocation would lose its logical communicative force and take the poet in an a-temporal and a-historical frame by means of revelation of the arcane and ineffable.

This achievement risked, of course, isolating the poet outside of history and the concerns of society. As Montale has always maintained, isolation in the interior space of poetry is always the only refuge against life, especially in those histori-

---

[26] Alfredo Giuliani, "Prefazione 1965" in *I Novissimi, Poesie per gli anni '60*, Einaudi, Turin, 1965, p. 8.

[27] Francesco Flora, *La poesia ermetica*, Laterza, Bari, 1936. For *Frontespizio* see the anthology edited by Luigi Fallacara, Landi, Rome, 1961, and for *Campo di Marte* the anthology *Solaria, Letteratura e Campo di Marte*, edited by Alberto Folin, Canova, Treviso, 1973.

cal moments when the poet is particularly impotent to bring about meaningful changes, for

> art is the form of life of one who truly doesn't live: a sort of compensation or a surrogate. Which is not to justify the poet's deliberation to live in an ivory tower: the poet makes no effort to renounce life. It is life that takes it upon itself to elude him.[28]

Equipped with new understanding of the poetic language and better understanding of the hermetic lesson, critics and literary historians were better disposed to understanding Camillo Sbarbaro.

In 1955 the poet Giovanni Giudici declared the Ligurian poet "our contemporary." Giudici was then about thirty years old and Sbarbaro was a poet "che naviga verso i sessanta" ("who sails toward his sixties"). In making Sbarbaro his contemporary Giudici did not wish to start an "anti-arcane" or "anti-hermetic" controversy, especially since he recognized the positive contributions brought to the younger generation of poets by that pre-World War II poetics of *troubar clus*. Neither did he wish to raise Sbarbaro to some kind of *maestro*, to launch some kind of *sbarbarismo* among the already many "isms" of Italian and European literary history. Instead, according to Giudici, Sbarbaro was ever so modern because his *Pianissimo* contained a

> solution, or, at least, the beginning of a solution to certain problems that are in part the same of the poetry of the young in 1955.[29]

In those poems—Giudici continued—simplicity spelled things out without the flirtatiousness of so much literature, without the fear of naming things exactly as they are, with no pretense of "evocation" or any poetic declamation, and by so doing handed the reader a "naked document of a sentimental biography."[30]

---

[28] In "Intenzioni (Intervista immaginaria)" in *La Rassegna d'Italia*, *op. cit.*. See also Jonathan Galassi, *op. cit.*, p. 296.

[29] Giovanni Giudici, "Il nostro coetaneo Sbarbaro" in *La Fiera Letteraria*, 13 November 1955.

[30] *Ibidem*.

As we will see, others will echo this judgement of Camillo Sbarbaro, but for now it is sufficient to conclude that the reason for his continued readership (his standing and fortune have increased in the last twenty years and today he may well be one of the most read minor poets of the century) is directly related to our new understanding and appreciation of the early 20th-century avantgarde movements and the poetic movements that followed.

Camillo Sbarbaro

Though nearly all he wrote is either directly or indirectly autobiographical, critics have always noted a "symptomatic poverty of exterior events" in the life of Camillo Sbarbaro. The poet was born in Santa Margherita Ligure on January 12, 1888, the older of two children. His sister Clelia was to be his lifelong companion in what seems to be somewhat of a recurrence of an Italian trend: the return of the poet to the family "nest" (Pascoli is the classic example).[1]

Sbarbaro's childhood, spent in the tranquillity and beauty of Ligurian coastal towns around Genoa and Savona, was soon marked by tragedy and personal loss: his mother, Angiolina Bacicalupo (1866–1893) died at the age of twenty-seven after a protracted struggle with tuberculosis when the

---

[1] The official biography of Sbarbaro is Gina Lagorio's *Sbarbaro un modo spoglio di esistere*, Saggi Blu, Garzanti, Milan, 1981, previously *Sbarbaro contro-corrente*, Guanda, Parma, 1973. A brief biographical account was given by his sister Clelia "Camillo Sbarbaro nei ricordi della sorella" in *Paragone* (Letteratura), no. 250, December 1970, also as appendix to *Poesie*, Vanni Scheiwiller, Milano, 1971, 1973, now in *Poesia e prosa* a cura di Vanni Scheiwiller, Mondadori, Milan, 1979. Previously most anthologies and dictionaries lamented a paucity of biographical data. A typical biographical sketch is in *Poeti italiani del Novecento* a cura di Pier Vincenzo Mengaldo, Mondadori, Milan, 1978, pp. 317–321.

poet was only five years old; his father, Carlo (1839–1912), who was nearly fifty when he married Angiolina, soon developed poor health, along with a nearly total loss of hearing, due to an earlier industrial accident in which he was involved, and later, even eyesight. The age and health of the father became important factors in the poet's development and outlook toward life.

The poet received a solid classical education, begun at home under the supervision of his father who held three degrees in architecture and engineering, then continued in the parochial schools of the Salesian fathers and in the public Ginnasio Cristoforo Colombo in Genoa and the Liceo Chiabrera in Savona. The poet excelled in the classics, in French and in botany.

Having decided not to attend the university for lack of a strong desire to continue traditional forms of study, and to be near his sister and his ailing father in need of his financial support, the poet took clerical employment with the steel manufacturing firm of Siderurgica in Savona, and later with the Ilva in Genoa.[2] The life of a *travet* did not agree with the shy, reclusive young poet.

It was during his high school days that Sbarbaro wrote his first poems. *Resine* (*Resin*) appeared in Genoa in 1911 thanks to the intervention of his school friends who paid for its publication with the editor Caimo.[3]

Between 1911 and 1913 Sbarbaro also composed *Pianissimo*, his first major work, one which expresses both his aliena-

---

[2] *Ilva*, the Latin name for the island of Elba, site of Italy's scarse iron mines, became by extension the synonym of *Alti forni and acciaiertie d'Italia*. The *Siderurgica* of Savona merged with a number of other companies. Sbarbaro was indebted for his employment as a clerk and secretary to the director Dr. Rietti to the Fera brothers, friends of the family and rich Jewish stockholders of the company.

[3] *Resine* contained rather traditional poems, all later repudiated by Sbarbaro. More recently the critic Carlo Torchio has analyzed the language of *Resine* in an attempt to extablish more accurate links on the relevance of linguistic models used in those early years of the century in *Sigma*, March 1968. "Il pino" is the only poem that stands out for its relevance to the theme of nature in Sbarbaro's poetry.

tion from an urban scene and employment situation for which he had no forbearance or talent and his tacit suffering over the imminent and inevitable death of his father.

Sbarbaro abandoned his clerical position at the Ilva at the first reasonable opportunity. That opportunity came with World War I. In 1916 the poet volunteered as a Red Cross attendant and, drafted the following year, was first an infantryman, and, soon after, a lieutenant. He served with the 27th Infantry Division in the northeast corner of the Trentino Alto Adige where he remained after the end of the war until the summer of 1919. Upon his return he edited and compiled his first volume of *Trucioli* (*Shavings*), his *poèmes en prose* in which he continued the themes of *Pianissimo*, and which he published in Florence with Vallecchi.

Except for brief periods of employment in a couple of prominent private schools in Liguria, Sbarbaro held practically no other traditional job and lived mostly by his pen, by private teaching of Latin and Greek, and by translating. At the same time he dedicated himself to the study and collection of lichens, a field in which he excelled and achieved international recognition.

While staunchly antifascist in the 20's and 30's (his refusal to join the party and to take a pledge cost him his employment at the Jesuit Istituto Arecco in Genoa), Sbarbaro, like Eugenio Montale, never opposed the regime publicly.

In 1928 he published with Ribet of Turin, *Liquidazione* (*Clearance*), new prose that reflected the stylistic directions of *La Ronda*.[4] A long period of silence followed as the poet was denied publication of a new edition of *Trucioli* in the late 30's by

---

[4] *La Ronda* (1919–1922) was a literary review largely under the direction of Vincenzo Cardarelli. It had a vast influence on the writers of the twenties and thirties. It advocated a return to very strict classicist style in reaction to the immediacy and spontaneity more typical of the Italian earlier avantgarde movements. It also represented a movement toward prose and away from poetry. Leopardi's *Operette morali* were the model advocated in the attempt to recapture a perfect blend of poetic standards imposed on a descriptive prose style. Emilio Cecchi, one of the founders of *La Ronda*, was one of the first critics of Sbarbaro's *Pianissimo*.

the fascist Ministero della Cultura Popolare (MinCulPop). The final edition of *Trucioli* was issued by Mondadori in 1948.

For that volume Sbarbaro won in 1949 the Saint Vincent Prize. In 1956 he won the Etna-Taormina Prize for his volume of *Rimanenze* (*Remains*), which collected poems from the early 20's and 30's. In 1961 he received the highest Italian academic honor, the Feltrinelli Prize of the Accademia Nazionale dei Lincei, for his literary and scientific work as lichenologist. In their decision the members of the jury pointed out that Sbarbaro's "fragments," so typical of the poets of *La Voce*, assume a concentration that turns them to lyric and are by now the property of a new literature and poetry: the one that finds its highest expression in Ungaretti and Montale. In Sbarbaro the Academy wanted to recognize "a talent, or perhaps even a sort of genius of antirhetoricism: a virtue one can never reward enough."[5]

Except for a very few trips abroad and some limited travel within Italy, Sbarbaro spent most of his life in the region of Liguria. From there he was able to conduct extensive research into lichens from all over the world, and to contribute considerably to its cataloguing and study.

He was also an avid reader of classics and has given us very handsome translations of Euripides, Aeschylus and Pythagoras. Of French 19th and 20th century writers he preferred master writers like Flaubert, Balzac and Maupassant, as well as "decadent" writers like Huysmans, Villiers de l'Isle-Adam, Barbey d'Aurevilly.

Sbarbaro was a man of few but faithful friendships, shunned public attention and had little tolerance for literary circles and intellectual or political groups. In 1951 he retired with his sister to Spotorno, the town of his mother's family, where the Bacicalupos had at one time been landowners.

The poet was essentially rediscovered in the early 50's when the Venetian editor Neri-Pozza reissued a revised edi-

---

[5] Accademia dei Lincei, Rendiconti delle adunanze solenni, seduta del 13 giugno 1962, vol. VI, fascicolo 5.

tion of *Pianissimo* along with the original 1914 text. To the attention of critics and readers Sbarbaro responded with a small avalanche of tiny booklets with the very telling titles of *Grocce (Drops), Contagocce (Eyedrops), Primizie (First Fruits), Fuochi Fatui (Will-o'-the-wisp), Bolle di sapone (Soap Bubbles), Vedute di Genova 1921 (Sights of Genoa 1921), Quisquilie (Trifles).* In 1966, thanks to Angelo Barile, Sbarbaro's lifelong friend and confidant, the poet was also able to publish his letters from the front during World War I under the title of *Cartoline in franchigia (Postcards on Leave).* He died in Savona on October 31, 1967, a few months before his eightieth birthday.

If Sbarbaro's life was "symptomatically free of exterior events" it was nonetheless rich with friendships and old family ties, quietly but consistently cultivated over a lifetime. Out of this network of relationships Sbarbaro's friendship with Eugenio Montale, the 1975 Nobel Laureate, and his friendship with the De Bosis Vivante family, are particularly noteworthy.

Montale has himself provided substantial documentation of his devotion to the Ligurian poet in the "Poems for Camillo Sbarbaro" in *Gli ossi di seppia* (1925), in his 1920 review of *Trucioli,* in the necrology "Ricordo di Camillo Sbarbaro," and in a number of interviews and autobiographical reflections (see appendix for some of those texts).

Montale and Sbarbaro met about 1920 in their native Liguria through their mutual friends Angelo Barile, the Baratono brothers Adelchi and Pierangelo, and other minor writers and intellectuals. For a while they belonged to a bohemian group of *scapigliati* headed by the boisterous and eloquent Ceccardo Roccatagliata Ceccardi.[6] They saw each other frequently until 1928 when Montale moved to Florence and eventually to Milan. Their friendship lasted throughout their lives and they continued to meet from time to time, often at Solaia, the villa on the estate of the De Bosis Vivante family.

---

[6] Ceccardo Roccatagliata-Ceccardi (1872–1919) was the author of *Sonetti e poemi* (1910) and the posthumous *Sillabe ed ombre.*

Leone Vivante was a prominent philosopher with intellectual and social ties to England and the United States. One of his first works bears the introduction of T. S. Eliot. His wife, Elena De Bosis Vivante was a painter and in spirit very close to the personality of the Ligurian poet. Their friendship is documented in a volume that Sbarbaro assembled from letters he received from Elena. He called the volume *Autoritratto (involontario) di Elena De Bosis Vivante.*[7]

Elena was the daughter of a brilliant and prominent poet of the 19th century, Adolfo De Bosis, whose *Convito* (1885–1907) was among the most important poetry reviews at the turn of the century. Her brother Lauro, a bright young poet well known in the United States, a friend of Thornton Wilder, disappeared while dropping antifascist literature from a small plane over Rome.[8] Sbarbaro's friendship with Elena is also remembered in a very thoughtful article "Of Love and Friendship" written by her son Arturo Vivante for the the *New Yorker* in 1973.[9]

Another important friendship Sbarbaro developed was in the late 50's with the novelist/critic Gina Lagorio, who became his biographer. In her volume, originally published in 1973 by Guanda of Parma and reissued more recently by Garzanti, Lagorio challenges the prevailing opinions of many critics, but especially Sbarbaro's most important interpreter, Giorgio Bàrberi Squarotti.[10]

---

[7] The *Autoritratto* was printed at the poet's expense by the typography Valdonega of Verona for the editor Vanni Scheiwiller of Milan. In reviewing the book for the *Corriere della sera* (April 19, 1964), Montale suggested that since Italian literature is poor in diaries and epistolaries, it will be precious to future historians. Montale's review is now contained in his volume *Sulla poesia,* Mondadori, Milan, 1976, pp. 327–328.

[8] On Lauro De Bosis (1901–1931) see the Foreword by G. M. Trevelyan in *The Golden Book of Italian Poetry*, chosen and edited by Lauro De Bosis, Oxford University Press, London, New York, 1932 (1933), and the very recent Iris Origo, *A Need to Testify: Portraits of Lauro De Bosis, Harcourt, Brace, Jovanovich, New York, 1984.*

[9] *The New Yorker*, May 26, 1973, pp. 41–45.

[10] Giorgio Bàrbari Squarotti, *Camillo Sbarbaro*, Mursia, Milan, 1971, and "La città di Sbarbaro" in *Atti del congresso nazionale di studi su Sbarbaro*, Resine, Genoa, 1974, also in *Gli inferi e il labirinto*, Cappelli Bologna, *(continued, page 22)*

Squarotti's psychological analysis of Sbarbaro's work had ignored, beyond reason, any biographical data of the poet. The critic held that, as in the *Autoritratto* of Elena, so in all his other booklets Sbarbaro had constructed his own personality. The result was a complete mystification of the real person and the poetic persona. Gina Lagorio's many promotions of the Ligurian poet, including her excellent volume *Sui racconti di Sbarbaro* (*On Sbarbaro's Short Stories*), have corrected many misunderstandings about Sbarbaro, but most of all, have reinstated to its proper function and role the significance of biographical data in the work of critical analysis.[11]

In 1973 a Congress of Studies on Camillo Sbarbaro was held in Spotorno to discuss his poetry only.[12] Today Sbarbaro is recognized as a very important poet of the early 20th century and one whose importance goes well beyond his most obvious accomplishments. He emerges as an exemplary figure faithful to a concept of poetry and artistic prose that rises from the most personal and intimate experience without ever betraying the slightest hint of sentimentality nor displaying the bourgeois myth of "inspiration."

In his "Recollections of Sbarbaro" Montale quite appropriately reminds us that Rimbaud was the "addiction" of Sbarbaro's adolescence.

> He was a man of *terra firma* and of few but faithful friendships. It is also my impression that, all in all, his was the life of a successful, perhaps even a happy man. Fate had granted him the gift of expression and for him that was enough . . .

(*continued from page 21*) 1974, and now in *Letteratura Italiana: Il Novecento. I Contemporanei*, vol. II, Marzorati, Milan, 1979.

[11] *Sui racconti di Sbarbaro*, Guanda, Parma, 1973. The volume includes the following short stories: From *Scena Illustrata*, "L'ultima scoperta del dottor Patrice" (May 1, 1909); from *La Riviera Ligure*, "Giornata di Pioggia" (July 1913), "La bottega di profumeria" (March 1914), "La casa nuova" (September 1914), "La zia Catta" (December 1914), "Lily Dargle'e" (February 1915), "Madre" (February 1915), "L'intrusa" (February 1915), "In carrozza" (April 1915), "Congedo" (April 1915), "Il chierico" (June 1915), "Nelle tasche del babbo" (July 1917); from *La Voce*, "Tom" (June 26, 1913); from *Lacerba*, "La seconda vita di Teodoro B." (February 15, 1914), "Libertinaggio" (April 17, 1915).

[12] *Atti del congresso di studi su Sbarbaro, op. cit.*

He led the life of a just man, a man who never asked anything from the world and who tolerated poverty, if not indigence, because every other form of wealth would have offended his sense of common dignity, of decency.[13]

This same sense of dignity and separation between the man and the poet is echoed by Pier Vincenzo Mengaldo:

no other writer in out century has been able to practice with his firmness and dignity the equally distinct separation between the producer of verses and the private citizen, to live with such acute awareness of the modern decentralization of the poetic function[14].

Of Sbarbaro's art and writing habits Montale pointed out that:

his art was made up of brief fulgurations and the drug that brought him to these happy moments was life, life felt as something inexplicable but nonetheless no less worthy of being accepted. Writing meant for him waiting for the moment when the dictate of inspiration matured. Whose dictation? Regardless, Camillo never submitted totally to the irrational and kept always at a distance from any groups and literary tertulias.[15]

Chronology

1888 Born January 12 in Santa Margherita Ligure.

1893 The poet's mother dies of tuberculosis. Camillo is only 5 and his sister Clelia 4 years old. Their aunt Maria Zita Bacicalupo (1871–1953) has already been taking care of the children. The family moves to Voze, later a favorite place of the poet.

1894 The family moves to Varazze. Earliest education of the children under their father's direction.

1896 Sbarbaro attends elementary schools under the Salesian fathers till 1902.

---

[13] "Ricordo di Sbarbaro" in *Corriere della sera*, November 5, 1967, now in *Sulla poesia, op. cit.*, and available also in Camillo Sbarbaro, *Poesia e prosa, op. cit.* For a translation of Montale "Recollections of Sbarbaro" see Jonathan Galassi, *The Second Life of Art, op. cit.*.

[14] *Poeti Italiani del Novecento, op. cit.*, pp. 319–320.

[15] "Recollections of Sbarbaro," *op. cit.*

1902 Attends the Ginnasio Cristoforo Colombo in Genoa from 1902 to 1904.

1903 Benedetto Croce launches one of the most important publications of the first half of the century, *La critica*. The purpose of the journal is to revive Italian culture by criticizing the positivists who saw erudition as an end unto itself. Croce's orientation was toward Neo-hegelian idealism.

Giovanni Papini (using the pen name of Gianfalco) starts the avantgarde publication *Il Leonardo* (1903–1907), is later joined by Giuseppe Prezzolini (Giuliano il Sofista). Sbarbaro will eventually come in contact with these and other movements of the peninsula.

1905 Filippo Tommaso Marinetti and Sem Benelli start a publishing house and a review, *Poesia*, dedicated to the propagation of futurist works. The advancement of free verse advocated by *Poesia* is important to the formation of poets of Sbarbaro's generation.

1908 Papini and Ardengo Soffici start another journal, *Il commento*, which fails after the first issue on Feb. 16.

Prezzolini, with Soffici and Papini, starts *La Voce*, the most important publication of the period; "Vociani" are the major writers, including Sbarbaro who contributed to the periodical. Toward the end it was directed by Giuseppe De Robertis and was known as *La Voce Bianca*. It ceased in 1917.

1909 Sbarbaro receives his diploma from the Liceo Chiabrera in Savona, attended from 1904. In those same years he composes his earliest poems in a style typical of Giosué Carducci. Extremely withdrawn, comes under the protective care of his life long friend Angelo Barile. Spends summers in Spotorno with his maternal grandparents in total freedom to write and explore nature. Begins to correspond with various writers and botanists of his region and with his teacher Adelchi Baratono.

Marinetti publishes the first Futurist Manifesto in *Le Figaro* of Paris February 20.

1910 The condition of the poet's father begins to deteriorate.

Sbarbaro is forced to abandon the joy of creative leisure for the necessity of employment. He has elected not to attend the university. Employed by Siderurgica of Savona as a clerk.

1911 His former classmates at the Liceo Chiabrera publish at their expense the poet's earliest poems under the title of *Resine* (*Resin*). Sbarbaro writes his first short stories (published in 1973 by his biographer and friend Gina Lagorio). Transferred from Savona to Genoa following the fortunes of the Siderurgica which together with three other companies is absorbed by Ilva.

1912 Death of his father Carlo after a long illness, a major factor in the composition of *Pianissimo*. First contribution to *Riviera Ligure* (Adelchi Baratono has written Angelo Novaro, the editor, on behalf of the young poet).

1913 Papini and Soffici launch *Lacerba*, an organ of futurist ideas. Sbarbaro contributes a number of *frammenti* and for a while shares the ideals of the journal.

1914 Angelo Barile intervenes on behalf of the poet, with Prezzolini of *La Voce*. A letter written on January 19 (published by Domenico Astengo in *I libretti di mal'aria* on May 20, 1977) asks for assistance in publishing 32 poems by the young poet. Prezzolini invites Sbarbaro to Florence. Brief stay. The poet meets many writers and intellectuals at the elegant *Caffé Paskowski* and at *Le Giubbe Rosse*. Prefers the more informal *Bar della Rosa*. Publication of *Pianissimo*.

1916 Partly because of the monotony of his employment and the war, Sbarbaro joins the Red Cross. Has no convictions about the war. By contrast most other writers of his generation exhalted war as "the only hygiene of the world" (Marinetti).

1917 Is recruited in February and assigned to the 12th regiment of the infantry. On May 15 undertakes officer training in Sandrigo and ends up as lieutenant in the

27th Infantry Division in the northeast corner of the Trentino, where he remains till Summer 1919. Unlike Piero Jahier, Giuseppe Ungaretti and various other contemporaries, Sbarbaro has little commitment to the war and sees only minor action. He even tries to resign his officer status, and bears the war the way he supported any other unpleasantness, with stoicism and resignation.

1919 The return to civilian life is particularly difficult for the poet especially amidst economic difficulties, social and political unrest. Belongs to a group of *scapigliati* headed by the Ligurian poet Ceccardo Roccatagliata Ceccardi. They meet in the Caffé Diana in the Galleria of Piazza Manin in Genoa. Begins sporadic employment as a private tutor and as teacher of Latin, Greek and Italian in a number of private schools.

1920 Second brief stay in Florence on the occasion of Vallecchi's publication of his *Trucioli*. Meetings with old friends and acquaintances from 1914. But things have changed: Dino Campana is now in an asylum; Papini has moved from uncompromising atheism and the most irreverent iconoclasticism to devout Catholicism, which culminates in the publication of his *Storia di Cristo* (1920). Back in Liguria Sbarbaro continues to teach and to do botanical research on lichens and other moss from his region and later from all over the world. His *Trucioli* receives the attention of Eugenio Montale who reviews the book in *L'Azione* of Genova on Nov. 10. This is a crucial year in the career of the poet, and his friendship with Montale may have been a significant turn for the better. Is invited to write for *L'Azione*, the radical independent paper of Genoa.

1922 With Montale, Sergio Solmi and Giacomo De Benedetti he is on the editorial board of *Primo Tempo*, an outstanding but short-lived Turin literary journal started that May.

1924 Quietly but staunchly anti-fascist, Sbarbaro becomes

increasingly more withdrawn especially when, after the murder of Matteotti, Mussolini abolishes parliamentary opposition and imposes his "leggi eccezionali fasciste" marking the end of constitutional government and of civil rights. Later he is forced to give up employment as teacher of Latin and Greek at the Istituto Colasanzio in Cornigliano and at the Jesuit Istituto Arecco in Genoa for his refusal to comply with the required fascist membership and pledge of allegiance.

1928 Publishes *Liquidazione*, more short compositions reflecting the newer requirements of style prescribed by *La Ronda*. The collection includes "Delli Ammaestramenti a Polidoro" which Montale defined the best Fidenzian prose of the century.

Sells in Stockholm his first important catalogue of lichens. Travels to Holland and Germany. In Rome becomes reacquainted with Leone Vivante. Through him Sbarbaro meets Elena De Bosis Vivante, sister of Lauro, both children of Adolfo De Bosis. The friendship with Elena, like the one for Montale, offers the poet the kind of social link he has needed since the death of his father. Later Montale and Sbarbaro will be frequent visitors to Solaia, the villa near Siena, where the De Bosis/Vivante family had settled on their vast estate.

1931 Collaborates on the literary journal *Circoli* (1931–1939) directed by Adriano Grande.

Angelo Barile publicly invites Sbarbaro to reissue *Pianissimo*, long out of print. The poet refuses, wishing to revise the volume.

1937 The Vivante family is forced to flee to England to avoid persecution of Jews imposed in Italy by Mussolini's new racial laws. Sbarbaro has an opportunity to follow his friends to England where he has been offered a teaching position. His hesitation and failure to be issued a passport from the authorities (he had voted against the party in the last election) keep the poet from leaving Italy.

1938 The Ministero della Cultura Popolare (MinCulPop), the political arm of the Fascist censorship, halts the publication of a new volume of *Trucioli* to be published by Vallecchi of Florence. Difficulties are incurred every time Sbarbaro receives packages of lichens or plants from abroad. He is the only serious scholar of botany in Italy.

1940 Invasion of Albania, breaking the 1926 treaty between the two countries, had virtually plunged Italy into WWII already in 1939. Genoa is the first Italian city to be heavily bombed because of its important seaport and depots. Following the outbreak, the poet at first refuses to leave the city. Finally, on February 9, he takes his sister Clelia and his aunt Benedetta to a small house in the orchards of Spotorno, is called but found ineligible for return to active military duty. Begins a vast activity as translator mostly from French and Greek. For a while this will be his main livelihood.

1943 For Einaudi of Turin translates Flaubert's *Salambò*.

1944 First draft of *Fuochi Fatui* (*Will-o'-the-wisp*), particularly those pieces relating to the war. Sbarbaro and his family are forced to move further into the interior by the German occupation troops in anticipation of possible invasion by Allied forces. Translates Euripides' *The Cyclope*, Joris Karl Huysmans' *A Rebours*, Stendhal's *The Charterhouse of Parma*, Sophocles' *Antigone*. When even the interior is bombed the poet returns to Spotorno where the house in the orchards has been demolished. There are civilian deaths everywhere.

1945 Gradual return of the population to Genoa as German troops withdraw. Sbarbaro feels increasingly isolated. Translates Flaubert's *Trois Contes*, *Les diaboliques* of Barbey D'Aurevilly, Maupassant's *The Port and Other Stories*, Villiers de L'Isle-Adam's *Unusual Stories and Cruel Tales*.

1948 Mondadori publishes the final edition of *Trucioli* which includes compositions from 1914 to 1940. Garzanti issues *Resine* under the "Opera Prima" series of 20th century Italian authors.

1949 With Bruno Barilli receives the Saint-Vincent Prize. Meets Ungaretti. Translates Poulaille and Aeschylus.

1950 Sells to the University of Chicago an important and large catalog of lichens.

1951 Retires with his sister and aging aunt Benedetta to Spotorno thus fulfilling a youthful wish. Continues private teaching of Latin and Greek.

1952 Date of publication of several translations (see bibliography).

1954 At the urging of many friends the poet finally agrees to let the Venetian editor Neri Pozza publish *Pianissimo*. Revisions on the famous volume had begun in the thirties and 8 poems had already appeared in *Poesia* in July 1946 (pp. 42–48). The volume was to include the 1914 edition followed by the new text.

1955 Publication of *Rimanenze* (*Remnants*), poems from the 20's and 30's. The *Fiera Letteraria* dedicates part of the November 13 issue to Sbarbaro.

1956 Receives the Etna-Taormina Prize with Jules Supervielle. New edition of *Rimanenze; Fuochi Fatui* is published by Vanni Scheiwiller (All'insegna del pesce d'oro) in Milan.

1957 With Massimo Bontempelli and Luigi Gigli translates *The Theatre* of Crommelynck for the editor Bompiani of Milan.

1958 New expanded edition of *Fuochi Fatui*. Collects in the volume *Primizie* (*First Fruits*) a small number of poems missing in previous volumes.

1960 In *Scampoli* (*Remnants*) published by Vallecchi of Florence he collects a number of *trucioli* and stories from newspapers and weekly magazines.

1961 A new edition of his *Poesie*, edited by Vanni Scheiwiller, appears in Milan. The poet has eliminated a number of poems and most of *Primizie* except the poem "Organetto" ("Street-organ").

1962 Donates his papers and remaining catalogues of lichens to the Museo di Storia Naturale di Genova. In December is awarded with Bruno Cicognani, Giuseppe De Robertis and Carlo Emilio Gadda the Antonio Feltrinelli Prize of the Accademia Nazionale dei Lincei, Italy's highest recognition.

1963 Death of Elena De Bosis Vivante. Sbarbaro edits and compiles her letters to him in an *Autoritratto (involontario)* of this exceptional artist and personality. The poet publishes the first of a number of tiny booklets, this one with the telling title of *Gocce* (*Drops*).

1966 Thanks to Angelo Barile, his friend from childhood, who had saved his letters, the poet is able to publish a "youthful book in his old age," his letters from the front during WWI. He calls them *Cartoline in franchigia* (*Postcards on Leave*).

1967 After a brief illness Sbarbaro dies in Savona the 31st of October.

Selected Bibliography

Works by Camillo Sbarbaro

Resine, Caimo, Genoa, 1911, then in "Opera Prima," Garzanti, Milan, 1948.

Pianissimo, La Voce, Florence, 1914.

Trucioli (1914–1918), Vallecchi, Florence, 1920.

Liquidazione, Ribet, Torino, 1928.

Trucioli (1914–1940), Mondadori, Milan, 1948, second printing 1963.

Pianissimo (1914 and 1954 editions), Neri Pozza, Venice, 1954.

Rimanenze, Scheiwiller, Milan, 1955, second edition 1956.

Fuochi Fatui, Scheiwiller, Milan 1956, second edition enlarged 1958; Third edition enlarged Ricciardi, Milan-Naples, 1962.

Primizie, Scheiwiller, Milan, 1958.

Scampoli, Vallecchi, Florence 1960.

Poesie, includes the two versions of *Pianissimo*, part of *Primizie, Rimanenze*, Scheiwiller, Milan, 1961, 1971.
Gocce, Scheiwiller, Milan, 1963.
"Il Nostro" e nuove gocce, with Montale's 1920 essay about Sbarbaro's *Trucioli* and an iconography by Vanni Scheiwiller, Milan, 1964.
Contagocce, Scheiwiller, Milan, 1965.
Cartoline in franchigia, Nuove Edizioni Enrico Vallecchi, Florence, 1966.
Bolle di sapone, Scheiwiller, Milan, 1966.
Vedute di Genova 1921, Scheiwiller, Milan, 1966.
Quisquilie, Scheiwiller, Milan, 1967.
Licheni, un campionario del mondo, Nuove Edizioni Vallecchi, Florence, 1967.
Ricordo di Giorgio Labò, Scheiwiller, Milan, 1969.
Poesie, final edition, Scheiwiller, Milan, 1971.
Poesia e prosa, edited by Vanni Scheiwiller with two essays by Eugenio Montale, Mondadori, Milan, 1979.
La trama delle lucciole. Lettere ad Angelo Barile (1919–1937), edited by Domenico Astengo and Franco Contorbia, Edizione S. Marco dei Giustiniani, Genova, 1979.
"Le Ultime Lettere di Camillo Sbarbaro" to the English critic and translator Seppe Lind, in *L'Osservatore politico letterario*, October, 1971.
"Lettere a *Diogene*," in *Resine*, June 1972.
"Tre vecchi Trucioli" (with a note by Domenico Astengo), in *Resine*, September, 1973.
"Lettere inedite di Carlo Emilio Gadda e di Camillo Sbarbaro ad Aldo Camerino" (with a note by Maria Corti), in *Strumenti critici*, no. 27, 1975.
Autoritratto (involontario) di Elena De Bosis Vivante da sue lettere, edited by Camillo Sbarbaro, Stamperia Valdonega, Verona, 1963.

Translations by Camillo Sbarbaro

G. Flaubert, *Salambò*, Einaudi, Torino, 1943; Mondadori, Milan 1959; Einaudi, Torino, 1961 (with a preface by Camillo Sbarbaro).
Sophocles, *Antigone*, Bompiani, Milan, 1944; also 1945.
J. K. Huysmans, *Controcorrente*, Gentile, Milan, (n.d.); also 1963; *A rovescio*, Scheiwiller, Milan, 1968 (with a note by Camillo Sbarbaro and a recollection by Eugenio Montale); *Controcorrente*, Rusconi, Milan, 1972, introduction by Carlo Bo; *Controcorrente*, Garzanti, Milan, 1972.
Stendhal, *La certosa di Parma*, Einaudi, Turin, 1944; 1961 (with a preface by Camillo Sbarbaro; 1963 and 1965.

J. Supervielle, *La figlia del mare aperto*, Gentile, Milan, 1945.

J. Barbey D'Aurevilly, *Le diaboliche*, Bompiani, Milan, 1945.

G. De Maupassant, *Il porto e altri racconti*, Bompiani, Milan, 1945, 1946.

G. Flaubert, *Tre racconti*, Bompiani, Milan, 1945, and 1946.

Ph. A. P. Villiers de l'Isle-Adam, *Storie insolite e racconti crudeli*, Bompiani, Milan, 1945, with an introduction by Camillo Sbarbaro.

Euripides, *Il Ciclope*, Editrice Genovese Lettere e Arti, Genova 1945; Scheiwiller, Milan, 1960; Einaudi, Torino, 1965 (with a preface by A. Angelini).

H. De Balzac, *La pelle di zigrino*, Einaudi, Turin, 1947; Mondadori, Milan, 1958.

H. Poulaille, *Il pane quotidiano*, Mondadori, Milan, 1949.

Aeschylus, *Prometeo incatenato*, Bompiani, Milan, 1949.

H. De Montherlant, *Quelle che prediamo fra le braccia*, in *Sipario*, no. 63, July, 1951.

R. Martin du Gard, *I Thibault*, Mondadori, Milan, 1951; Club degli Editori, Milan, 1965, Utet, Turin, 1966.

E. Zola, *Germinale*, Einaudi, Turin, 1951, also 1958; Editori Riuniti, Rome, 1958; Oscar Mondadori, Milan, 1970.

Euripides, *Alcesti, Il Ciclope*, Bompiani, Milan, 1952.

H. De Montherlant, *Malatesta*, in *Il gran maestro Santiago - La regina morta - Malatesta*, Bompiani, Milan, 1952 by Massimo Bontempelli.

J. Green, *Varuna*, Mondadori, Milan, 1953.

F. Crommelynck, *Teatro* (*L'intagliatore di maschere, Il cornuto magnifico, Gli amanti puerili, Trippe d'oro, Una donna che ha il cuore troppo piccolo, Caldo e freddo*) edited by M. Bontempelli, L. Gigli, and Camillo Sbarbaro, Bompiani, Milan, 1957.

Pythagoras, *I versi d'oro*, Scheiwiller, Milan, 1958, 1960, 1968.

H. De Montherland, *Il cardinale di Spagna - Port Royal*, Bompiani, Milan, 1961.

G. Flaubert, *Bouvard e Pécuchet*, Einaudi, Turin, 1964; Mondadori, Milan, 1968.

G. Pascoli, *Thallusa - Pomponia Grecina* (verse translation for RAI).

Criticism

Recent bibliographies of Camillo Sbarbaro criticism are in the following works: Camillo Sbarbaro, *Poesia e prosa*, op. cit., pp. XXXIII–XLVII, chronologically ordered; Gina Lagorio, *Un modo spoglio di esistere*, Garzanti, Milan, 1981, pp. 355–378; still useful, though superseded by the ones just mentioned, are the annotated bibliographies found in

Giorgio Bàrberi Squarotti, *Camillo Sbarbaro*, Mursia, Milan, 1971 which expanded the one contained in *I contemporanei*, Marzorati, Milan, 1963 (later revised and enlarged in the 1979 edition); and in Lorenzo Polato, *Sbarbaro*, La Nuova Italia, Florence, 1969, 1974.

The latest additions to the bibliography of Sbarbaro are the following articles:

Corrado Federici, "Indifference in Camillo Sbarbaro's *Pianissimo*", in *Canadian Journal of Italian Studies*, Vol. 2, nos. 1–2, Fall-Winter 1978–1979, pp. 92–104.

———, "Il grottesco nei *Trucioli* di Sbarbaro," in *Italica*, vol. 58, no. 4, winter 1981, pp. 301–306.

and reviews:

Gina Lagorio, *Sui racconti di Sbarbaro di Sbarbaro, Guanda, Parma, 1973,* in *Canadian Journal of Italian Studies*, vol. 1, no. 3, Spring 1978, pp. 236–239 (Vittorio Felaco).

Camillo Sbarbaro, *Poesia e prosa*, Mondadori, Milan, 1979, and *La trama delle lucciole*, Sabatelli, Genoa, 1979, in *Canadian Journal of Italian Studies*, Vol. 4, nos. 3–4, Spring-Summer 1981, pp. 322–324 (Vittorio Felaco).

Lastly, there exists an annotated edition of *Pianissimo* edited by Lorenzo Polato, Il Saggiatore, Milan, 1983.

Monographic Studies on Sbarbaro

Giacinto Spagnoletti, *Sbarbaro*, Cedam, Padua, 1943.

Adriano Guerrini, *Il significato di Sbarbaro*, Sabatelli, Genoa, 1968.

Lorenzo Polato, *Camillo Sbarbaro*, "Il Castoro", La Nuova Italia, Florence, 1969, 2nd edition 1974.

Giorgio Bàrberi Squarotti, *Camillo Sbarbaro*, Mursia, Milan, 1971.

Luciano Nanni, *L'idea di oggettivazione artistica in Camillo Sbarbaro*, Guida, Napoli, 1973.

Gina Lagorio, *Sui racconti di Sbarbaro*, Guanda, Parma, 1973, includes Sbarbaro's short stories never collected before.

———, *Sbarbaro, un modo spoglio di esistere*, Garzanti, Milan, 1981, revised and enlarged edition of *Sbarbaro controcorrente*, Guanda, Parma, 1973.

A Congress of Studies on Camillo Sbarbaro was held in Spotorno, Oct. 6–7, 1973; its proceedings were published in *Atti del Congresso Nazionale di Studi su Sbarbaro*, edited by Adriano Guerrini, Resine - Quaderni Liguri di Cultura, Genoa, 1974.

From *Primizie*

From *First Fruits*

I walk alone in the night
through deserted alleys
amidst the greatest squalor.
I am frightened
by the sound of unknown steps
echoing against the empty houses.

Thick clouds hang
on the houses and fill the air
like frayed edges along the eaves;
and the tiny yellow lights
of the gas lamps flicker
on the dampened pavement in the breeze;
one lonely shutter creaks
in the night.

In such traditional words
and movements
you pass by
youth that will never return.
And if you feel disgust

Da *Primizie*

Vo nella notte solo
per vicoli deserti
lungo squallide mura.
Al discorde rumor dei passi incerti
echeggiando le case come vuote,
trasalgo di paura.

Si sfilacciano contro i cornicioni
delle case che occupano l'aria
i nuvoloni;
e la fiammella gialla
del lampione traballa
su lastrici che caldo vento bagna;
un'imposta si lagna
solitaria.

In parole consuete
in consueti passi,
giovinezza, trapassi
—che non torni.
E se disgusto senti

for yourself, for your days
wasted, a foolish premonition
—nearly a certainty—
deludes you:
that your youth
may once again return,
poor foolish life.

Like all the others
who received from life
with each share of suffering
their share of bread,
driven like beasts
by necessity and lust
where darkness swallows them
—so and without tears
for the eyes are dry—
like all others
you who promised so much.

My soul hangs on me
like an old suit;
all that's around encumbers me;
each thing nearly
strangles me
and weighs me down
but will not let me cry . . .

And then quite suddenly
in that sultry silence of the night
an easy melody springs
from an organ in the street.
It's a dance motif:
each note ricochets
like a pearl on crystal,
then noisily fills the street.

Something fresh and new

di te stessa, dei giorni
inutili, t'illude
folle presentimento
—ed è quasi certezza—
che torni un'altra volta,
povera vita stolta,
la tua giovinezza.

Come gli altri come tutti
ch'ebbero dalla vita
per la parte di stenti
la lor parte di pane,
spinti come giumenti
dalla fame e la foia
dove il buio li ingoia
—così e senza pianto
ché gli occhi sono asciutti,
come gli altri come tutti
tu che potevi tanto.

Come il vestito vecchio
l'anima addosso mi pesa;
tutto intorno m'ingombra;
ogni cosa mi pare che mi copra
il fiato,
ogni cosa mi pare mi stia sopra
e non mi lasci piangere . . .

Quand'ecco nel silenzio afoso balza
da un organo sgorgando
facile melodia.

È un motivo di ballo:
ogni nota rimbalza
perla su cristallo,
fragorosa empie la via.

Qualche cosa di fresco di nuovo

runs through my blood . . .
I cannot say what I feel.

By sheer instinct I search in the dark
where the mysterious organ plays.
No longer do I walk
along the wall cautiously:
I move away instead
walking straight in the middle
with sure footing.

And when I pass by that wood
that trembles and sings, I feel
myself turning in that
instrument of sound:
every fiber changed
in tense metallic chords,
the whole body in shivers,
a bundle of nerves that vibrates.

Thus for the last time
I summon from within
my last turbid spirits.
An unusual pride
fills my breast;
bold and defiant I look around
and to myself I say: I want.

Oh mountains and woods,
solitudes vast as the eye can see,
crossed only by the shadow of a cloud
or overrun by wind;
morning smell of dew,
novelty only earth can secrete,
sudden splash
that drenches all,
and with each leaf even the soul revives;
running waters, fresh rustling of trees,

il sangue mi corre . . .
Indicibile, quello che provo.

E d'istinto io cerco nel buio
l'improvviso organetto ove suoni.
Non più ciondoloni
rasento il muro:
mi scosto, cammino
diritto, nel mezzo,
con piede sicuro.

E quando vicino gli passo,
al legno che trema e che canta, mi sento
mutato d'un tratto
nel sonoro strumento:
in corde metalliche tese
cambiata ogni fibra,
il corpo, percorso da brividi,
in fascio di nervi che vibra.

E come per l'ultima volta
i torpidi spiriti, i fiacchi
propositi chiamo a raccolta.
Il petto mi colma
insolito orgoglio;
intorno mi guardo spavaldo,
dico a me stesso: Voglio.

O mie montagne o boschi,
solitudini a vista d'occhio aperte
sulle quali va l'ombra della nuvola
e che il vento scorrazza;
odore al mattino di guazza,
novità della terra
sotto lo scroscio improvviso
quando tutto è intriso
e l'anima è nuova e la foglia;
correr d'acque stormir d'alberi fresco,

peach blossoming
in the barren countryside,
clear wintry skies,
what freshness
the mere thought of you
can pour
on my feverish thirst!

Nature great and green
in birth and death continuously engaged,
even silent you speak to me loudly;
Nature in which alone
man loses himself,
for the eyes never sated with looking
reveal him a stranger to himself;
starry spaces
in this thirst
you are surely my allies.

The gaze of my countenance
is clear now,
my arms are ready to fight.
I sense the ecstacy
of my new and real youth
like an icy wind upon my face.

When suddenly the waltz fades
and the organ closes
with a sharp break.

At once something inside of me fails,
something caves in . .
and the night which that sound
had cleared away and turned to day,
that vain night with its silence
and its shadows closes me in again.

I return weak and alone.

rifiorire del pesco
nella campagna spoglia,
cieli tersi invernali,
soltanto che vi pensi,
nella mia triste arsura
che frescura
versate!

Grande e verde
che muori e rinasci continua,
taciturna che dentro a gran voce mi parli,
Natura, ove perde
l'uomo se stesso,
estraneo a se stesso diventa per gli occhi
di guardare mai sazi,
spazi stellati,
nella sete di forza
mi siete alleati.

Chiaro lo sguardo
s'è fatto nel volto,
pronte alla lotta le braccia.
Sento l'ebrezza,
quasi vento gelato sulla faccia,
della mia nuova e vera giovinezza.

Quando il valzer precipita ed ecco
l'organetto si chiude
d'un colpo secco.

Subito qualche cosa vien meno,
qualche cosa in me frana . . .
E la notte che il suono avea sgombra
del buio e fatta giorno,
la vacua notte col silenzio e l'ombra
mi si richiude intorno.

Resto debole e solo.

My will sags
like a sail without wind;
every impulse dies:
exhultation, pride, everything.
I see myself going through deserted
streets vile, miserable and ugly.
A cat sneaks out of a dark portico
and stops in the middle of the street,
questions me with his big eyes;
meows at me, then quickly
skips away.

I return to the side
and walk along the wall
jumping in foolish fear
when my foot trips the pavement
or the sudden flash of a headlight
shines in the stillness of the wind.

What good is will
to my immense dreams
if it's founded on the unsteady
sands of my senses?

Midnight breaks above my head
and it seems to roar.
To one who roams
alone in the night
the hours fall
like stones to the heart.

Savona, 1910

Vela al mancar del vento,
la volontà s'affloscia;
ogni impeto cade,
l'esaltazione, la fierezza, tutto.
Mi vedo andare per deserte strade
vile miserabile brutto.

Sbuca da un nero portico e s'arresta
nel mezzo della via,
m'interroga con occhi larghi un gatto;
miagola a me, poi ratto
scivola via.

E mi butto da lato e rasento
di nuovo le mura,
se il piede nel lastrico inciampa
o nella pausa del vento
un fanale divampa
trasalendo di sciocca paura.

Volontà, che mi vali
per i miei sogni immensi,
fondata sulla sabbia
instabile dei sensi?

Si stacca sul mio capo
rombando mezzanotte.
A me che vo vagando
solo nella mia notte
cadono sul cuore
come pietre quell'ore.

Savona 1910

About *Primizie*

Primizie was published by Vanni Scheiwiller of Milan in 1958 during a surge of popularity for the early poets of the Italian *Novecento*. Although Sbarbaro had repudiated *Resine* (*Resin*, his *opera prima*, published by Caimo in Genoa in 1911), he permitted the collection of a few early poems. *Primizie* included "Organetto," the poem translated here, as well as "Felicità," "Cimitero di campagna," the Pascolian fragment "Stracci di nebbia lenti," an interview with Cinzia Fiore and a Spanish translation of "Lettera dall'osteria" by the poet Gerardo Diego.

"Organetto" ("Street organ") was the only composition from *Primizie* to be included in the 1960 and 1971 definitive edition of *Poesie*. It was discarded in the Mondadori anthology of 1979. Because the poem is important for the themes and the poetic concept of subsequent poems, it is presented here. The mute and dark cityscape of *Pianissimo* is first glimpsed in "Vo nella notte solo."

The poem was written in Savona in 1910, and appeared in *La Riviera Ligure* in October 1915. Although clearly a youthful composition, it has a remarkably compact plot. The *persona*, a youth on the verge of manhood, regards his adolescence as a wasted time that has offered him little preparation for the future. He sees himself and all other human beings motivated only by "necessity and lust," each creature enclosed in his own petty vice. The poem however, also advances the other major theme of *Pianissino,* that of the tranquillity that comes from nature. But nature is not the index of a classical *locus amoenus,* nor the equivalent of a Renaissance conception of an elaborate and lavish garden. Instead, the lone *organetto,* by the magic of its simple motif, points to a vision of nature undisturbed by the meddlesome, destructive acts of humanity. Though no one moves the handle, the *organetto* plays a simple tune that has the power to restore the will of the *persona* and lead him to a vision of mountain solitude in virgin woods "vast as the eye can see."

That invocation to the mountains is a clear reference to the D'Annunzian ode "Alle Montagne" in *Elettra,* the second volume of the much acclaimed *Laudi del cielo, del mare, della terra e degli eroi,* which included also *Maia* and *Alcyone.*[1]

The ode "Alle Montagne" was an invocation to the mystics and prophets who in mythology inhabit the mountains, privileged places of prayer and meditation. It expresses the augury that they will send to Italy a heroic poet-prophet. The second composition of *Elettra,* "A Dante," suggested that he had prophesied the revival of Italy's greatness. The other compositions contained explicit appeals to Italians to aspire to freedom from false doctrines (especially socialism) and to fight for individal liberty and national greatness through territorial conquest.

Sbarbaro's humble and personal poem is a sad refutation of the bombastic and self-assured *Laus Vitae* (subtitle of *Maia*) with which D'Annunzio could claim to have produced from the "furnace" of his spirit "the only poem of total life to have appeared in Italy since the *Comedy.*"[2]

---

[1] Gabriele D'Annunzio, *Elettra,* Treves, Milan, 1928, pp. 1–3. All of D'Annunzio's works are collected in 49 volumes of the *Opera Omnia,* Edizione nazionale (Istituto nazionale), Rome, 1927–1936. See also *Tutte le opere,* edited by Egidio Bianchetti, Mondadori, Milan, 1939–65.

[2] The remark was made by D'Annunzio in the preface of his tragedy *Più*

"Organetto" is also Sbarbaro's first significant attempt to define the polarities between city and country. The theme of the modern city with its alienating and dehumanizing forces that contribute to man's reification was a common expression of much European nineteenth century literature. But Italy provided very few expressions of this theme, with the notable exceptions of Renzo's extraordinary entry into the city in Alessandro Manzoni's historical novel *I promessi sposi* (*The Betrothed*), the incidental contribution of Francesco Mastriani in *I misteri di Napoli* (*The Mysteries of Naples*), the minor contribution of Giovanni Verga's descriptions of Milan, and some occasional *bozzetto* by Giacomo Leopardi, and later Giosué Carducci. For the most part Italian literature had not explored the changing and reifying evolution of its urban centers the way Engels had explored London and its crowds, or Eugène Sue *I es Mystères de Paris*, or even Baudelaire and Rimbaud in their separate visions of the modern city and its *evils*.

Sbarbaro had at his disposal the more recent model of D'Annunzio's "Città terribili" in the first book of the *Laudi*, *Maia;* cities of horror, of literally human *scum*, of hanging, papermaché moons, of lights more beautiful than the light of stars, and night that falls with the morbid odor of death. Here are some of those verses:

Gloria delle città
terribili, quando a vespro
s'arrestano le miriadi
possenti dei cavalli
che per tutto il giorno
fremettero nelle vaste
macchine mai stanchi,
e s'accendono i bianchi
globi come pendule lune
tra le attonite file
dei platani lungh'esse

---

che l'amore, which opened at the Costanzi in Rome, October 29, 1906. Quoted in *Alcyone*, a selection, edited with introduction and notes by J.R. Woodhouse, Manchester University Press, Manchester, 1978, p. 13.

le case mostruose
dalle cento e cento occhiaie,
e i carri sulle rotaie
stridono carichi di scoria
umana scintillando
d'una luce più bella
che la luce degli astri,
e ne' cieli rossastri
grandeggiano solitarie
le cupole e le torri!

Orrore delle città
terribili, quando sulle vie
arse cadono i larghi lembi
violacei della Sera
con un odore molle di morte,
e s'accendono su le porte
delle taverne i fanali
rossi che versano il sangue
luminoso al limitare
ove scoppierà la furente
rissa dopo l'ingiuria,
e i fuochi della lussuria
brillano negli occhi senili
della grigia larva che insegue
per l'ombra la vergine impube
con nel passo malfermo
l'indizio del morbo dorsale,
e il bardassa trae per le scale
già buie il soldato che ride,
e la libidine incide
l'enorme priàpo sul muro![3]

As Giorgio Bàrberi Squarotti clearly points out, D'Annunzio's descriptions demonstrate the poet's total involvement in the city of horror. That monstrous modern city, product of industrial civilization is viewed by D'Annunzio with a kind of delight, gratification and even rapture which are totally extraneous to Sbarbaro's experience.[4]

---

[3] *Maia*, Treves, Milan, 1928, pp. 218–220.

[4]Giorgio Bàrberi Squarotti, "La città di Sbarbaro" in *Atti del congresso nazionale di studi su Sbarbaro, op. cit.* pp. 54–56, and passim. The article was

It is in "Organetto" that the infernal city of *Pianissimo* is first outlined as a place in which the poetic *persona* fully participates in the horror and inhumanity. D'Annunzio dominates the forces of the terrible cities, Sbarbaro suffers intimately their alienation and reification. D'Annunzio's language matches perfectly the infernal reality of those cities; Sbarbaro attempts to deal with its reality by circumscribing the language of his description, reducing it to the barest elements of identification free of any rhetoric and any type of delectation.

For Sbarbaro, necessity and lust, fear, loneliness and tears dominate the only world in which the *persona* lives and no memory of any vision of an earlier spontaneity and sufficiency can correct that tragically negative perception; for when the waltz fades, so does something in the *persona,* who returns weak and alone, vile, miserable and ugly to walk alone through the deserted streets of the night cityscape.

This is a modernistic and De Chirichian conception of reality. Sbarbaro, by attempting to draw us closer to the earlier Leopardian vision of the universe, even the vision of the idyll, reduces to the barest essence the classical landscape of all poetry and reveals the corrosion that the other intervening poets, like Giacomo Zanella with his cosmic fantasy of the ode "Sopra una conchiglia fossile," and the *crepuscolari* had already exercised on it.

Sbarbaro has replaced the hopes and promises of the enlightened polis of Leopardi's "Ginestra" with the mechanical device of the *organetto* and the mere necessity of being. Leopardi's appeal to the *magnanimi* to unite in a common *cause celèbre* against the common enemy of natural destruction is missing in Sbarbaro, because for him nature is not the enemy of mankind, rather man is the anomalous creation that obstructs the normal life/death cycle of nature. Man has no hope of reversing his own need to exploit the environment, yet lives

---

reprinted in *Letteratura italiana, Novecento: I contemporanei,* Marzorati, Milan, 1979, and in *Gli inferi e il labirinto,* Cappelli, Bologna, 1974.

condemned to the memory of a different vision of things. The immense dreams cannot be fulfilled by sheer *will*, for the will is founded only on the unstable sands of the senses.

Sbarbaro, though ideologically close to nineteenth century culture, its sensibilities and philosophies, attempts to define modern man's predicament and maladjustment a decade before other major European writers such as Kafka, Musil, Svevo, Montale, Eliot.

Pianissimo (1914)

Pianissimo (1914)

> The purpose of poetry is to remind us
> how difficult it is to remain one person,
> for our house is open, there are no keys in the doors,
> and invisible guests come in and out at will.
>
> What I'm saying here is not, I agree, poetry,
> as poems should be written rarely and reluctantly,
> under unbearable duress and only with the hope
> that good spirits, not evil ones, choose us for their instrument.
>
> (Creslaw Milosz, "Ars Poetica?")

I do not know who I am, what soul I have.

When I speak with sincerity, I do not know what sincerity I am speaking with. I am varyingly someone other than an "I" of whom I do not know if he exists (if he is those others).

I feel beliefs which I do not hold. I am ravished by passions I repudiate. My constant study of myself is constantly pointing out to me breaches of faith by my soul toward some character which perhaps I never had nor does it think I do have.

I feel multiple. I am like a room with innumerable fantastic mirrors that distort by false reflections one single pre-existing reality which is not there in any of them and is there in them all.

As the pantheist feels he is tree [?] and even the blossom, I feel myself as different beings. I feel myself living alien lives, in me, incompletely, as though my soul shared in all human beings, incompletely, through a sum of non-"I"s synthesized in an afterthought "I."

(Fernando Pessoa, *Manuscript, 1915?*)

Pianissimo, a collection of poems unified by a distinctive similarity in tone and inspiration, is linked to the historical socio-political and literary moment in which it was conceived and developed. In *Pianissimo* autobiographical elements, vaguely disguised behind a poetic *persona*, and a polemical denial of traditional uses of poetry combine to reveal a reflection of the condition of the poet and his craft in Italian literature at the turn of the century.

The first part of *Pianissimo* was composed between 1911 and the winter of 1912 while the poet suffered quietly the imminent death of his father, to whom the entire work was dedicated. The second part was composed before May 1913. It was first published by *La Voce* of Florence in 1914.

Most of the poems of *Pianissimo* had already appeared in various journals of the time, such as *La Voce*, the major literary publication of the early decades of the century, *Il quartiere latino*, the biweekly founded by Ugo Tommei and Arcangelo Distaso, and *La Riviera Ligure*. *La Riviera Ligure* was owned and controlled by the Sasso/Novaro families, early entrepreneurs of Italian capitalism who successfully mixed business with literary aspirations. Other poems were unpublished and a few appeared composed exclusively for the collection.[1]

As in the case of *Resine*, *Pianissimo* too owes its publication to the interest and intervention of Sbarbaro's friends, particulary the poet Angelo Barile. In a letter to Giuseppe Prezzolini (the founder of *La Voce* and one of the editors of its companion publishing house in Florence) Barile described the

[1] The original publication of each poem is indicated, where applicable, in the comment. For a history of Italian publishing in the early decades of the century see: *La cultura italiana attraveso le riviste del novecento*, Einaudi, Turin, 1961. For the *Riviera Ligure* also A. Hermet in *La ventura delle riviste (1903–1940)*, Vallecchi, Florence, 1941, Giovanni Cattanei, *La Liguria e la poesia italiana del novecento*, Silva, Milan, 1966, and *La Riviera Ligure*, a cura di E. Villa and P. Boero, Canova, Treviso, 1975.

poet as one who because of his character and temperament would probably never publish, even if a good publisher could be found to accept the work of an unknown. Barile said that the collection included 32 poems (the final volume contained 29) "that have a compact inspirational and expressive unity," a poetry of "subdued and heart-felt interiority" so very appropriate to the literary life of their times.[2]

Sbarbaro's own recollections of how *Pianissimo* came to be published appear in *Fuochi Fatui* and in *Scampoli* (*Remnants*), (translated here for the reader's convenience). In the 1930's Sbarbaro was asked to reissue long out of print *Pianissimo*. But the poet refused thinking that he wanted to revise the entire work. A first revision of eight poems did in fact appear in the journal *Poesia* in July 1946[3] but it wasn't until 1954 that Neri Pozza of Vicenza published a revised, abridged version of the work together with the original 1914 edition.

In 1960 Vanni Scheiwiller issued another version, reflecting additional cuts; the 1914 edition was again retained. For some time critics studied the new versions trying to make some sense of the variants offered in each draft. The consensus was that in each omission and change Sbarbaro seemed to be attempting to conform the original text to the more recent poetic sensibilities of the hermetic school.[4] The only text recognized today is, nonetheless, the 1914 one, restored to the original intentions of the poet. A new edition of that text has just been published by Il Saggiatore of Milan, edited by Lorenzo Polato.

This brief history of the editorial fortunes of *Pianissimo*

---

[2] Barile's letter was published by Domenico Astengo in *I libretti di mal'aria*, May 20, 1977, but had already appeared in *Il tempo della Voce*, Longanesi-Vallecchi, Milan-Florence, 1960, p. 581.

[3] *Poesia*, July 1946, pp. 42–48.

[4] Analyses of the variants in Sbarbaro's poetry are: Giorgio Bàrberi Squarotti, "Sbarbaro 1914–1954" in *Itinerari*, Nos. 11–12, December 1954, then in *Astrazione e realtà*, Rusconi e Paolazzi, Milan, 1960; Aldo Camerino, "La poesia di Sbarbaro nelle versioni di *Pianissimo*," in *Il Gazzettino*, May 20, 1955.

cannot be complete without an examination of the history and development of Italian literature in the twentieth century.

By the early 1950's Sbarbaro was in effect totally forgotten, but the Neri Pozza edition of 1954 served to bring to the attention of critics and readers a writer whose work, despite the acceptance of his contemporaries and the sympathies of the hermetic critics who followed, had never received the attention it deserved. This discovery coincided with a widespread interest in finding the roots and the origins of Italian poetry in this century.

Today *Pianissimo* has found its place among the major poetic works of the early twentieth century, is regarded as one of the fundamental models of much of the earlier poetry of Eugenio Montale (*Gli ossi di seppia*) and has been acclaimed the most representative work of poetry to give the literature of the so-called *vociani* a more coherent and artistic form.

Yet Sbarbaro was not a *vociano*, though the label has often been applied to him almost antonomastically. With Piero Jahier he was considered the only poet of that literary movement of the early *Novecento* to survive the inexorable test of time. He had captured the full energies and ideals of that movement, its ethical, psychological tendencies, its preference for autobiographical themes, its moralism, in a similar fragmentary style that freed those qualities of all that was excessive and superfluous in a language that frustrated any avantgarde extremism.

Perhaps no one expressed this thesis more concisely and clearly than Gianni Pozzi in his *La poesia italiana del Novecento da Gozzano agli ermetici*.

> The importance of Sbarbaro's poetry rests in his having submitted, without any linguistic violence and avantgarde extremism the traditional syntax of poetic language to the urgency of self-confession, and its new moral exigencies; in his having expressed a poetic interiority that was in the air, by utilizing those modes of expression that, before the twentieth century crisis (Boine, Rebora) had seemed adaptable only to descriptive and narrative forms.[5]

---

[5] Einaudi, Turin, 1970, p. 84.

Pianissimo was thus regarded as the first formal, successful attempt of the literature of the century to formulate a poetry that expressed the most intimate sentiments of the soul without resorting to the more typical dramatic and harsh linguistic expressions of Giovanni Boine or Clemente Rebora, nor the expressionistic playfulness of Ardengo Soffici, nor the lyrical but ephemeral and visionary verses of Dino Campana.

As Pier Vincenzo Mengaldo has more recently demonstrated, associating Sbarbaro with *La Voce*

> does not hold especially on stylistic grounds, because in *Pianissimo* moralistic torment, unlike that of the most authentic *vociani*, is expressed without the exhibition of any linguistic violence, at the most it contains a sort of silent and suffocated violence that is entrusted to the articulation overtly prosastic and antimelodic of the verse, derived principally, as Cecchi had already noted, from the barest hendecasyllable verses of Leopardi . . . . So that *Pianissimo* turned out to be, along with the youthful verses of the similar, but more lively Saba, the first true example in Italy of a poetry capable of wringing the neck of the traditional rhetoric, without giving any appearance of wishing to do that: in other words the prosaism and the subdued tone of monologue are no longer an ironic echo, rather are presented as their own necessary and natural voice.[6]

Pianissimo is the story of alienation and the loss of a sense of personal identity on the part of the poetic persona, recounted aginst the backdrop of a mute and totally depersonalized city. The twenty-nine short poems, made up mostly of unrhymed hendecasyllables, the most widely used verse of Italian prosody, are divided into two distinct moments.

The first part shows the development of the poetic persona and is haunted by the imminent, inevitable death of the father. The memory of childhood is important yet memory is never nostalgia. Autobiographical themes and the construction of an ideal character combine to delineate the dimensions of a human tragedy, a sorrow without comfort or hope.

The second part of *Pianissimo* is dominated by the total abandon of the *persona* to the evils of the impersonal city. The

---

[6] *I poeti italiani del novecento, op. cit.*, p. 318.

character, now become a *flâneur*, a modern wanderer without aim or direction, has only one alternative: to follow the goddess perdition wherever she may lead.

This central theme of alienation and separation is in complete contrast to accepted socio-political, even religious ideas, and to the usual comforts of poetry. For *Pianissimo* is radically anti-rhetorical, rejects the various rhetorical solutions sung by decadent poets such as D'Annunzio and Pascoli, to turn instead to Leopardi and, through him to a type of nineteenth century literature of protest, but one emptied of anger, scorn and passion so as to approach a sort of detachment.

Pianissimo has most commonly been understood as a work of poetry that depicts the utter desolation and aridity of the soul and its petrification, a nihilistic concept of the world. It has also been seen as a vain and grotesque polemic against a world toward which the poet feels no affinity, a world dominated by necessity and lust, one in which virtue is impotent against the indifference of nature.

But seen more closely, especially in its historical background, and against the development of European literature, *Pianissimo* reveals that behind the human experience of failure, whether real or feigned, there is a poetry that we sense as both authentic and, in its own way, noble.

The prosaic and antimelodic tone of *Pianissimo* tends to obscure the literary, and occasionally erudite, substratum of its poems. The contemporary critics of Sbarbaro spoke immediately of Leopardi as the nearest inspiration of many of the themes and the poetic solutions discovered and developed by the Ligurian poet. Giovanni Boine, Emilio Cecchi, Pietro Pancrazi, and most of the hermetic critics that followed them identified in Leopardi an ideological, lyrical model of a timeless kind of poetry that stands outside of history; a poetry so personal and yet so anti-rhetorical as to resist critical intervention, even as it will be in Boine's words "remembered for millennia."[7]

---

[7] In "Plausi e Botte," in *La Riviera Ligure*, no. 34, October 1914, then in

The critics that followed them have confirmed this very telling ascendancy, even when, as Pier Vincenzo Mengaldo has done, they have tried to detail it to the least typical Leopardi of the "Rimembranze," "Aspasia," "La sera del dì di festa," etc. But Sbarbaro's culture was also heavily made up of nineteenth century French literature, and more recently critics have identified a substantial number of allusions to poets such as Charles Baudelaire, Arthur Rimbaud, Paul Verlaine, and Stéphane Mallarmé.

Sbarbaro was a very astute reader and translator of numerous other French novelists and prose writers, and his own style reflects many of the tendencies of the now nearly forgotten Jules Renard. Sergio Solmi first mentioned Renard in his 1949 review of Mondadori's definitive edition of *Trucioli* which had appeared the year before.[8] Renard's unsentimental narrative style eschews any causal-temporal architecture, to reveal a world of phenomenology in which things are just as they are, where bleakness and desolation are never ameliorated by the intervention of style, and are never sugar-coated in order to play up to middle class inappropriate sensibilities and phobias. It is very much the direction and the aim of Sbarbaro's style both in *Pianissimo* and *Trucioli*, the *poémes en prose* with which the poet seeks to continue his notations on the world in which he lives, as a distant but sensitive observer.

Like Renard and some of the writers of the *Mercure de France*, Sbarbaro works against both European romanticism and decadentism, as well as against Zola's type of naturalism. For him, in Italy, that means to oppose the style of D'Annunzio as well as the tradition of the *veristi* to come closer to the sensibilities of Federico Tozzi and Mario Puccini.[9] In so doing

---

Frantumi seguito da "Plausi e Botte," La Voce, Florence, 1918, 1921, now in *Il peccato e altre opere*, Guanda, Parma, 1971.

[8] Sergio Solmi, "I *Trucioli* di Sbarbaro," in *La Rassegna d'Italia*, March 1949, then in *Scrittori negli anni*, Il Saggiatore, Milan, 1963, and now reprinted by Garzanti, Milan, 1976.

[9] Federico Tozzi (1883–1920), best known for his novels *Con gli occhi chiusi* (With Eyes Closed), *Tre croci* (Three Crosses), *Il podere* (The Farm), *Bestie* (Animals), and *Gli egoisti* (The Egotists), shares with *(continued, page 62)*

he also abandons the artistic prescriptions of the *crepuscolari* and the futurists.

Sbarbaro's literary models indicate a preference for a literature of anti-establishment protest, of which the model of Leopardi is already a clear clue. Yet all of Sbarbaro's models are filtered through a process that tends to reduce their voices to the very essence of their tone. His is neither an echo nor the parody of his *auteurs*, but a whole new solution to the treatment of similar artistic aims. Of Baudelaire Sbarbaro retains the "extreme discretion" with which he captures something extreme, precisely as Walter Benjamin says of the French master.[10] Of Rimbaud he captures what Malcolm Cowley has identified as the ultimate lesson of the French *maudit*, child poet, that

> art is separate from life; the artist is independent of the world and superior to the lifelings.[11]

In trying to match Rimbaud's *dédoublement du moi*, Sbarbaro wishes to embrace the duality of the artist condemned to follow the inevitable course of his discovery. Sbarbaro himself was not a *maudit*, no one in Italy really was, not even Dino Campana. Rather he seeks to capture the very personal sense of impending alienation that was to become modern man's most acute and desperate *malaise*.

From the Italian *crepuscolari*, *Pianissimo* retains a loose narrative style, but one in which both plot and character are reduced to their barest hint. The character becomes the mere

---

(continued from page 61) Sbarbaro a nonrhetorical literary language and an unsentimental view of life, now considered important elements of the literature of the early Novecento in Italy. His *Opere* were published by Vallecchi of Florence (1961–1970). To my knowledge only *Three Crosses* has been translated into English, Moffat Yard, New York, 1921.

Mario Puccini (1887–1957), like Tozzi, brought to his writing the difficult experiences of his childhood. As a contributor to *La Voce* he also shared a new sense of artistic prose antithetical to the aestheticism of D'Annunzio.

[10] Walter Benjamin, "On Some Motifs in Baudelaire," in *Illuminations*, edited and with an introduction by Hannah Arendt, translated by Harry Zohn, Harcourt, Brace & World, New York, 1968, but originally published by Suhrkamp Verlag of Frankfurt in 1955.

[11] Malcolm Cowley, "The Death of Dada" in *Exile's Return, A Literary Odyssey of the 1920's*, Penguin Books, New York, 1969, p. 144.

persona whose inevitable tendency to reification is interrupted only by the occasional illusion of the double, to be resolved in an act of total resignation and indifference.

Nearly all of these elements are contained in the opening poem of *Pianissimo,* which thus functions as a preamble: the weariness of the soul, its resignation, its total separation from the body, and a world made up of things that are merely what they are, irrelevant unrelated phenomena of a completely depersonalized universe in which events no longer touch us, one in which the "siren of the world" has lost its voice.

The preamble represents an interior monologue, the soliloquy of the soul which is a literary *topos* of western poetry from Petrarch to D'Annunzio. With it Sbarbaro establishes the confessional tone of the entire collection. Petrarch's "Mira quel colle o stanco mio cor vago,"[12] the D'Annunzian plot of the soul amidst the tedium of life and fear of death in the "Esortazione" of the *Poema Paradisiaco*[13] or "Meriggio," the poem from *Alcyone* in which we read:

> Non suona
> voce, se ascolto

and, further down:

> Perduta é ogni traccia
> dell'uomo. Voce non suona,
> se ascolto. Ogni duolo
> umano m'abbandona,
> non ho più nome.[14]

remind us that the tradition of meditation and interior reflection is clearly observed in the *incipit* of the preamble of *Pianissimo*.

In Sbarbaro, however the soliloquy acquires no self-gratification and no self-satisfaction; the *topos* is emptied of all that can be seen as self-pleasing and delectable as the poet operates instead a kind of *reductio ad essentiam* that leaves

---

[12] Francesco Petrarca, *Canzoniere*, Sonnet CCXLII, Einaudi, Turin, 1972, p. 306.

[13] In *Tutte le opere*, edited by Egidio Bianchetti, *op. cit.*, p. 617

[14] *Ibidem*, p. 742

behind no pretensions and no declamations in order to create a situation of purely mental dimensions harnessed within a very personal and heart-felt meditation.

A similar process of simplification characterizes the urban setting of *Pianissimo*. The theme of the infernal city, already announced in "Organetto," expressed the very personal way in which the poet treats a phenomenon that others had already viewed with personal interest and only in order to exploit it. From Engels' *The Condition of the Working Class in England*, which is also an analysis of the condition of life of the masses in the capital city of London, Eugène Sue's *Les Mystères de Paris*, and its Italian counterpart by Francesco Mastriani *I misteri di Napoli*, to the way the city was viewed by *crepuscolari* and futurists, it is clear that Sbarbaro's analysis aims at totally different results. With a process of urbanization that was surpassing all previous historical precedents, the crowd, the masses, throngs of people along impersonal and silent sidewalks had become more than another subject of the writer's and the intellectual's attention.

Walter Benjamin in his essay "On Some Motifs in Baudelaire" observes:

> The crowd—no subject was more entitled to the attention of the nineteenth-century writers. It was getting ready to take shape as a public in broad strata who had acquired facility in reading. It became a customer; it wished to find itself portrayed in the contemporary novel, as patrons did in the paintings of the Middle Ages. The most successful author of the century met this demand out of inner necessity. To him crowd meant—almost in the ancient sense—the crowd of the clients, the public. Victor Hugo was the first to address the crowd in his titles: *Les Misérables*, *Les Travailleurs de la mer*. In France Hugo was the only writer able to compete with the serial novel. As is generally known, Eugène Sue was the master of this genre, which began to be the source of revelation for the man in the street. In 1850 an overwhelming majority elected him to Parliament as representative of the city of Paris. It is no accident that the young Marx chose Sue's *Les Mystères de Paris* for an attack. He early recognized it as his task to forge the amorphous mass, which was then being wooed by an aesthetic socialism, into the iron of the proletariat.[15]

---

[15] *Op. cit.*, p. 168.

According to Benjamin, Baudelaire's interest in the masses and the crowds of the metropolis is anything but exploitive. Exploiting the masses is

> external to him; indeed, it is easy to trace in his works his defensive reaction to their attraction and allure.[16]

Similarly, Sbarbaro's city, its masses and crowds that shove us but do not know us, is never protrayed with any complacent gratification. In speaking of Baudelaire's masses Walter Benjamin, without changing a word, could be describing those of Sbarbaro's in *Pianissimo*.

> The masses had become so much a part of Baudelaire that it is rare to find a description of them in his works. His most important subjects are hardly ever encountered in descriptive forms. As Dujardin so aptly put it, he was 'more concerned with implanting the image in the memory that with adorning and elaborating it.' It is futile to search in *Les Fleurs du mal* or in *Spleen de Paris* for any counterpart to the portrayals of the city which Victor Hugo did with such mastery. Baudelaire describes neither the Parisians nor the city. Forgoing such description enables him to invoke the ones in the form of the other. His crowd is always the crowd of a big city, his Paris is invariably overpopulated. It is this that makes him so superior to Barbier, whose descriptive method caused a rift between the masses and the city. In *Tableaux Parisiens* the secret presence of a crowd is demonstrable almost everywhere. When Baudelaire takes the dawn as his theme, the deserted streets emanate something of that 'silence of a throng' which Hugo senses in nocturnal Paris . . . The mass was the agitated veil; through it Baudelaire saw Paris. The presence of the mass determines one of the most famous components of *Les Fleurs du mal*.[17]

Sbarbaro's mute and desolate city, like Baudelaire's *fourmillant cité*, where the irritating *foules* can only reaffirm man's inescapable loneliness, is the result of modern life. But while Baudelaire's city is characterized by boredom or ennui,[18]

---

[16] *Ibidem*, p. 169.

[17] *Ibidem*, pp. 169–170.

[18] Georges Bataille, "Baudelaire," in *Literature and Evil*, translated by Alastair Hamilton, Urizen Books, 1981, reprint of Calder & Boyars Ltd., 1973, pp. 19–44. So also Northrop Frye in *T.S. Eliot, An Introduction*, University of Chicago Press, Chicago, 1963, 1981, p. 51.

Sbarbaro's is the way it is for no clearly defined physical or metaphysical reason. Like the world of Renard's novels and short stories, Sbarbaro's world is such that the poet refuses to offer his own cerebral interpretation or to impose his own solutions. The poet's task is, instead, to tell of the phenomena that make up that universe.

In *Pianissimo*, by refusing all accepted ideas, the historical, socio-cultural, and even religious comforts normally available to man, Sbarbaro in essence walls himself in, precisely as he describes in the first composition of *Trucioli* in which he characterizes the persona as a vine so accustomed to the less than ideal pavement of the alley that if transplanted might die altogether. Thus *Pianissimo* offers no manifesto, no explicit political ideas; on the contrary, its aim is to separate poetry from rhetoric, morality, philosophy, psychology, and from the patriotic songs that Italian poets from Petrarch to the more recent Leopardi, Carducci and D'Annunzio had always sung.

Pianissimo seeks to confirm that poetry is the exclusive product of imagination and fantasy, but not of the romantic imagination with its instinctive force that makes havoc of nature. On the contrary, the poet's imagination must put nature in order and offer one harmonious intellectual perception of the universe. Baudelaire had wished to be the decypherer and translator of those universal analogies, to capture for us the *correspondances* of nature; Sbarbaro likewise seeks to divest nature of all conventional and romantic ideas to reveal a very simple even childish emotion that focuses instead on the liberating powers of the environment.

From that nature, so naked, so divested of any outside will or reason, come the instincts of the persona, the only force moving toward man's inevitable perdition. Here is how Georges Bataille explains this same process in Baudelaire:

> Evil, which the poet does not so much perpetrate as he experiences its fascination, is indeed Evil since the will, which can only desire Good, has no part in it. Besides it hardly matters whether it is Evil. If the contrary of will is fascination, if fascination is the destruction of the will, to condemn behavior regulated by fascination on moral grounds may be the only way of really liberating it from the will. Religion, castes, and, more recently, romanticism, had been a

means of seduction. But these very means of seduction began to use trickery, and obtained the approval of a will which was also prepared to use trickery. Poetry, therefore, which hoped to seduce the senses, had to limit its objects of seduction to those regulated by the will (conscious will which insists on such conditions as survival and satisfaction). Ancient poetry limited the liberty implicated in poetry. In the turgid mass of these waters Baudelaire opened a trough of cursed poetry which no longer assumed anything and which submitted itself to a fascination incapable of giving satisfaction, a fascination which was purely destructive. Thus poetry turned away from extrinsic requirements, from the requirements of the will in order to satisfy one single intimate requirement which connected it with that which fascinated, which made it the opposite of will.[19]

Like Baudelaire's, Sbarbaro's denuncation of will is quite explicit:

non voglio non desidero, neppure
penso.

("I want not, desire nothing, neither/do I think.") Except that he wishes for every experience of the day to weigh on him and for sorrow to seize him boldly in order to place him in the very center of life, so that he can experience all perversions and walk through the world held by the hand of the goddess perdition. Not even the image of his father, symbol of personal dignity and sacrifice, can distract the poet from his total negation of human values if his wish is to have as sad an end as his father. For all virtue is useless against the indifference of life, a realization that confirms that man's fate is one of solitude and separation.

In the infernal city where the musty odor of dark undergrounds overcomes the "smell of grass in the sun," and where "myriads of beings sealed in themselves like tombs" brush against us without ever knowing us, only the wish to shed one's own name can still seize us. Of all things man has cared about, not the smallest remembrance will remain. The only fitting wish is then to be inert like "a very ancient ruin" that

---

[19] Georges Bataille, *op. cit.*, p. 41.

sees the hours follow one another and men change their direction the way the skies at dawn take color and lose it again by night.

It is not man's unwillingness to act upon his own history that is represented, but modern man's incapacity to do so without denying much that civilization refuses to recognize as insignificant, or refuses to place in its correct perspective.

Sbarbaro's Introduction to the 1954 Neri Pozza Edition of *Pianissimo*

My first cry as a poet must have taken place in the house in Savona to which we had just moved: it was a poem published in an issue of *Illustrazione Popolare*, one which my father transcribed in his own hand, my father who, while denying I could possibly be the author, by doing so betrayed his hope that it may be true. The name that figured under the poem was that of Gabriele D'Annunzio. With the implied merit, so blatantly excessive of that attribution, began my literary career. Poor dad.

My first collection of verses (which a very optimistic editor reprinted a few years ago in a number of copies which, though limited, still seems disproportionate to the nationwide demand) came to maturity in the first two years of high school. More than writing them, I mulled them over in my mind during the long solitary walks that as a boy I used to take. To each composition I ascribed great importance, until a new one took its place in my esteem. The last one was always the best; it always left me shaken and certain that I would never write anything quite so good as that. On account of these verses I became popular among my fellow students, and it was they who had the slim book printed at their expense and even gave

Il mio vagito di poeta deve ancora trovarsi in qualche casa a Savona, dove finì in occasione d'un trasloco: una poesia inserita a titolo antologico in un'annata dell "Illustrazione popolare", dove di sua mano la trascrisse mio padre, il quale, mentre negava potessi esserne io l'autore, tradiva così la sua speranza che lo fossi. Il nome che vi figurava sotto era quello di D'Annunzio. Con la lode palesemente eccessiva implicita in quella attribuzione s'iniziava la mia carriera letteraria. Povero babbo.

I primi versi (che un editore ottimista ristampò anni fa in un numero di copie, per quanto esiguo, sproporzionato al fabbisogno nazionale) li maturai nei primi due anni di liceo. Non li scrivevo, li ruminavo nelle lunghe passeggiate solitarie che da ragazzo avevo l'abitudine di fare. A ogni componimento annettevo grande importanza, finché uno nuovo non lo soppiantava nella mia stima. L'ultimo era sempre il definitivo; mi lasciava spossato e con la certezza di non poter più far nulla che gli stesse a paro. Per quei versi venni in fama tra i condiscepoli e furono essi a stampare di loro tasca il libretto e a imporgli il

it a title: *Resine* (*Resin*). My title was more modest: *Bolle di sapone* (*Soap Bubbles*),[1] with which I meant to indicate the casualness and the inconsistency of those verses. Its appearance excited me when, walking down the Corso, I saw my name so prominently in the window of the major bookstore; a review by Angelo Barile appeared in installments in the local paper, *Letimbro*, while the small sum of 16 lire was an impetuous warning that the returns of my literary activities would always be modest.

To that minor outburst (when *Resine* came out in 1911 those poems were already a few years old) followed a period of drought, one from which I did not suffer; in fact I hardly felt it. The adventure, quite excusable after all at the age of 18—I said to myself—is over. The booklet soon became quite foreign to me, like a fallen leaf to the tree. This must be that vacation I always promised myself after the birth of each poem, I repeated to myself.

After a few years of this drought, one night while lying glutted in bed, "stretched out as in a coffin," this realization came spontaneously to my lips:

> Be silent, my soul, weary as you are
> of pleasure and suffering . . .

I was taking conscience of myself; my second book of verses was about to be born: I uttered silently to myself a sort of disconsolate confession in which, along with the surfacing of turbid instincts and sexual nausea, I lived the anticipated mourning for the death of my father, a death seen now as inevitable and near.

Something I sent to *La Voce*—The Florentine periodical that one awaited like a lover—pleased Soffici and I received a warm letter from Prezzolini, and a little later in 1914 they published my little book.

Sottovoce (*Whispering*) (that was my title; Soffici proposed

---

[1] Sbarbaro will eventually publish a book entitled *Bolle di sapone* in 1966 (see bibliography).

titolo: Résine (il mio era più modesto: "bolle di sapone" e dei versi voleva denunciare la casualità e l'inconsistenza.) La sua uscita mi procurò l'ebrezza, passando per il Corso, di sbirciare il mio nome bene in vista nella vetrina del maggior libraio; una recensione di Angelo Barile comparsa a puntate sul locale "Letimbro", e un ricavo di lire sedici, tempestivo avvertimento che i miei proventi letterari sarebbero sempre stati modesti. A quello sgorgo (nell'undici, quando uscì, Resine aveva già qualche anno) seguì un periodo di siccità, una siccità di cui non soffrii, anzi neanche avvertivo: l'avventura, scusabile mi dicevo a diciott'anni, era chiusa; il libretto, diventato a me estraneo come all'albero la foglia caduta; giunta la definitiva vacanza che, a ogni parto, m'ero invano promessa.

Da alcuni anni durava la tregua, quando una notte che coi sensi sazi giacevo a letto "lungo disteso come in una bara", mi venne da sé alle labbra la constatazione: Taci, anima stanca di godere e di soffrire . . . Prendevo coscienza di me; nasceva il mio secondo libretto di versi: una specie di sconsolata confessione fatta a fior di labbro a me stesso, dove sull'affiorare di torbidi istinti e di nausee sessuali dominava il lutto, patito in anticipo, per la morte che vedevo prossima di mio padre. Qualcosa che mandai alla "Voce"—il periodico fiorentino che si attendeva a quel tempo come un'amante—piacque a Soffici e ebbi una calda lettera di Prezzolini che poco dopo, nel quattordici pubblicò il libretto.

Sottovoce (era il mio titolo; Soffici proponeva "Grisaglie":

instead *Grisaglie*:[2] an unusual word he would have introduced personally, he told me) stirred the curiosity of Papini[3] who was reading the proofs and criticized it miserably to my face, line by line, in a little café in Piazza San Marco. My total lack of reaction, the readiness with which I accepted his choice of title *Pianissimo* (the idea came to him during a concert by Giannotto Bastianelli,[4] and he rushed to convey it to me), but above all the total lack of interest I showed for the typographical layout (in contrast to the gloom of the content he had wanted a pink cover) astonished him, and he told me so.

It wasn't all indifference; it was also distance, aided by the tiny manuscript I had in my pocket. When later Papini read it, (we were in the printing shop of *Lacerba*[5]), he handed those few sheets of paper to the printer. That's how I landed on my *terra firma*, prose.

This book, which I never thought would be reprinted, has come to light again because of the interest of Aldo Came-

---

[2] *Grisaglie*, plural form of *grisaglia*=wool pattern made up of black and white dots which thus create a gray pattern. From the French *grisaille* which derives from the adjective *gris*=gray.

[3] Giovanni Papini (1881–1956), Florentine poet, novelist, essayist and editor (*Leonardo—Regno—La Voce—Lacerba*), his many talents pushed him to want to try everything. Intellectually he may represent the worst elements of his generation. *Un uomo finito* (*The Failure*, 1912) was his most important book, an autobiographical document in which failure is attributed to the desire to try to accomplish too much, while avoiding any intellectual responsibility for his own errors in judgement.

[4] Giannotto Bastianelli (1883–1927), musician and critic, contributed also to *La Voce*.

[5] *Lacerba*, literary and political review founded by Giovanni Papini and Ardengo Soffici in 1913 upon their leaving *La Voce*. Soon the journal took on very clearly defined futurist orientation. It ceased publication in 1915. Sbarbaro contributed mostly *trucioli*:

1913: June 15, no. 12 "Torbidità"
1914: February 15, no. 4 "La seconda vita di Teodoro B."
May 15, no. 10 "La vite," "Caffé"
June 1, no. 11 "La croce"
August 1, no. 15 "Appelli," "Il fantoccio"
1915: January 31, no. 5 "Capstan"
April 17, no. 16 "Libertinaggio," "La ballerina"

avrebbe introdotto lui la parola, mi disse) incuriosì Papini che lo lesse in bozze e a quattr'occhi me lo stroncò verso per verso in un caffeuccio di piazza San Marco. La mancanza in me di reazione, la prontezza con cui accettai il titolo *Pianissimo* da lui suggerito (gliene venne l'idea durante un concerto di Giannotto Bastianelli e si affrettò a comunicarmelo), ma sopratutto il nessun interesse che mostravo per la veste tipografica (per contrasto con la tetraggine del contenuto lui voleva una copertina rosa) lo stupirono e me lo disse. Non era tutta indifferenza; era anche distacco e s'alimentava di due o tre foglietti manoscritti che avevo in tasca. Quando più tardi Papini li lesse (si era nella tipografia di "Lacerba") li passò al proto. Ero così approdato alla mia terraferma, la prosa.

Questo libretto che non credevo di ristampare rivede la luce per iniziativa di Aldo Camerino. Sono passati da quando

rino.[6] Forty years have passed since it first appeared. And yet something in me must still feel close to these verses, for I have gone over them many many times hoping to free them of all that is superfluous and to substitute for approximations precisely what I wanted to say, and which my inexperience had prevented me from saying.

Pianissimo is my voice from when I was alive; since then—that is to say since I learned to appease myself with the color of the sky—it is a voice that stings me every time I hear it.

---

[6] Aldo Camerino, critic and editor. See "Lettere inedite di Carlo Emilio Gadda e di Camillo Sbarbaro ad Aldo Camerino", with a note by Maria Corti, in *Strumenti critici*, no. 27, 1975.

uscì quarant'anni. Eppure a questi versi deve ancora rispondere in me qualcosa se a tante riprese vi tornai sopra, col desiderio di liberarli del troppo e nella speranza di sostituire all'approssimativa l'espressione precisa di ciò che volevo e l'inesperienza m'aveva impedito di dire.

Pianissimo è la mia voce di quando ero vivo; da allora—e cioè da quando imparai a appagarmi d'un colore del cielo—una voce che mi scotta ognivolta che la riodo. (Premessa alla ristampa, '54.)

I

1

Be silent, my soul, weary as you are
of pleasure and suffering—from one
to the other you move resigned.
No voice of yours I hear if I listen:
not of regret for my miserable childhood,
nor of anger or hope
and not even of tedium.
                                        You lie
with the body, silent,
full of a desperate resignation.

We should not be surprised,
my soul, if the heart
should stop, if all breathing
stopped . . .
                        Instead we walk,
we walk, you and I, like somnambulists.
And the trees are trees, houses
mere houses, the women
passing by just women, and all is what
it is, only what it is.

The vicissitudes of joy and pain
do not touch us. The siren of the world
has lost its voice, and the world is a great
desert.
            In this desert
with dry eyes I stare at myself.

I

–1–

Taci, anima stanca di godere
e di soffrite (all'uno e all'altro vai
rassegnata).
Nessuna voce tua odo se ascolto:
non di rimpianto per la miserabile
giovinezza, non d'ira o di speranza,
e neppure di tedio.
                Giaci come
il corpo, ammutolita, tutta piena
d'una rassegnazione disperata.

Non ci stupiremmo,
non è vero, mia anima, se il cuore
si fermasse, sospeso se ci fosse
il fiato . . .
        Invece camminiamo,
camminiamo io e te come sonnambuli.
E gli alberi son alberi, le case
sono case, le donne
che passano son donne, e tutto è quello
che è, soltanto quel che è.
La vicenda di gioia e di dolore
non ci tocca. Perduto ha la voce
la sirena del mondo, e il mondo è un grande
deserto.
      Nel deserto
io guardo con asciutti occhi me stesso.

This poem, which functions as a preamble to the entire collection, appeared originally in *La Riviera Ligura* in March 1913 with the title of "Pausa" ("Pause"). The internal monologue, marked by the very distinct call to silence and meditation, represents the soliloquy of the soul to which the poetic *persona* is contrasted in an unusual doubling effect. This immediate and emphatic contrast recalls a similar stylistic device in Charles Baudelaire's poem "Le Goût du Neant" in *Les Fleurs du Mal*.

Résigne-toi, mon coeur; dors ton sommeil de brute.
Esprit vaincu, fourbu! Pour toi, vieux maraudeur,
L'amour n'a plus de goût, non plus que la dispute;
Adieu donc, chants de cuivre et soupirs de la Flûte!
Plaisirs, ne tentez plus un couer sombre et bourdeur!

Le printemps adorable a perdu son odeur![1]

The theme of resignation and sleep replaces the sense of pleasure no longer conceivable, and thus denotes the end of music, which Sbarbaro takes up with the siren of the world, changing the last verse, to match D'Annunzio's verse in *Maia*: "O diversità, sirena / del mondo, io son colui che t'ama." But the entire stanza is worth reviewing here. Sbarbaro's verses are in total contrast to the D'Annunzian *Laus Vitae*, a hymn to life, that "terrible gift of god," viewed by the decadent poet with passionate involvement. From the preamble the Ligurian poet wishes to make it very clear that his cry is of a different imprint. Here is the first stanza to D'Annunzio's composition to the siren of the world:

Nessuna cosa
mi fu aliena;
nessuna mi sarà
mai, mentre comprendo.
Laudata sii, Diversità
delle creature, sirena
del mondo! Talor non elessi

[1] "Le Goût du Néant" in *Les Fleurs du Mal et Autres Poèmes*, Garnier-Flammarion, Paris, 1964, p. 97, vv. 5–10. All other quotations from Baudelaire will be from this edition unless otherwise indicated.

perché parvemi che eleggendo
io t'escludessi,
o Diversità, meraviglia
sempieterna, e che la rosa
bianca e la vermiglia
fosser dovute entrambe
alla mia brama,
e tutte le pasture
co' lor sapori,
tutte le cose pure e impure
ai miei amori;
però ch'io son colui che t'ama,
o Diversità, sirena
del mondo, io son colui che t'ama.[2]

Sbarbaro's poem is made up of 26 verses, mostly hendecasyllables. Rather than actual divisions in stanzas, the poem relies on frequent pauses (hence its title "Pausa" is justified stylistically as well as thematically) and a number of *enjambements* to give it an elasticity, like the opening and closing of an accordion, appropriate perhaps to the disconsolate tone of the entire composition and of *Pianissimo* as a whole.

The siren, of course, recalls the Homeric episode of Ulysses and the song of the sirens. By contradicting and denying the use D'Annunzio makes of the *myth*, Sbarbaro seems to empty that singular image of all its allure and turn it instead into a mere "sign" of the voyage of the tale. The song loses its immediacy and acquires the connotation of narration, of fiction; it changes from *song* to *episode*, from myth to reality.

At a conference held in 1978 on the theme "The Levels of Reality," Italo Calvino drew inspiration precisely from the same Homeric episode to show how in a literary work various levels of reality can intertwine even as they remain distinct and separate. The credibility of such a literary text is based—he said—on what Coleridge defined as "suspension of disbelief," which is the condition of success of any literary invention,

[2] Gabriele D'Annunzio, *Laudi del cielo, del mare, della terra e degli eroi, Libro I, Maia*, Treves, Milan, 1928, pp. 18–19.

even when it is openly situated in the realm of the fantastic and the incredible. The "I," the subject of the phrase: *I who write*, becomes the "I" of a character of a novel, of the "I" of a mythical author, just like Homer.[3]

Calvino distinguishes the Homeric episodes in which Ulysses narrates directly in the first person and those in which the third person is used. The third person narrative acquires a psychological and affective dimension missing in the first person narrative, which contains instead a more primitive, mythological repertory of natural and supernatural events in which common mortals meet face to face supernatural creatures such as monsters, Cyclopes, sirens, enchantresses, men and women changed into beasts, etc. To these two levels must be added the only level that is outside of both narrations: the ideal place of the narration, be it the court on the island of the Phaeacians, or villa in the Florentine frame of Boccaccio's *Decameron*. We may believe or not the internal elements of the narrations but we cannot reject the elements that stand outside of the narration.

This apparent digression has been necessary to demonstrate that to a poet/classicist like Sbarbaro this distinction is quite relevant and significant for it offers us a clear clue to the *fictional* world of *Pianissimo* and to the doubling of the poetic *persona* on which he relies from time to time, and that is crucial to the entire structure of the *opus*.

To further demonstrate the significance of this to the modernist writer, we need only recall Blanchot's essay "The Song of the Sirens: Encountering the Imaginary."[4] For Sbarbaro the silence of the siren is a rejection of literary "gimmicks," the refusal to participate in a work of fiction or lie, it is

---

[3] Convegno Internazionale sul tema "I livelli della realtà" held in Florence on September 11–13, 1978 in which participated scientists and critics as well as writers. The intervention by Calvino from which I have summarized the main ideas appeared in *Il corriere della sera*, September 12, 1978, p. 3.

[4] In *The Gaze of Orpheus*, translated by Lydia Davis, edited with an afterword by P. Adams Sitney, Station Hill Press, 1981, pp. 105–13.

a very dramatic and effective way to impress on the reader the fact that his is a modest and barely audible story, the monotonous narration of a very personal anguish. He can thus dismiss the muse without detracting from the value of his meditation or diminishing his concentration. For this reason critics from Giovanni Boine on have always remarked that in *Pianissimo* we confront a poetry that defies criticism, without ever stopping to speak to us.

2

At times, while I walk alone in the sun
and look at the world with my clear eyes
where all appears so fraternal:
air, light, blade of grass, insect,
a sudden chill touches my heart.

I seem to be like a blind man seated
on the shore of an immense river.
Beneath, the rapid waters whirl past,
but he does not see them: a little sun
he catches blissfully. And if at times
the murmur of the waters reaches him,
he mistakes it for a mere buzzing of the ear.

For I seem, in living this
poor life of mine, to skim another
as if in a dream, and that dream
is my present life.

As if lost I am then overtaken
by a childish fright.
I sit
all alone on the edge of the road
and stare at my miserable mean world
and caress with trembling hand the grass.

This poem too appeared in *La Riviera Ligure*, March 1913, with the title "Paura" ("Fear"). The poem relies on the familiar nineteenth century *topos* of the double to create a sense of impending disaster and the alienation of the *persona*. The dream is what gives the *persona* the sense of a double existence.

The opening adverbial expression "talor" recalls Baudelaire's use of "parfois" in the poem "J'ai vu, parfois, au fond

–2–

Talor, mentre cammino solo al sole
e guardo coi miei occhi chiari il mondo
ove tutto m'appar come fraterno,
l'aria la luce il fil d'erba l'insetto,
un improvviso gelo al cor mi coglie.

Un cieco mi par d'essere, seduto
sopra la sponda d'un immenso fiume.
Scorrono sotto l'acque vorticose,
ma non le vede lui: il poco sole
ei si prende beato. E se gli giunge
talora mormorio d'acque, lo crede
ronzio d'orecchi illusi.

Perché a me par, vivendo questa mia
povera vita, un'altra rasentarne
come nel sonno, e che quel sonno sia
la mia vita presente.

Come uno smarrimento allor mi coglie,
uno sgomento pueril.
                                        Mi seggo
tutto solo sul ciglio della strada,
guardo il misero mio angusto mondo
e carezzo con man che trema l'erba.

d'un théâtre banal . . . ,"[1] while the setting and the posture of the *persona* is clearly reminiscent of Giacomo Leopardi's verses in "Aspasia":

                                        su l'erba

[1] See "L'Irréparable," v. 41, *op. cit.*, p. 80.

qui neghittoso immobile giacendo,
il mar la terra e il ciel miro e sorrido.[2]

and in "La vita solitaria":

Talor m'assido in solitaria parte,
sovra un rialto, al margine d'un lago[3]

Later in *Pianissimo* the image of water and even Leopardi's implied precipice return as central images of the distortions that now characterize the contrasts between city and country.

The expression "occhi chiari" of course, has a definite Petrarchan sound, but the phrase has probably greater affinity to Baudelaire's *Fleurs du Mal*, where, as Walter Benjamin has noted in his well known essay on the father of modern poetry, the eyes have lost their main function in the arid city landscape.

> The greater Baudelaire's insight into this phenomenon, the more unmistakably did the disintegration of the aura make itself felt in his lyrical poetry. This occurs in the form of a symbol which we encounter in the *Fleurs du Mal* almost invariably whenever the look of the human eye is invoked . . . What is involved here is that the expectation roused by the look of the human eye is not fulfilled. Baudelaire describes eyes of which one is inclined to say that they have lost their ability to look. Yet this lends them a charm which to a large, perhaps predominant, extent serves as a means of defraying the cost of his instinctual desires. It was under the spell of these eyes that *sexus* in Baudelaire detached itself from *eros*.[4]

In Sbarbaro the eyes are always the mirror of the *persona*, the mirror of a world totally free of passionate reflections, a mirror of resignation, and later in *Rimanenze* even a mirror in which the "eyes of others dare not look." They see a reality

---

[2] Giacomo Leopardi, "Aspasia" in *Canti*, a cura di Niccolò Galli e Cesare Gàrboli, Einaudi, Torino, 1972, pp. 231–238, vv. 110–112.

[3] *Ibidem.*, pp. 125–131, vv. 23–24.

[4] Walter Benjamin, "On Some Motifs in Baudelaire" in *Illuminations, op. cit.*, p. 191.

that others are not able to see, they serve to fill in the story of each human ghost that walks along the cityscape, they touch gently the blade of grass, and the head of a child with equal tenderness. Like Baudelaire's, Sbarbaro's eyes cannot invent reality, they are not exactly myopic, but they certainly cannot see worlds of fantasy; neither writer would have made it in science fiction. Yet every description they give us has the otherness of a science fiction novel.

Finally the image of the caressing of grass is also Leopardian but here it stands to signify the poet's total abandon and his solidarity with the simplest and most fleeting of elements.

3

I awaken from a light sleep
alone in the heart of the night.
All around
the house is silent as if empty, far away
shine the lights of a silent port.
So cold and removed are those lights
and so great is the silence in the house
that I raise myself on my elbows listening.
A sudden terror suspends my breathing,
my eyes open wide in the night:
my life is separate from the rest of the earth
and I am alone in the world.

Then the memory of the familiar streets,
of the names and the faces of every day
reemerge out of sleep,
and smiling at myself I settle down again.

But though the fear is vanished in sleep
a deep chill persists in my soul.
I walk among men staring
at each one attentively,
curious of them, but as a stranger.
And no one do I have in whose hands
to place mine in complete trust
and with whom to forget myself.

So much so that if waters and trees did not exist
nor all the things of this mute world
which accompany my life on earth,
I think that I would die of solitude.

This walking among strangers,

–3–

Mi desto dal leggero sonno solo
nel cuore della notte.
                                        Tace intorno
la casa come vuota e laggiù brilla
silenzioso coi suoi lumi un porto.
Ma sì freddi e remoti son quei lumi
e sì grande è il silenzio nella casa
che mi levo sui gomiti in ascolto.
Improvviso terrore mi sospende
il fiato e allarga nella notte gli occhi:
separata dal resto della casa
separata dal resto della terra
è la mia vita ed io son solo al mondo.

Poi il ricordo delle vie consuete
e dei nomi e dei volti quotidiani
riemerge dal sonno,
e di me sorridendo mi riadagio.

Ma, svanita col sonno la paura,
un gelo in fondo all'anima mi resta.
Ch'io cammino fra gli uomini guardando
attentamente coi miei occhi ognuno,
curioso di lor ma come estraneo.
Ed alcuno non ho nelle cui mani
metter le mani con fiducia piena
e col quale di me dimenticarmi.

Tal che se l'acque e gli alberi non fossero
e tutto il mondo muto delle cose
che accompagna il mio viver sulla terra,
io penso che morrei di solitudine.

Or questo camminare fra gli estranei

this emptiness all around frightens me
and to think it will be forever.

Yet my eyes remain so cruelly dry.

The images that dominate this still youthful poem are: sleep, the night, an empty house, the lights of a distant port, and the utter separation felt by the poet at a particular moment when sensibilities and awareness are sharpened.

The poet's memories in the drowsiness of the night are of small comfort to him, for they are of faces and names never personalized by a fraternal touch. In *Pianissimo*, memory almost always has the value of a return to infancy and youth, to the closed and sad experience of a household in which the tragedy of the mother's early death and the "senility" of the father determined an existence different and sadder than that of other people. It is worthwhile to remember Cesare Pavese's acute remarks on the role of memory and infancy in twentieth century literature.

> Modern art is a return to infancy. Its perennial motive is the discovery of things, a discovery that can happen, in its purest form, only in the memory of childhood. This is the effect of the pervading consciousness of the modern artist (historicism, notion of art as a self-sufficient activity, individualism) which makes him live from the age of 16 on in a state of tension, that is to say, in a state no longer disposed to assimilation, no longer naive. And in art one expresses well only what was assimilated naively. The artist can do no more than to turn and seek inspiration from that period when he was not yet an artist, and that is infancy.[1]

That is why, reading Lukàcs, Pavese noted:

> Nineteenth century art encounters the development of situations (bildungsroman, historical cycles, careers, etc.); in the twentieth

---

[1] Cesare Pavese, *Il mestiere di vivere*, Einaudi, Torino, 1952, p. 213. The diary is available in English, *The Burning Brand: Diaries 1935–1950*, translated by A. E. Murch, Walker, New York, 1961.

questo vuoto d'intorno m'impaura
e la certezza che sarà per sempre.

Ma restan gli occhi crudelmente asciutti.

> century, art is encountered in the static essence. The hero used to be different at the beginning that at the end of the story; now he is always the same. In the nineteenth century infancy was the preparation of man; in the twentieth infancy is contemplated in itself.[2]

The pivotal importance of Sbarbaro in a delineation of the theme of infancy in the poetry of our century has been recognized by many other poets and critics. Montale's own definition of Sbarbaro "estroso fanciullo" in the poems he dedicated to his co-regional poet in *Gli ossi di seppia,* is already a very explicit clue. More recently the poet Andrea Zanzotto has given us a brilliant and scholarly review of this theme in "Infanzie, poesie, scuoletta" in *Strumenti Critici.*[3] His few observations on Sbarbaro are worthy of further elaboration. Certainly all of *Pianissimo* and *Trucioli* present a poetic *persona* that has all the characteristics of a perennial child for whom adulthood is viewed as a stage of life constantly scorned or rejected, one for which it feels a complete lack of preparation and aptitude.

---

[2] *Ibidem.*, p. 326.
[3] *Strumenti Critici*, 20 February, 1973, pp. 52–77.

4

I am leaving the house of pleasure.
                                                            I start out
along an echoing pavement in the night.
I feel no remorse or agitation,
I am just immensely tranquil.
                                                   And yet
something has changed in me, something
outside of myself.
                                Because the city seems to me
to have become immensely vast and empty,
a city of stone that no one inhabits,
in which Necessity alone
moves the cars and marks the hours.

To these symmetrical and deserted streets,
to these mute houses I am similar.
I share in their indifference,
in their immobility.
                                  I seem
to be deaf and opaque like them,
to be made of stone like them.

Because my father and my sister are
far away, as if dead so many years already,
as if buried in memory.
And the name of a friend some vague name.

Between me and them has come
my sin similar to an immanent boulder.
And even if I did find out that my father is dead,
thinking of whom my heart used to cry
only at the thought of being far away,
now that the days of life together are counted,
if they did tell me that my father is dead,
I sense so well I would not cry now.

—4—

Esco dalla lussuria.
M'incammino
per lastrici sonori nella notte.
Non ho rimorso o turbamento. Sono
solo tranquillo immensamente.
Pure
qualche cosa è cambiato in me, qualcosa
fuori di me.
Chè la città mi pare
sia fatta immensamente vasta e vuota,
una città di pietra che nessuno
abiti, dove la Necessità
sola conduca i carri e suoni l'ore.

A queste vie simmetriche e deserte
a queste case mute sono simile.
Partecipo alla loro indifferenza,
alla loro immobilità.
Mi pare
d'esser sordo ed opaco come loro,
d'esser fatto di pietra come loro.

Chè il mio padre e la mia sorella sono
lontani, come morti da tanti anni,
come sepolti già nella memoria.
Il nome dell'amico è un nome vano.

Tra me ed essi s'è interposto il mio
peccato come immobile macigno.
E se sapessi che il mio padre è morto,
al qual pensando mi piangeva il cuore
di essere lontano ora che i giorni
della vita comune son contati,
se mi dicesser che mio padre è morto,
sento bene che adesso non potrei piangere.

I am as if placed outside of life,
myself a machine that obeys,
like the car and the street, necessary.

But I cannot grieve.

I walk
the echoing pavement in the night.

This poem has led many critics to insist mistakenly on a kind of *saison en enfer* lived by the Ligurian poet, though in a more subdued and provincial fashion than the daring Arthur Rimbaud. However even Carlo Torchio, who has catalogued nearly all the echoes of Rimbaud in Sbarbaro's poetry and prose, has noted that Sbarbaro captures the essence of the French poet without retaining those excesses contrary to his personality and life style.[1]

Torchio identified in "Esco dalla lussuria" a sort of parallel composition to "Mauvais sang." Yet while Rimbaud could sing in his poem:

> Oh! Tous les vices, colère, luxure
> magnifique la luxure.

Sbarbaro's composition was not at all meant as an ode to *luxure*. A visit to a brothel in this city of stone which he has created in his poem, is an empty social convention that in Sbarbaro's moralistic vision can turn us likewise into inanimate rock.

The poem is not at all an attempt to relive the brothel experience but concerns the resulting reflections. It may even be a "fiction," a mere prop in what is a portrayal of the making of an alienated personality. It is significant that in *Pianissimo*

---

[1] "Rimbaud e Sbarbaro" in *Studi Francesi*, no. 40, 1970, pp. 51–52.

[2] Arthur Rimbaud, *Complete Works, Selected Letters*, Translation, Introduction and Notes by Wallace Fowlie, The University of Chicago Press, Chicago, 1966, p. 174.

Son come posto fuori della vita,
una macchina io stesso che obbedisce,
come il carro e la strada necessario.

Ma non riesco a dolermene.

Cammino
per lastrici sonori nella notte.

---

lussuria, pleasure and sexual prowess are never raised to the allegorical and regenerative levels claimed by decadents like D'Annunzio. They remain the expression of what they are, their essence is determined by other factors which remain beyond the individual's control.

"I am leaving the house of pleasure" is instead, a hymn to those modernist goddesses Indifference and Immobility. The house of pleasure may offer a momentary distraction but remains another expression of man's alienation from himself.

In Rimbaud's *Une saison en enfer* we have all the possible *alchimie du verbe,* an art form that as Jean-Pierre Richard writes

> rejects all manifestations of depth, and it is this which marks his real divorce from Baudelaire. His visions display themselves on a shallow screen; filmstrips supremely thin and yet unbreakable for there is nothing behind them, neither volume nor abyss nor being nor nothingness nor god nor the infinite. . .[3]

In Sbarbaro we have instead, the suspension of all drama; there is no denial of god, nor of the abyss, nor of the infinite. Simply the affirmation of indifference and immobility. This cautiousness justifies the accusation originally made by Piero Gobetti and more recently reiterated by Marziano Guglielminetti, that in Sbarbaro, in the end, we have no more and no less than the "cantor of the same old weariness" of life.[4] Yet at

---

[3] Quoted in " 'Trouver une Langue' The anti-paysage of Rimbaud" in *The Poetics of Indeterminacy: Rimbaud to Cage,* by Marjorie Perloff, Princeton University Press, Princeton, 1981, pp. 65–66.

[4] Piero Gobetti in *Ordine Nuovo,* quoted in *(continued, page 96)*

seventy years of distance from the appearance of *Pianissimo* we recognize how much more effective is the quiet imprecation of Sbarbaro's indifference than the aggressive nihilism of Rimbaud.

Another comparison of Sbarbaro's indifference with Montale's later personification of it in *Gli ossi di seppia* reveals another interesting observation. Montale repeats and elaborates the previous use of indifference, and gives it a divine quality, while retaining his own position of doubt, and his own approximation of definition:

> Bene non seppi, fuori del prodigio
> che schiude la divina indifferenza:
> era la statua nella sonnolenza
> del meriggio, e la nuvola, e il falco alto levato.[5]

Sbarbaro stands at equal distance between the Rimbaudian hymn to *luxure* and the spiritual calm and measured equilibrium of Montale's verses. For his is an attempt to overcome the drama that intimately involves him. The equidistance from the two models is confirmed by the poet's insistence on reification, the process by which he is made like the city, a process that clearly identifies the lack of distance in the author's own personal experience.

Giorgio Bàrberi Squarotti has insisted that Sbarbaro expresses this process of reification in *Pianissimo* but, ignoring any biographical data about the author, has linked that process to a sort of pathological inability on the poet's part to participate in life in any traditional and substantive way.[6]

Of course the poem offers only a provisional solution to the theme of meaningfulness of human existence, but that limitation does not detract from its effectiveness. The mixing

---

(continued from page 95) Marziano Guglielminetti, "Per un'interpretazione della poesia di Sbarbaro" in *Atti del Convegno Nazionale di Studi su Sbarbaro*, Resine, Quaderni Liguri di Cultura, Genoa, 1974, p. 41, now also in *Sbarbaro poeta, ed altri liguri*, S. F. Flaccovio, Palermo, 1983, p. 40.

[5] Eugenio Montale, *Gli ossi di seppia*, 1925, now in *Tutte le poesie*, Mondadori, Milan, 1977, p. 54.

[6] Giorgio Bàrberi Squarotti, *Camillo Sbarbaro, op. cit.*

of a personal history with the theme of the new urbanism, far from giving the poem a provisional tone, makes it a fine document, like an old print that still captures our attention and in its understatement and control reveals an artist.

5

I love life but not just for
the sudden flames that surge in the night
and not even for the sudden aspects
of earth and sky in which
I drown my horrible sadness:
but for the roses that have yet to blossom,
or that wither already; for the desire
that leaves but a handful of flies
just as in our fables when we were children;
for the regret that each one bears
to our yesterdays; for the indifference
of all to our most divine dreams;
for not being able to live anything
but the moment like the sheep
that nibble through the world
on this grass or that,
neglectful of all else;
for the remorse that we all share
of having lived life uselessly,
like dregs in the bottom of the glass;
for the great joy of crying;
for the eternal sadness of loving;
for the infinite darkness that benights us . . .

for all this bitterness I love you, Life.

Of this poem, in which the central figure is the personification of *Vita, Desiderio, Amore,* Giorgio Bàrberi Squarotti has spoken of the opposition to the D'Annunzian theme of celebration of life as experience and possession.[1] As we have seen in the note to the first poem, D'Annunzio's exuberant and

---

[1] Giorgio Bàrberi Squarotti, *Camillo Sbarbaro, op. cit.*, pp. 56–57.

–5–

Non, Vita, perché tu sei nella notte
la rapida fiammata, e non per questi
aspetti della terra e il cielo in cui
la mia tristezza orribile si placa:
ma, Vita, per le tue rose le quali
o non sono sbocciate ancora o già
disfannosi, pel tuo Desiderio
che lascia come al bimbo della favola
nella man ratta solo delle mosche,
per l'odio che portiamo ognuno al noi
del giorno prima, per l'indifferenza
di tutto ai nostri sogni più divini
per non potere vivere che l'attimo
al modo della pecora che bruca
pel mondo questo o quello cespo d'erba
e ad esso s'interessa unicamente,
pel rimorso che sta in fondo ad ogni
vita, d'averla inutilmente spesa,
come la feccia in fondo del bicchiere,
per la felicità grande di piangere,
per la tristezza eterna dell'Amore,
per non sapere e l'infinito buio . . .

per tutto questo amaro t'amo, Vita.

pantheistic hymn to life was a celebration of all experiences which enabled the poet to sing in praise of *Diversità*. Without attempting to mock D'Annunzio, that is to say without resorting to irony, Sbarbaro in this poem wished to sing of life an altogether different tune. His reaction is largely in line with that of the majority of anti-D'Annunzian poets and thinkers, especially in his region of Liguria. The tone of the poem recalls Giovanni Boine's *Frantumi*, the general situation of his novel *Il peccato*, while the *amaro* has its original imprint in Clemente Rebora's *Frammenti lirici*.[2]

Other critics have pointed out the similarities to Baudelaire's analogous treatment of the negative elements of life, and the presence of Pascoli's image of the *infinito buio*.[3]

According to the taste of the time this poem would have pleased many a critical ear. Today we might react negatively to the stilted, more typically nineteenth century format and theme of the hymn to life. Yet Sbarbaro does not offer us a mere parody of a popular, though minor theme from another century, rather he attempts its reversal in a more modern and critical perspective.

(commentary continues next page)

6

Sleep, sweet brother of Death,
that from life briefly frees us
then quickly releases us in its prey
like a cat toying with its ball of yarn;
till my life justifies that of my sister,
and I shall leave a sign
that I too lived,
I will content myself with you
and your deceit.

Come, comforter of the afflicted.
Abolish for me all space and time
and dissolve in nothingness this meager self.
No child did ever at his mother's bosom
rest as I in your arms myself abandon.

When one sleeps one no longer knows.

---

[2] Giovanni Boine, *Frantumi*, La Voce, Florence, 1921, p. 68; Clemente Rebora, *Frammenti lirici, XLII*, La Voce, Florence, 1913.

[3] Lorenzo Polato, *Camillo Sbarbaro: Pianissimo*, Il Saggiatore, Milan, 1983, pp. 53–54.

The poem is one long stanza of unrhymed hendecasyllables. One main verb at the end, *t'amo*, is the key to the entire syntactic construction (the English text, of course, anticipates the verb). There is no discernible pattern to the "reasons" the poet adduces to the love of life, but the centrality of *indifferenza* and *sogni più divini* is not altogether casual. Significant also is the reference to the "handful of flies" which the poet ascribes to the fables of childhood. It is another reference to the centrality of fiction and narration, as well as another reference to his own childhood, even if indirect and impersonal.

–6–

Sonno, dolce fratello della Morte,
che dalla Vita per un po'ci affranchi
ma ci rilasci tosto in sua balìa
come gatto che gioca col gomitolo;
di te, finché la mia vita giustifichi
la vita della mia sorella e un segno
che son vissuto anch'io finché non lasci,
io mi contenterò e del tuo inganno.

Vieni, consolatore degli afflitti.
Abolisci per me lo spazio e il tempo
e nel nulla dissolvi questo io.
Nessun bambino mai così fidente
s'abbandonò sul seno della madre
com'io nelle tue mani m'abbandono.

Quando si dorme non si sa più nulla.

The classical *topos* of sleep as symbol of death explains the more compact and traditional formulation of this composition. The poem was eliminated in the 1954 Neri-Pozza edition and in the 1960 edition of *Poesie* by Vanni Scheiwiller, as perhaps redundant. In fact the images of the cat and the mouse, the child asleep at his mother's bosom, as well as the themes of affliction, and abandon to the comforter are all in other poems, beginning with "Organetto."

The wish to leave a mark of one's existence, proof of the literary interests of *Pianissimo*, balanced (continued, next page)

7

Father, even if you were not my father,
and a total stranger to me,
for yourself I would love you.
I remember one late winter morning
when from your window you discovered
on the opposite wall the first violet
and you brought us the news in delight.
Then you took the ladder on your shoulder
and leaned it against the wall outside.
We children were at the window.

Another time I recall
when you were chasing through the house
my sister still small
(stubborn, she had done I know not what)
But when you reached her, yelling loudly,
out of fear your heart nearly stopped,
and you who had seen yourself chasing
your little daughter, pulled her frightened
to your chest unsteadily,
and with caresses in your arms

against the personal history of negation and failure, while poorly developed, is central to the entire composition. It demonstrates, in my opinion, the conscious use the poet is making of literary *topos*.

Baudelaire, of course, among other modern poets had kept alive this sort of treatment of the subject in "Le léthé":

> Je veux dormir! dormir plutôt que vivre!
> Dans un sommeil aussi doux que la mort,
> J'étalerai mes baisers sans remord
> Sur ton beau corps poli comme le cuivre.[1]

–7–

Padre, se anche tu non fossi il mio
padre, se anche fossi a me un estraneo,
per te stesso egualmente t'amerei.
Ché mi ricordo d'un mattin d'inverno
che la prima viola sull'opposto
muro scopristi dalla tua finestra
e ce ne desti la novella allegro.
Poi la scala di legno tolta in spalla
di casa uscisti e l'appoggiasti al muro.
Noi piccoli stavamo alla finestra.

E di quell'altra volta mi ricordo
che la sorella mia piccola ancora
per la casa inseguivi minacciando
(la caparbia avea fatto non so che).
Ma raggiuntala che strillava forte
dalla paura ti mancava il cuore:
ché avevi visto te inseguir la tua
piccola figlia, e tutta spaventata
tu vacillante l'attiravi al petto,
e con carezze dentro le tue braccia

---

[1] Charles Baudelaire, *Les Fleurs du Mal*, *op. cit.*, p. 164.

you enveloped as if to protect her
from that evil you of a while before.

Father, even if you were not my father,
and a total stranger to me,
you among all men,
for your very childlike heart I would love.

This poem, one of the most frequently anthologized, first appeared in *La Riviera Ligure* in September 1912, along with "Padre che muori tutti i giorni un poco." The poet's father, Carlo, died that same year in November.

The first two stanzas of the poem tell of two distinct exempla that echo, as in a refrain, the love that no extraneity could temper or alter. The elimination of time, warranted by the literary construction of the exemplum, is achieved by bringing the past to the memory of the present. The episodes recalled serve not to illustrate the father as ancestor and guide, but to create a sense of intimacy that is much more in tune with the rest of *Pianissimo*.

Sbarbaro often treats the theme of the father, as for example, in the short stories "Tom" and "Congedo"[1], in *Trucioli*, and in *Fuochi Fatui*.[2]

The memory of the father has none of the characteristics that are central to the treatment of the father in poems by Giovanni Pascoli. In Pascoli the memory and the *deeds* of the father represent an attempt to recapture the games and rituals of infancy in a constant return to the family and the paternal home as to a "nest." The more concrete and realistic the memories, the more they become mere titillations of a symbolic world of ghosts as the adult poet places his energies at the

---

[1] Sbarbaro's short stories are collected in *Sui racconti di Sbarbaro*, edited by Gina Lagorio, Guanda, Parma, 1973. "Tom" had originally appeared in *La Voce*, June 26, 1913, "Congedo" in *La Riviera Ligura*, in April 1915.

[2] See *Trucioli*, Vallecchi, Florence, 1920, pp. 110–111; pp. 131–132; *Fuochi Fatui*, Ricciardi, Milan-Naples, 1962, p. 16 and *passim*.

l'avviluppavi come per difenderla
da quel cattivo ch'era il tu di prima.

Padre, se anche tu non fossi il mio
padre, se anche fossi a me un estraneo,
fra tutti quanti gli uomini già tanto
pel tuo cuore fanciullo t'amerei.

service of the child, mysteriously grown in physical appearance but without real emotional development.[3]

In Sbarbaro there are no apparent residues from the *crepuscolàri* who went as far as calling themselves *fanciulli* in their attempt to recapture that time when they were not artists to better express what was naively absorbed. Unlike Rimbaud, Sbarbaro does not view adulthood as a total negation of poetic creativity present only in the child and the adolescent, albeit only as self-annihilation and destruction. As Zanzotto has noted, in Sbarbaro the memory and the entire relationship to the father represent a realization of being forced into an adulthood from which he saw no escape.

Gianni Pozzi comments thus on Sbarbaro's use of memory:

> Even memory, and the desperate yet delightful melancholy that it produces in his verses has quite an original function in his poetry: to feed the humble, familiar microcosm of feelings; that is hardly reconcilable with the haughty sentiments of the hermetic poets.[4]

And the critic Giacinto Spagnoletti similarly notes that in Sbarbaro's poetry there are nearly no nostalgic moments, no regrets, no happy memories in which to reflect his own desperation.

> For him there is no Past, that typically Leopardian time, that can be reduced to a psychological function of consolation. His aridity is

---

[3] Andrea Zanzotto, "Infanzie, Poesie, Scuoletta," *op. cit.*, pp. 61–64.

[4] *La Poesia Italiana del Novecento—Da Gozzano agli Ermetici*, Einaudi, Turin, 1965, 1970, p. 89.

> surrounded only by inert stares along the roads, on men . . . Yet in this poem that stands out in *Pianissimo*, the affectionate portrait of the father takes on all the colors of a desperate nostalgia; it permeates each verse to the point of transforming the memory into something eternal and immutably certain. This time the strongest of his sentiments has prevailed over the reasons of his arid quotidian torment.[5]

Sbarbaro has in this poem, as in his other one on the father, captured the total dignity and moral stature of the father without compromising his own sense of reality and dignity; he has captured all of his affection and respect for the man without resorting to fake sentiment- *(continued next page)*

8

Now that you mean nothing to me, now
that you no longer make me either suffer
or enjoy, you are the habit of all my days.
You resemble a lake all the same.
I move along the shore in a daze.
I want not, desire nothing, neither
do I think.
                I touch myself to test if I exist.
And being and not being, like the water
and the sky of the lake, blend together.
My pain becomes that of another
and life is neither glad nor sad.

I hate you, assiduous companion of all my days,
you do not distract me from my life, but make me
instead, like sleep, an inanimate thing
that barely comes close to life.

---

[5] *Poeti del Novecento*, Edizioni Scolastiche Mondadori, Milano, 1952, 1977, pp. 126–127.

alism; he has captured his quiet indignation and disillusion without giving in to invective or anger. By contrast Dylan Thomas' wonderful poem on the death of his father "Do not go gentle into that good night" is rhetorically and structurally a poem that stirs deep emotions of rage inside all of us at the death of a loved one.[6] Sbarbaro's poems tend not to sublimate or externalize for us the feelings we cannot uncover for ourselves, rather they lead us to internalize our feelings so we may dwell on them without rhetoric, without the aid of any other emotion except our sorrow.

–8–

Ora che non mi dici niente, ora
che non mi fai godere né soffrire,
tu sei la consueta dei miei giorni.
Assomigli ad un lago tutto uguale
sotto un cielo di latta tutto uguale.
Assonnato mi muovo sulla riva.
Non voglio non desidero, neppure
penso.
          Mi tocco per sentir se sono.
E l'essere e il non esser, come l'acqua
e il cielo di quel lago si confondono.
Diventa il mio dolore quel d'un altro
e la vita non è lieta né triste.

T'odio, compagna assidua dei miei giorni,
che alla vita non mi sottrai, facendomi
come il sonno una cosa inanimata,
ma me la lasci solo rasentare.

---

[6] The poem by Dylan Thomas was first published in Marguerite Caetani's *Botteghe Oscure* in November 1951. The poem is a *villanelle* and for its text see: *Dylan Thomas: The Poems*, Edited with an Introduction and notes by Daniel Jones, J. M. Dent & Sons Ltd., London, 1971, pp. 207–208.

Since I am resigned to live, I want
every hour of the day to weigh on me,
to touch my flesh most vitally.
I want sorrow to hold me tight
and place me in the center of life.

Now that you mean nothing to me, now
that I no longer suffer or enjoy
I await resigned that you go away.

This poem directly addresses *consuetudine* and *dolore*, key expressions of Sbarbaro's moralistic conception of the world between the two centuries. Once more the traditional construction of the poem (the more typical hendecasyllable interrupted only by an occasional shorter verse, and the intentionally isolated *penso* of line 8) reveals a world of necessity and resignation, indifference and immobility in which will, desire, and even thought are totally negated because of their intrinsic inadequacy to alter the ultimate outcome of man's inevitably alienated condition.

The dominant image is again that of the somnambulist along the shore in that twilight zone of being and not being, like the water and the sky that blend on the horizon of a lake of sameness in which even sorrow seems to become that of another and life is neither glad nor sad. *(continued, next page)*

9

With both joy and fear I see you
every day decrease, my Sorrow.
Like the lover who awakes to spy
the face of the lover still asleep
and senses the irreparable coldness
for he sees those two bodies so near
become each day more estranged,
every day I awaken to discover

Poiché son rassegnato a viver, voglio
che ogni ora del dì mi pesi sopra,
mi tocchi nella mia carne vitale.
Voglio il Dolore che m'abbranchi forte
e collochi nel centro della Vita.

Ora che non mi dici niente, ora
che non mi fai godere né soffrire,
io rassegnato aspetto che tu passi.

This annullment of the oldest dichotomy, being and not being, like sadness and gladness, like water and sky help to destroy the distinction of interiority and exteriority to expose the *persona*'s senses to every stimulus. In this context pain can only give an illusion of importance, even if negative.

These concepts echo those of Giovanni Boine in *Frantumi* to highlight the first original stirrings of European existentialism in Italy. In Sbarbaro, perhaps better than in any other writer of the period, those concepts are utilized in the fullest documentation of a particular existential crisis. It is to his more mature representations of that crisis that we must look for some answers to the issues that affected every poet and artist of the early Italian *Novecento*. A similar treatment of *dolore* is in Clemente Rebora's Frammenti Lirici (no. LV in particular).

–9–

Io ti vedo con gioia e con paura
ogni giorno scemare, mio Dolore.
Come l'amante che al risveglio spia
il volto dell'amante addormentata
e sente il freddo dell'irreparabile
ché i due corpi così vicini vede
farsi ogni giorno più tra loro estranei,
ogni mattino che mi sveglio scopro

your face more pale, Sorrow,
till one day will appear in your place
the wan face of Consuetude.

You once deluded a little
my aridity and made my clear eyes
see less through turbid tears,
and my whole life reduced to each moment,
now that I have learned to love only you,
oh Sorrow, ephemeral as ever,
you irreparably pass by.
And were it so granted, perhaps
I would not have the courage to recall you.

But my true life comes away with you
for when I do not suffer, neither do I live.

In this poem the poet expresses further the theme of the previous poem: even pain and sorrow can be made null by habit. The one sensation, proof of true existence, which comes to interrupt the *persona*'s aridity, has also proved illusory and fleeting. Now even the courage to recall it has diminished, and the *persona* is caught inescapably in his own *accidia*.

Noteworthy again is Sbarbaro's prosopopoeia of *Dolore* in the more typical style of the *crepuscolari*, but common also in D'Annunzio.

For an example of the theme of separation from life see Rimbaud's first of the "Délires," "La vrai vie est absente" in *Une saison en enfer.*[1]

For another similar way in which the poets of Sbarbaro's

---

[1] Arthur Rimbaud, *Complete Works, op. cit.*, pp. 186–188.

Quelle vie! La vraie vie est absente. Nous ne sommes pas au monde. Je vais où il va, il le faut. Et souvent il s'emporte contre moi, *moi, la pauvre âme*. Le Démon! — C'est un Démon, vous savez, ce n'est pas un homme.

il tuo volto più pallido, Dolore,
finché un mattino al posto tuo m'appaia
il volto scialbo della Consuetudine.

Tu che illudesti per un po' la mia
aridità ed ai miei chiari occhi,
di pianto intorbidandoli, lasciasti
vedere meno bene, e mi facesti
tutta la vita vivere nell'attimo,
adesso che ho imparato a amarti solo,
o Dolore tu anche passeggero,
irreparabilmente te ne vai.
E se mi fosse dato, non avrei
forse il coraggio di chiamarti indietro.

Ma la mia vera vita con te viene
perché quando non soffro neppur vivo.

generation repeatedly associated Life and Sorrow (*Vita e Dolore*) see Umberto Saba's "Città vecchia," which appeared in *La Riviera Ligure* in July 1911, a publication Sbarbaro was certain to read from cover to cover.[2]

---

[2] Umberto Saba, "Città vecchia" in *Trieste e una donna*, now in *Antologia del Canzoniere*, Introduzione di Carlo Muscetta, Einaudi, Turin, 1963, 4th ed. 1972, p. 30.

Spesso, per ritornare alla mia casa
prendo un'oscura via di città vecchia.
Giallo in qualche pozzanchera si specchia
qualche fanale, e affollata è la strada.

Qui tra la gente che viene che va
dall'osteria alla casa o al lupanare,
dove son merci ed uomini il detrito
di un gran porto di mare,
io ritrovo, passando, l'infinito
nell'umiltà.
Qui prostituta e marinaio, il vecchio
che bestemmia, la femmina che bega,

(continued, page 112)

10

Sometimes while I walk alone
through the streets of the noisy city
I forget my destiny of being one
among others, and, oblivious
even of myself, I look
at the people with wide estranged eyes.

It is then that a childish vague sense
of suffering and anxiety seizes me
like a hand weighing down my heart.
Bald headed old men, unaware
eyes of children, common faces
of people born to labor and reproduce,
sly faces blissfully stupid,
ambiguous faces of priests, painted
faces of prostitutes,
impress themselves painfully in my brain.
And I know the deceit by which they live,
the suffering that placed that crease
upon their lips, the hopes always
frustrated,
and the uselessness of their bitter
lives and their ultimate destiny: darkness.

Each one of them carries with him
his condemnation: yet they go on
forgetful of this and everything, each
totally engaged in the fleeting moment,
distracted only by his favorite vice.

(continued from page 111)
il dragone che siede alla bottega
del friggitore,
la tumultuante giovane impazzita
d'amore,
sono tutte creature della vita

–10–

Talor, mentre cammino per le strade
della città tumultuosa solo,
mi dimentico il mio destino d'essere
uomo tra gli altri, e, come smemorato,
anzi tratto fuor di me stesso, guardo
la gente con aperti estranei occhi.

M'occupa allora un puerile, un vago
senso di sofferenza e d'ansietà
come per mano che mi opprima il cuore.
Fronti calve di vecchi, inconsapevoli
occhi di bimbi, facce consuete
di nati a faticare e a riprodursi,
facce volpine stupide beate,
facce ambigue di preti, pitturate
facce di meretrici, entro il cervello
mi s'imprimono dolorosamente.
E conosco l'inganno pel qual vivono,
il dolore che mise quella piega
sul loro labbro, le speranze sempre
deluse,
e l'inutilità della lor vita
amara e il lor destino ultimo, il buio.

Ché ciascuno di loro porta seco
la condanna d'esistere: ma vanno
dimentichi di ciò e di tutto, ognuno
occupato dall'attimo che passa,
distratto dal suo vizio prediletto.

---

e del dolore;
s'agita in esse, come in me, il Signore.
Qui degli umili sento in compagnia
il mio pensiero farsi
più puro dove più turpe è la via

I feel as uneasy as the person
who sees one chasing butterflies along the edge
of a precipice, or looks upon a strange gang
of convicts blissfully smiling.
Then, for one fleeting moment,
I truly become frightened
seeing that men are so many.

In this poem the high and low tones of *Pianissimo* most conclusively reveal that Sbarbaro, like Gozzano, Rebora, Boine, D'Annunzio, and later even Montale, are particularly sensitive to the Baudelairean lesson of *Les Fleurs du Mal* and *Les Petits Poèmes en Prose*, which also influence Sbarbaro's *Trucioli.*[1] The high tone of the meditation and reflection on which the entire poem is predicated, are sharply contrasted to the low tone of the realistic description of city life. The interior monologue of the *persona* is in sharp contrast with the actual existential scene. The realization of such horrible overpopulation ("seeing that men are so many") causes an immediate sense of fright.

The low tones of this "atrocious image of humanity" recall a similar distortion of humanity in Baudelaire's "Le Jeu," similar after all, to the scene by Saba we just quoted in the notes to the previous poem. The estrangement from this tragicomic reality of the city is aptly conveyed not only with the familiar edge of a precipice, but also with the very Rimbaudian gang of blissful convicts.[1]

The campactness of the recurring images creates in *Pia-*

---

[1] In *Les Fleurs du Mal* compare the theatrical passage of distorted human faces and the poet's personal conclusion in "Le Jeu":

> Et mon coeur s'effraya d'envier maint pauvre homme
> Courant avec ferveur à l'abîme béant,
> Et qui, soûl de son sang, préférait en somme
> La douleur à la mort et l'enfer au néant! (*op. cit.*, p. 117)

For Rimbaud compare "L'Impossible" in *Une saison en enfer, op. cit.*, pp. 200–204.

Provo un disagio simile a chi veda
inseguire farfalle lungo l'orlo
d'un precipizio, od una compagnia
di strani condannati sorridenti.
E se poco ciò dura, io veramente
in quell'attimo dentro m'ampauro
a vedere che gli uomini son tanti.

nissimo a very unusual urban geography, quite different from Saba's *Città vecchia*, which retains the familiarity of the daily return home. In Sbarbaro the cityscape hardly ever contains the familiarity of the residential place. It is always a fictional world, but alien and frightful, a scene more fitting to a science-fiction novel for the sense of otherness it conveys.

11

Under curious stares, tears
don't break out suddenly while I speak
of foolish things—I remember
my walks under an overcast sky,
without a friendly hand to comfort me;
and the uselessness of what I say
and what I do makes my heart heavy.

A hand running through my hair irritates me.
Too often in my youth
I hid my tears by laughing,
for the pity of men humiliates me.
And that other I that always
comes along would like to raise his head
amid my tears and laugh frenetically.

While on my knees I look at my father;
don't come down, oh tears, rapid and warm.
With his weak eyes my father looks at me
without batting an eye and discovers anew
the restless child whose hand he used to hold
and who grew by his side nearly unknown.

But in the dark corners of a room
or in the solitude of the woods
oh sweetness of crying all alone!
At every sudden burst
I lean to the nearest post in total
abandon as if I were about to die
while with heavy tears
my face lights up in gratitude.

Thus in the goodness of heaven
I am as naked as at birth;
behind the thin veil of tears
only then am I truly I.

–11–

Lacrime, sotto sguardi curiosi
non mi scoppiate a un tratto mentre parlo
di vane cose (mi sovviene a un tratto
del mio cammino sotto cieli bui,
non avendo una mano che m'incuori;
e l'inutilità di ciò che dico
di ciò che faccio mi fa grave il cuore).

M'irrita la carezza nei capelli.
Io troppe volte in giovenezza risi
per ricacciare dentro le mie lacrime,
ché la pietà degli uomini mi umilia.
E quell'altro mio io il quale sempre
m'accompagna, vorrebbe quando piango
alzar la faccia e ridere frenetico.

Mentre guardo mio padre ginocchioni
non mi colate giù rapide e calde.
Mi guarda il padre coi suoi poveri occhi
senza battere ciglio e scopre nuovo
l'irrequieto che tenea per mano
e che gli crebbe presso sconosciuto.

Ma nell'anglolo buio d'una stanza
o nella solitudine d'un bosco
oh dolcezza di pianger tutto solo!
Al sostegno più prossimo m'appoggio
nell'improvvisa piena
abbandonatamente come fossi
per morire e tra mezzo grosse lacrime
mi brilla il viso di riconoscenza.

Allora sotto la bontà dei cieli
io sono nudo come quando nacqui;
dietro il sottile velo delle lacrime
allora sono solamente io.

This poem alternates a discourse of the present with reflections of the past (the already expressed need of a friendly hand and the uselessness of one's words) even as it reviews the father/son relationship. The invocation of the tears, nearly a personification, creates a certain distance in the poem, a distance behind which the critic Lorenzo Polato has identified a technical solution reminiscent of Paul Valery's "L'Ineffable," for indeed our tears are the expression of our inability to counter with words the oppression of what we truly are.[1]

12

Implacable as they are, my eyes are
always limpid, even when they cry
no friendship can deceive them.
When we speak loudly or
suddenly keep silent,
they see the evil that gnaws at us.
With the sound of our voices we want
to create between us that which is not;
when we are quiet we don't know what to say
and that silence opens a vast abyss.
To embrace each other will not help
if we remain separate to our eyes.

Not even you can deceive them,
Sorrow. When you release your hold,
my father and my sister too
frightfully disappear.

At times at the sight of a pup
licking another while they play
a cruel envy torments my heart.

---

[1] Lorenzo Polato, *op. cit.*, p. 84.

(continued from page 118)

The explicit use of the double in this poem becomes the perfect objective correlative of the *persona's* alienated condition. It is not by irony that laughter and tears are brought together, but by the similarity of their solution.

For a similar *incipit* involving the subject of tears by another contemporary of Sbarbaro, see Corrado Corazzini's "Elegia."[2]

–12–

I miei occhi implacabili che sono
sempre limpidi pure quando piangono
Amicizia non vale ad ingannare.
Quando parliamo troppo forte o quando
d'improvviso taciamo tutti e due,
vedono essi il male che ci rode.
Col rumor della voce noi vogliamo
creare fra di noi quel che non è;
quando taciamo non sappiam che dirci
ed apre degli abissi quel silenzio.
Allacciarci non giova con le braccia
se distinti restiamo ai nostri occhi.

A ingannarli non vali neppur tu,
Dolore. Quando allenti la tua stretta,
il mio padre e la mia sorella anch'essi
s'allontanano paurosamente.

Certe volte vedendo una bestiola
che lecca una bestiola e gioca seco,
mi morde il cuore una crudele invidia.

---

[2] In *Poesie edite e inedite*, Einaudi, Turin, 1968, p. 135–37

With my own eyes I see that I am denied
the joy of loving someone.

As in the opening poem of *Pianissimo,* in this poem the eyes have total dominion over any other sensory mechanism. It is the eyes that reconstruct the reality outside of the *persona* and occasionally create the impression of a double existence. Our words—seems to say the poet—cannot fill the void created by the insufficiency of our alienation; our gestures, also like our emotions, lack the spontaneity and the perfect adequacy of the activities of puppies. *(continued on next page)*

13

At times when I think of my life
forever retracing its own steps,
like day and night repetitious
in all its loathings and desires,
or when my desolate satiety
meets the desire that whispers
at the corner of the street; then comes
to mind the image of a ladder
that we climb up and down without pause
like curious children in some foolish game;
a new kind of clairvoyance opens wide
my eyes on Life, so that it seems to me
that I see it for the first time.
I see thus that nothing in life
is good and nothing sad, but that all
is to be accepted in the same way;
and I think that one must resign oneself,
for all things are made equal by necessity.

But since in that moment I see so
clearly that I can no longer delude
myself to cross that circle
in which Necessity encloses us,
and since I also sense

Con gli occhi vedo che mi sei negata,
gioia di voler bene a quelcheduno.

Sorrow, like sleep and habit can only confirm the illusion of one's existence, for it brings into perfect view, once more, the reality of the father dying and the loneliness of the family, the unfullfilled dreams of the sister. All this is a reminder to the poet of his own inability to resign himself to the unpleasant and inevitable scenario, and thus proves the accuracy of Montale's and Zanzotto's analyses of the poet, that he is reluctant to embrace an adult world for which he has little preparation and talent.

–13–

A volte, quando penso alla mia vita
la qual ritorna sempre sui suoi passi
e come il dì e la notte si ripete
nei suoi disgusti e nei suoi desideri,
o quando la mia triste sazietà
incontra il desiderio che vocifera
al canto della strada, e mi si affaccia
l'immagine alla mente d'una scala
che saliamo e scendiamo senza tregua
come ragazzi in qualche gioco sciocco;
una chiaroveggenza nuova allarga
sulla Vita i miei occhi, tal che parmi
di vederla com'è la prima volta.
Vedo allora che nulla nella vita
è buono e nulla è triste, ma che tutto
è da accettare nello stesso modo;
e penso che convenga rassegnarsi
ché tutto eguaglia la necessità.

Ma poiché in quel momento è così chiara
la mia vista, che di varcare il cerchio
nel quale la Necessità ci chiude
più non m'illudo, e poiché anche sento

that I could not accept it all:
the tenderness of my sister
and the voracious possession of a woman,
from my heart blossoms a sudden
sincere desire to die.

In this reflection on life (again personified along with necessity) the very old image of a classical European *topos*, that of the ladder we climb restlessly everyday, dominates the night cityscape with its desires and loathing, and the desolate satiety experienced at the corner of the street. It is quite telling that Sbarbaro links the climbing up and down to the game of children. The clairvoyance too is that original one of the innocent yet all-seeing child, once more reminiscent of the twilight poets.

A very similar image of the ladder is in Baudelaire's "L'Irrémédiable" in *Les Fleurs du Mal*:

Un damné descendant sans lampe,
Au bord d'un gouffre dont l'odeur
Trahit l'humide profondeur,
D'éternels escaliers sans rampe,
Où veillent des monstres visqueux
Dont les larges yeux de phosphore
Font une nuit plus noire encore
Et ne rendent visible qu'eux;[1]

We have already mentioned in the introduction the remarkably central theme of clairvoyance in the poetry of the turn of the century. Gozzano in "Totò Merùmeni" declares clairvoyance the major characteristic of the man of the century. By totally personifying that process by which all illusions fall, Sbarbaro reaches the inevitable conclusion that all is to be accepted equally. Yet since he cannot escape the "circle / in which Necessity encloses us" he is once more overtaken by a "sincere desire to die."

His inevitable incapacity to embrace adulthood in its contemporary and universally accepted prescription, is dem-

---

[1] Charles Baudelaire, *Les Fleurs du Mal, op. cit.*, p. 100.

che accettar così tutto non potrei,
la tenerezza per la mia sorella
e l'ingordo possesso della femmina,
su dal cuore mi sboccia un improvviso
sincero desiderio di morire.

onstrated by the admission that he cannot accept indiscriminately brotherly tenderness and sexual domination of the female. This element of personal disposition is not without its significant poetic application when we consider the rather "pantheistic" conception of the woman in D'Annunzio, Baudelaire and even Goethe ("Ah, in another age you were my sister or my wife").[2] If Sbarbaro is incapable of embracing adulthood it is also true that his rejection of certain well-established decadent concepts place him in the context of an emerging, though not yet fully developed feminism.

D'Annunzio's constant confusion and blending of the woman/sister and the woman/prostitute (in "Pamphila" he says: "tu sei la mia sorella di quest'ora," a verse Sbarbaro will echo in another poem, as we will see) goes as far as raising a courtesan's love to the mythical capacity of satisfying the desires of the divinity ("Pamphila" in *Poema Paradisiaco*). In *Maia* that same prostitute holds at baptism the most famous *meretrix* of Pirgo.[3]

Sbarbaro totally demystifies the theme of eros to unveil the profound anguish pervading it. Yet this process of reducing and demystifying the whole thing has none of the irony or the parody to which Gozzano subjected the same topic: the woman/lover/goddess/sister.[4]

---

[2] The remark by Goethe appears in the context of the "tale" in Maurice Blanchot's essay "The Song of the Sirens" in *The Gaze of Orpheus, op. cit.*, p. 113.

[3] This contrast between Sbarbaro's treatment of the prostitute and D'Annunzio's is more thoroughly presented in Marziano Guglielminetti, *Sbarbaro poeta e altri liguri*, S. F. Flaccovio, Palermo, 1983, pp. 30–32.

[4] Guido Gozzano wrote parodies of "Pamphila" in his poems of Carlotta, Speranza and Cocotte, respectively in "L'amica di nonna Speranza" and "Cocotte". For both texts see: *The Man I Pretend to Be, op. cit.*, pp. 98–121.

14

Now that my lust is placated
I am left totally empty,
with not even the desire to die.
I know not if in the world there is one
who thinks of me or if my father lives.
Any thought of it I eschew.
For now all sorrow would seem
badly contrived to me.
I sense that I have crossed the boundary
within which one is human enough to suffer,
and that good sorrow I no longer deserve,
for to suffer guilt is truly good.

I let the breeze caress me,
the lights shine on me,
and the passing crowd push me,
heedless like a ship without anchor
or sail, its carcass to the waves.
And I await thus, without thought
or desire, that again,
by the eternal vicissitudes of things,
the will to live may return.

The first part of *Pianissimo* does not contain the relative abandon of the second part, which is more compact and perhaps more sustained poetically. In this poem Sbarbaro returns to the theme of *lussuria* as sexual drive and physical necessity of the senses. But the emptiness of the senses once *lussuria* is placated confirms the feeling of alienation and does nothing to

–14–

Adesso che placata è lussuria
sono rimasto con i sensi vuoti,
neppur desideroso di morire.
Ignoro se ci sia nel mondo ancora
chi pensi a me e se mio padre viva.
Evito di pensarci solamente.
Ché ogni pensiero di dolore adesso
mi sembrerebbe suscitato ad arte.
Sento d'esser passato oltre quel limite
nel qual si è tanto umani per soffrire,
e che quel bene non m'è più dovuto,
perché soffrire della colpa è un bene.

Mi lascio accarezzare dalla brezza,
illuminare dai fanali, spingere
dalla gente che passa, incurioso
come nave senz'ancora né vela
che abbandona la sua carcassa all'onda.
Ed aspetto così, senza pensiero
e senza desiderio, che di nuovo
per la vicenda eterna delle cose
la volontà di vivere ritorni.

alleviate the memory of his family drama, the dying figure of his father. It is not a question of sorrow, the poet tells us, for it would be too good to feel sorry for oneself. Only total abandonment to the life of the city can now ease the feeling of emptiness, an explicit reference to the stance the poet's poetic *persona* will assume in the second part of the collection.

15

Sometimes awakening in the morning I feel
such an acute loathing for living
that in that very instant
I would gladly agree to dying.

The awakening is to me like another birth;
for my mind, washed clean by oblivion
and returned virgin again in sleep,
looks upon its existence with curiosity.
Then suddenly the emergence of old experiences,
like sands at the passing of the tide,
make so clear the absurdity of living
that my mind refuses again to live and would
much rather plunge into the limbo
whence it has just come.

In that moment, I am like the man
that awakens on the edge of a precipice,
and with his hands desperately
but hopelessly tries to go back.

Like the precipice, the desperate light
of morning fills me with terror.

D'Annunzio's *Maia* had reestablished the theme of the awakening, another classical *topos* reelaborated by the decadents, and by the Italian twilight poets:

> Io nacqui ogni mattina. Ogni mio risveglio
> fu come un'improvvisa
> nascita nella luce:
> attoniti i miei occhi
> miravano la luce
> e il mondo . . . [1]

---

[1] Gabriele D'Annunzio, *Maia*, in *Laudi del cielo, del mare, della terra e degli eroi*, *op. cit.*, p. 21.

–15–

Svegliandomi il mattino, a volte provo
sì acuta ripugnanza a ritornare
in vita, che di cuore farei patto
in quell'istante stesso di morire.

Il risveglio m'è allora un altro nascere;
ché la mente lavata dall'oblio
e ritornata vergine nel sonno
s'affaccia all'esistenza curiosa.
Ma tosto a lei l'esperienza emerge
come terra scemando la marea.
E così chiara allora le si scopre
l'irragionevolezza della vita,
che si rifiuta a vivere, vorrebbe
ributtarsi nel limbo dal quale esce.

Io sono in quel momento come chi
si risvegli sull'orlo d'un burrone,
e con le mani disperatamente
d'arretrare si forzi ma non possa.

Come il burrone m'empie di terrore
la disperata luce del mattino.

Sbarbaro's poem instead represents not so much a mockery of the old theme as a recreation of it, once more in tune with the alternative scenario offered by *Pianissimo*. Sleep, oblivion, memory, the mind washed clean as in a *tabula rasa*, serve to make the affirmation that each reawakening is a rebirth. Unfortunately, that initial curiosity with which the poet's *persona* faces life anew quickly dissipates when the same previous experiences reemerge like sands when the tide is low. It is then that the absurdity of life cancels altogether that initial enthusiasm to live again.

The simplicity of the poem, despite the forced negative tone, remains significant particularly for the boldness and originality of its images: the edge of a precipice, the absurdity of life, the desperate light of morning.[2]

Also worthy of mention is Sbarbaro's *(contined, next page)*

16

Always absorbed only in myself and in my world
as if in sleep, I move among men.
If one shoves me with his elbow I take no notice,
and if at all things I stare intently
I almost always do not see.
Anger overcomes me if someone
distracts me from myself. All voices bother me.
I love only the voice of things.
All that is necessary and habitual,
all that is life irritates me,
as the twig irritates the snail,
and like the snail I withdraw in myself.

The life that suffices all others
would not suffice me.
And truly
if I did not have another world of my own
in which to take refuge from life,
if beyond misery and sadness,
necessity and consuetude
I did not remain true to myself
Oh how I would rather not exist!
But a strange sensation follows me
always upon every step and comforts me:
I seem to pass as if by chance
through this world . . .

---

[2] The "desperate light of morning" may be the inspiration to Cesare Pavese's *Verrà la morte e avrà i tuoi occhi*, Einaudi, Turin, 1950.

central metaphor of land and sea, "come terra scemando la marea," a device which seems to confirm Montale's contention that the poet was a man of *terra firma*.

—16—

Sempre assorto in me stesso e nel mio mondo
come in sonno tra gli uomini mi muovo.
Di chi m'urta col braccio non m'accorgo,
e se ogni cosa guardo acutamente
quasi sempre non vedo ciò che guardo.
Stizza mi prende contro chi mi toglie
a me stesso. Ogni voce m'importuna.
Amo solo la voce delle cose.
M'irrita tutto ciò che è necessario
e consueto, tutto ciò che è vita,
com'irrita il fuscello la lumaca
e com'essa in me stesso mi ritiro.

Ché la vita che basta agli altri uomini
non basterebbe a me.
E veramente
se un altro mondo non avessi, mio,
nel quale dalla vita rifugiarmi,
se oltre le miserie e le tristezze
e le necessità e le consuetudini
a me stesso non rimanessi io stesso,
oh come non esistere vorrei!
Ma un'impressione strana m'accompagna
sempre in ogni mio passo e mi conforta:
mi pare di passar come per caso
da questo mondo . . .

Giacomo Leopardi in "La sera del dì di festa" had observed:

> . . . a pensar come tutto il mondo passa,
> e quasi orma non lascia.[1]

That is the conclusion that Sbarbaro draws for us in this poem, which contrasts the urban world with the other, that of nature, to which he hopes to remain true. That is why the poet ignores the crowds of the city, the noises and the voices of humans, to declare his love for the "voice of things," the perfect objective correlative of man's inevitable reification. His formula, of course, changes completely the classical *topos* of *ubi sunt* by switching the reference from time to place.

In the poet's admission of irritation at all that is necessary, many critics have insisted, sometimes vehemently, upon Sbarbaro's inability to participate in the most ordinary of societal obligations. Yet Sbarbaro did not abstain from the usual, mandatory responsibilities of everyday life; his complaint is like the Biblical lamentation that all is *(continued, next page)*

17

Father, you who die a little every day,
whose mind weakens while with wide open
eyes you no longer see but your children,
and no thought have you for yourself, nor regret;
if I think of the courage with which
you have lived, the scorn you have held
for all that is small and mean,
beneath the rough appearance
the instinctive poetry of your soul,
the love you felt for your mother,
your ungrateful sister, and for our mother
dead,

---

[1] Giacomo Leopardi, *Canti*, *op. cit.*, p. 110.

vanity. Only nature provides a sense of eternity and reliability, which recalls Gozzano's famous stanzas:

> Ah! La Natura non è sorda e muta;
> se interrogo il lichene ed il macigno
> essa parla del suo fine benigno . . .
> Nata di sé medesima, assoluta,
> unica verità non convenuta,
> dinnanzi a lei s'arresta il mio sogghigno.
>
> Essa conforta di speranze buone
> la giovinezza mia squallida e sola;
> e l'alchenio del cardo che s'invola,
> la selce, l'orbettino, il macaone,
> sono tutti per me come *personae,*
> hanno tutti per me qualche parola . . .
>
> Il cuore che ascoltò, più non s'acqueta
> in visīoni pallide fugaci,
> per altre fonti va, par altra meta . . .
> O mia musa dolcissima che taci
> allo stridío dei facili seguaci,
> con altra voce tornerò poeta![2]

–17–

Padre che muori tutti i giorni un poco,
e ti scema la mente e più non vedi
con allargati occhi che i tuoi figli
e di te non t'accorgi e non rimpiangi,
se penso la fortezza con la quale
hai vissuto, il disprezzo c'hai portato
a tutto ciò che è piccolo e meschino,
sotto la rude scorza
l'istintiva poesia della tua anima,
il bene c'hai voluto alla tua madre,
alla sorella ingrata, a nostra madre
morta,

---

[2] "Pioggia d'agosto" in *The Man I Pretend to Be, op. cit.*, p. 162.

your whole life sacrificed,
and then I look at you the way you are now,
I silently wring my hands.

Against the indifference of life
I see virtue as equally useless,
and I feel strongly as I never have
the sense of our solitude.

Thus I confess to all, father, you
who smile when you see me and tremble
when some attention I show you,
what a coward I was toward you.

And if memory lightens my burden
it would be better if it weighed
forever on my heart unconfessed.

I, a mere beardless lad, looked at you
in anger, father, for your old age.
Rage against you would seize me . . .

Father who held us on your knees
in the room turning dark,
by the window where we used to count
the first lights dotting the hillside,
vying strongly to be first,
forgiveness I ask but not with tears
—for it would be too sweet to cry—
but with the bitter ones I ask
that fain would flow from my eyes.

Only one thought comforts me,
to be able to see without tears:
as a child at the thought that
you too, like all other men
had to die
in disbelief all alone and quiet

tutta la vita tua sacrificata,
e poi ti guardo così come sei,
io mi torco in silenzio le mie mani.

Contro l'indifferenza della vita
vedo inutile anch'essa la virtù,
e provo forte come non ho mai
il senso della nostra solitudine.

Io voglio confessarmi a tutti, padre,
che ridi se mi vedi e tremi quando
d'una qualche attenzion ti faccio segno,
di quanto fui vigliacco verso te.

Benché il ricordo mi si alleggerisca,
che più giusto sarebbe mi pesasse
inconfessato sempre sopra il cuore.

Io giovinetto imberbe, t'ho guardato
con ira, padre, per la tua vecchiezza.
Stizza contro te vecchio mi prendeva . . .

Padre che ci hai tenuto sui ginocchi
nella stanza che s'oscurava, in faccia
alla finestra, e contavamo i lumi
di cui si punteggiava la collina
facendo a gara a chi vedeva primo,
perdono non ti chiedo con le lacrime
che mi sarebbe troppo dolce piangere,
ma con quelle più amare te lo chiedo
che non vogliono uscire dai miei occhi.

Un pensiero soltanto mi consola
di poterti guardar con occhi asciutti:
il ricordo che piccolo pensando
che come gli altri uomini dovevi
morir pure tu, il nostro padre,
solo e zitto nel mio letto la notte

I would cry in my bed at night.
Since my eyes are now want to cry,
those childish tears console me,
father, for in those tears, it seems,
I may have left my childhood.

If I could promise one thing,
if only I could trust myself
and of myself hád no fear,
one thing I would promise:
to live as bravely as you have,
sacrificed to others as you did,
poor father, for the fierce joy
to die sadly like you.

For a discussion of this poem the reader is directed to the comment on the first poem addressed to the father, no. 7, "Father, even if you were not my father."

18

Perhaps one day, sister, we will retire
to a small house in the mountains
and there pass the rest of our lives.
Our father will be with us even dead.
We'll see him move about the house.
And then he'll understand all the suffering
that we lived united by the hand,
you, my sister, life without love,
I, life without illusions.

And I will work at the other task
for which I live, to leave this world
a sign that I too have lived.
And when the illusions will not suffice,
to live in art many lives,
your suffering will silence mine.

io di sbigottimento lagrimavo.
Di quello che i miei occhi ora non piangono
quell'infantile pianto mi consola,
padre, perché mi par d'aver lasciato
tutta la fanciullezza in quelle lacrime.

Se potessi promettere qualcosa
se potessi fidarmi di me stesso
se di me non avessi anzi paura,
padre, una cosa ti prometterei:
di viver fortemente come te
sacrificato agli altri come te
e negandomi tutto come te,
povero padre, per la fiera gioia
di finir tristemente come te.

–18–

Forse un giorno, sorella, noi potremo
ritirarci sui monti, in una casa
dove passare il resto della vita.
Sarà il padre con noi se anche morto.
Noi lo vedremo muoversi per casa.
E allora capirà tutto il dolore
che traversammo uniti per la mano,
tu, la vita, sorella, senza amore,
io la vita, sorella, senza inganni.

Ed io lavorerò allora all'altro
scopo pel quale vivo, di lasciare
un segno al mondo che son stato anch'io.
E quando l'illusione non mi basti
di vivere nell'arte molte vite,
il tuo dolore farà muto il mio.

To feel closer to each other every day
we will remember what once was;
and we'll review the places that we saw
as children held by our father's hand.
And if our lives should appear empty,
and the regret of a different life
should at times seize us by our throats,
we will go to the only comforter.
For days we'll lay our hands
open upon the grass,
nearly glad to exist for that alone.
And we'll live in the company
of out elder brothers: rivers and woods,
appeased to our destiny.

So that this may come true, I promise
that my sorrow will stay with me forever,
in fact that it may grow each day.

This the dream I dream with my eyes open.

There is little in this poem that goes beyond the most explicit autobiographical elements that in *Pianissimo* constantly intertwine with true poetic inspiration. Besides reminding us of the similarities between the brother/sister relationship in Sbarbaro and other poets like Pascoli, Leopardi and Carducci, the poem reveals also how the Ligurian poet maintains a rapport between himself and the poetic *persona* he has created.

The desire to leave proof of one's existence, the many lives of art, as he calls it, is evidence that *(continued, next page)*

Per sentirci ogni giorno più vicini
ricorderemo a volte ciò che fu;
e andremo a ripassar pei luoghi dove
passammo a man di nostro padre piccoli,
perché il nostro alimento è l'amarezza.
E se vuota ci paia l'esistenza
e se il rimpianto di tutt'altra vita
alla gola ci afferri qualche volta,
alla consolatrice unica andremo.
Delle giornate intere noi staremo
con le due mani aperte sopra l'erba,
quasi lieti d'esistere per quello.
E vivremo così in compagnia
dei maggiori fratelli, i fiumi e i boschi,
pacificati con la nostra sorte.

Perché ciò sia, sorella, io faccio patto
che il mio dolore duri quanto me,
anzi di giorno in giorno mi s'accresca.

Questo il sogno che faccio ad occhi aperti.

the poet sees within what is left of his family, the center of work and commitment, even if they are a constant reminder of their personal tragedy every time the memory of the father is recalled.

It is a naive and youthful statement, so blatantly explicit that it is the antithesis of the elaborate poetic identities of other poets whose themes and subjects he retraces. In the end it is the absolute vulnerability that dominates the *dramatis persona* he has chosen, not one to hide behind, rather one behind which to construct the ideal biography of the alienated man.

19

My heart swells for you, Earth,
like sod in spring.
I am back.
My eyes are new. All that I see
is as never seen before;
even the simplest and commonest things
move me and give me joy.

In you, Oh earth, I am cleansed as in waters
in which one forgets all that one is.
My misery I leave behind
like the snake leaves behind his skin.
I am no longer myself but another.
I am from myself set free.

Earth, you are for me so full of grace.
As long as I can see myself still near
to you, childlike, and my own pain
in you I can dissolve like the cloud
fading in the sun,
I will not curse the day that I was born.

Here I sit on the ground
with both hands open on the grass,
looking lovingly all around.
And in so doing sweet, warm tears
gently streak down my face.

Winter 1912

Though the poem is dated Winter 1912, it appeared in *La Riviera Ligure* with the title of "Grazia" in March 1913.

The emotions expressed and the tenderness for the earth not only find similar echoes in Goethe's Faust and other literature of the nineteenth century, but reflect *(continued, next page)*

–19–

Il mio cuore si gonfia per te, Terra,
come la zolla a primavera.
                                        Io torno.
I miei occhi son nuovi. Tutto quello
che vedo è come non veduto mai;
e le cose più vili e consuete,
tutto m'intenerisce e mi dà gioia.

In te mi lavo come dentro un'acqua
dove si scordi tutto di se stesso.
La mia miseria lascio dietro a me
come la biscia la sua vecchia pelle.
Io non sono più io, io sono un altro.
Io sono liberato di me stesso.

Terra, tu sei per me piena di grazia.
Finché vicino a te mi sentirò
così bambino, fin che la mia pena
in te si scioglierà come la nuvola
nel sole,
io non maledirò d'esser nato.

Io mi sono seduto qui per terra
con le due mani aperte sopra l'erba,
guardandomi amorosamente intorno.
E mentre così guardo, mi si bagna
di calde dolci lacrime la faccia.

inverno 1912

the changing sensibilities toward ecology and the new cult of environmental preservation.

Unlike D'Annunzio's poem "O rus!" in the *Poema Paradisiaco,* in which a romanticized catalogue of rural scenes and of country virtues express a desire to return to simplicity, Sbarbaro's celebration of the earth does not transform the earth into a refuge. In turning to the earth Sbarbaro does not flee from himself, nor does he reject totally the city and its institutions, rather he seeks a way to realize his own essence.[1]

"Grazia," the title of the poem, is also the key word in the composition. In the double meaning of the word is the poet's realization of a newly acquired freedom:

> Io non sono più io, io sono un altro.
> Io sono liberato di me stesso.

The statement stands not only in contrast to Gozzano's "Signorina Felicita" but also to Rimbaud's in Lettre à Izambard of 13 May 1871.

Invoking the simplicity of Felicity, Gozzano declared:

> Ed io non voglio più essere io!
> Non più l'esteta gelido, il sofista,
> ma vivere nel tuo borgo natio,
> ma vivere alla piccola conquista
> mercanteggiando placido, in oblío
> come tuo padre, come il farmacista . . .

---

[1] Gabriele D'Annunzio, *Poema Paradisiaco*, in *Tutte le opere*, op. cit., pp. 129–132.

Ed io non voglio più essere io![2]

Like Felicity he will no longer question if the earth is round, or meditate on Nietzsche. And Rimbaud's *autre* seeks to dissolve the identity of the poet in order to make it become truly responsible for humanity, even for the animals.[3] Sbarbaro's new self holds fewer pretensions; it is merely the recapturing of an identity that risks diffusion and annihilation in any other form of life. Once more a literary model has been reduced to its essential elements and its content brought to bear directly on the poetic *persona*.

Very similar for the dramatic tone and the resulting declaration of non-identity is Carlo Michelstaedter's treatment of the same theme:

Sta sotto il cielo sulla buona terra
questo che ch'io chiamo "io," ma ch'io non sono.
No, non sono questo corpo, queste membra
prostrate qui fra l'erba sulla terra
più ch'io non sia gl'insetti o l'erbe o i fiori.[4]

---

[2] Corrado Gozzano, *The Man I Pretend to Be, op. cit.*, p. 88.

[3] For the letter A Georges Izambard see *Complete Works, op. cit.*, pp. 302–305. For the discussion of the self in Rimbaud, especially contrasted to the romantic self, see Marjorie Perloff, *The Poetics of Indeterminacy:* Rimbaud to Cage, *op. cit.*, pp. 59–66.

[4] "Risveglio", 1910, in *Opere*, Vallecchi, Florence, 1958, p. 385.

II

20

Be silent my soul. These are the sad
days when without will one lives
the days of desperate expectation.
Like the naked tree in midwinter
growing sad in the deserted yard,
I don't expect to grow new leaves
and doubt I ever did.
Going along the road so very much alone
among people who shove but do not see,
I almost believe my total separation.
I press to hear where there is a throng,
I pause by the windows dazzled
and turn at the rustling of a skirt.
At the voice of a blind storyteller,
at the sudden flash of a neck
foolish tears drip from my eyes
that spark with sudden cupidity.
For all my life is in my eyes:
all that goes by moves them
like the weakest wind the deadliest waters.

I am but a resigned mirror
reflecting all things along the way.
Within myself I dare not look
for I would find nothing . . .

And come night I stretch out
in my bed as in a coffin.

II

—20—

Taci, anima mia. Son questi i tristi
giorni in cui senza volontà si vive,
i giorni dell'attesa disperata.
Come l'albero ignudo a mezzo inverno
che s'attrista nella deserta corte
io non credo di mettere più foglie
e dubito d'averle messe mai.
Andando per la strada così solo
tra la gente che m'urta e non mi vede
mi pare d'esser da me stesso assente.
E m'accalco ad udire dov'è ressa
sosto dalle vetrine abbarbagliato
e mi volto al frusciare d'ogni gonna.
Per la voce d'un cantastorie cieco
per l'improvviso lampo d'una nuca
mi sgocciolan dagli occhi sciocche lacrime
mi s'accendon negli occhi cupidigie.
Ché tutta la mia vita è nei miei occhi:
ogni cosa che passa la commuove
come debole vento un'acqua morta.

Io son come uno specchio rassegnato
che riflette ogni cosa per la via.
In me stesso non guardo perché nulla
vi troverei . . .

E, venuta la sera, nel mio letto
mi stendo lungo come in una bara.

The second part of *Pianissimo* develops further the theme of urban abandon and perdition even as we continue to realize that in Sbarbaro these themes are being redressed in such a way as to sensibly draw attention to the intimate suffering of the *persona*. We have seen this *reductio ad essentiam* every time we have compared Sbarbaro to D'Annunzio, to Rimbaud, even to Baudelaire, and certainly to most other contemporaries of his in Italy. Only Saba and Ungaretti, along with Sbarbaro do not match the linguistic "violence," that is to say the use of discordant and expressionistic vocabulary and syntactic constructions, of so many other poets.

The opening poem of the second part parallels the preamble of the first part with a new address to the soul. The sad days, days of a desperate expectation, are mostly a reference to the state of mind and spiritual condition of the *persona* described in the first part. Here the persona is more determined to follow its inevitable destiny toward perdition. The naked tree growing sad is the image the poet casts to describe a rather congenital condition of spiritual dwarfism, a stunted growth that is about to be projected as normalcy in modern man. The tree is also an image Sbarbaro resumes in *Trucioli* in some of the most memorable *poèmes en prose* he has written.

This poem appeared in *La Voce* 16 January 1913 with the title "L'attesa" ("Waiting"). In those early years of the century, but especially on the eve of one of the greatest disasters in history, there was indeed a mood of expectation, the sense of an inevitable pending doom, an ominous anxiety. It is evident in so much literature of the period and it is an important factor in the subsequent formulations of modernism. All avantgarde artists sensed it and reacted to it, even exploited it.

In Sbarbaro's poetry this anxiety takes on such a personal and sincere tone that even today the images of this poem speak directly to our understanding of the very essence of poetry and the poet's world. Furthermore we recognize in the simple outline of those images the logical antecedents of our contemporary myths of displacement and alienation. The blind storyteller, whether it be the ancient Homer or a contemporary street singer, translates perfectly the distance that still dominates the present reality of our myths. "The flash of a neck" still translates life lived in one's eyes, that induces the poet to call himself "a mirror" reflecting all things, and to all things resigned. Corazzini had used a very similar construction in his "Desolazione del povero poeta sentimentale" when he said:

> Io sono, oramai,
> rassegnato come uno specchio.[1]

And Corrado Govoni, likewise, sees an estranged world as through a lens:

> E mi par vivere in un mondo
> ch'io vedo a traverso una lente,
> un mondo estraneo.

Sbarbaro is among the first poets of the century to translate that anxiety and its resulting anguish without rhetoric, without any literary forcing of the issue, and without exploiting it. Instead he is willing to explore the very limits of poiesis by personalizing that condition of expectancy to the point of living with acute awareness the modern decentralization of the poetic function.

---

[1] Sergio Corazzini, *Piccolo libro inutile*, 1906, now in *Poesie edite e inedite*, a cura di Stefano Jacomuzzi, Einaudi, Turin, 1968, p. 117.

[2] In "Il piano," *Fuochi d'artifizio*, 1905, now in *Poesie (1903–1959)*, a cura di Giuseppe Ravegnani, Mondadori, Milan, 1961, pp. 99–100.

21

A mere child when the singing of drunks
first reached my ear in the night,
I would quickly rise from my books;
forgetful of them, my stuffy room
I opened wide to the night air
and leaned outside the window
and drank the song like a strong wine.
Then with what eyes I turned to see
my room at first, then the whole house
where all the lights were already out!
More than once on that cold slate,
in the wind that passed through my hair,
in the rain that soaked my face,
I cried some senseless tears.

Now even that illusion is gone,
now that I know how bitter is the mouth
that sings wide toward the sky;
still if it wakes me from my sleep,
that singing of drunks in the street,
I sit up and listen without breath,
suspended by a sudden emotion;
so I go to place again my face
in the wind that ruffles my hair
for I'd like to renew that bitter rapture,
the shiver that once ran through my body
and the lost blessing in which I no longer
believe, to cry like then . . .
                                        But nothing
except some foolish tear comes from my eyes.

Like the previous one, this poem appeared originally in *La Voce* on 16 January 1913 with the title of "Canto degli ubriachi." This is another composition that allows us to peer into the autobiographical antecedents of the poet's condition;

–21–

Piccolo quando un canto d'ubriachi
giungevami all'orecchio nella notte
d'impeto su dai libri mi levavo.
Dimentico di lor, la chiusa stanza
all'aria della notte spalancavo
e mi sporgevo fuor della finestra
a bere il canto come un vino forte.
Con che occhi voltandomi guardavo
la chiusa stanza e dopo lei la casa
dove già tutti i lumi erano spenti!
Più d'una volta sulla fredda ardesia
al vento che passava nei capelli
alla pioggia che m'inzuppava il viso
io piansi delle lacrime insensate.

Adesso quell'inganno anche è caduto.
Ora so quanto amara sia la bocca
che canta spalancata verso il cielo.
Pur se ancora mi desta dal mio sonno
quel canto d'ubriachi per la via
ad ascoltar mi levo con sospeso
dall'improvvisa commozione il fiato,
e vado ancora a mettere la faccia
nel vento che i capelli mi scompigli.
Rinnovare vorrei l'amara ebrezza
e quel sottile brivido pel corpo,
e il ben perduto cui non credo più
piangere come allora . . .
                                        Ma non m'escono
che scarse sciocche lacrime dagli occhi.

it is implied that the aristocratic though impoverished household of the poet's childhood gave the singing of drunks in the streets a strange aura of charm and appeal, for it ostensibly differed from the quiet, sleepy house in which a deaf, aging father required that people speak in whispers and accentuate the movement of the lips.

This is the narrative element of the poem. The memory of Leopardi is of course an inevitable stop to any poet who wished to turn into poetry the feelings of the child/poet confined by the restrictions of home. Leopardi too had sought to flee the oppressive home environment. For Leopardi, however, the memory of childhod is always filled with nostalgia and regret, emotions that bring a kind of romantic comfort to the desolate life of the poet. For Sbarbaro, as we have seen, memory never holds any nostalgic comfort, and here the song

22

Obscure desires at times
ferment in my poor blood.
I walk the city by night, alone;
the odor of musty underground warehouses
supplants the smell of grass in the sun.

I graze by the myriads of beings
sealed in themselves like tombs,
and I knock on unknown doors and climb
stairs worn by generations.
The woman waiting by the gate,
the drunk vomiting against the wall,
I look upon with fraternal eyes.
My nostrils ever ready to smell Crime,
at times are startled by the headlights
like bloodshot eyes at the end of an alley.

It's then that the fear of dying grows in me
without having yet enjoyed what there is

of drunks in the streets can only bring back the same sense of guilt for what the poet perceives as a lack of affection and sensitivity toward the ailing condition of his father.[1]

The youthful restlessness and the agonized escape are turned into a song of modern man's negative condition. The image of the drunk is, of course, a central one in *Pianissimo,* as in "Lettera dall'osteria" and in various *Trucioli.* The raising of the elbow, the image used in closing the last poem of the collection, is a fitting euphemism for drinking, and one of a very few ironic touches.

–22–

Nel mio povero sangue qualche volta
fermentano gli oscuri desideri.
Vado per la città solo la notte,
e l'odore dei fondaci al ricordo
vince l'odor dell'erba sotto il sole.

Rasento le miriadi degli esseri
sigillati in se stessi come tombe.
E batto a porte sconosciute. Salgo
scale consunte da generazioni.
La femmina che aspetta sulla porta
l'ubriaco che rece contro il muro
guardo con occhi di fraternità.
E certe volte subito trasalgono,
nell'andito malcerto in capo a cui
occhi di sangue paiono i fanali,
le mie nari che fiutano il Delitto.

Mi cresce dentro l'ansia di morire
senza avere il godibile goduto

[1] For Leopardi's treatment of the theme see: "La sera del dì di festa" (especially vv. 43–46), "Ricordanze," and perhaps "A Silvia."

to enjoy nor suffered all there is to suffer.
I'm seized by the will to shed my name
like a useless encumbrance.
And, with my only companion Perdition,
go through the world lighthearted and free.

The obscure desires the poet speaks of in this poem may turn out to be mere reflections of literary references from a cultural baggage heavy with French *maudit* models. Carlo Torchio, as we have already noted, sees a similarity between Rimbaud's "Mauvais sang" and Sbarbaro's *povero sangue*. Besides this similarity in which these two very different poets echo one another, there is in the poem a common desire to shed one's name. This form of anonymity could have come to Sbarbaro through Giovanni Boine in his *Frantumi,* and through a number of other *vociani* for whom also the shedding of one's name is a declaration of the poet's alienation from the world. The origin of this literary *topos* in Italy is still under scrutiny by both literary historians and critics. Stefano Giovanardi in *La presenza ignota, Indagini sulla poesia simbolista italiana fra otto e novecento* (1982) has focused on the many links that exist between the French symbolists and the Italian poets of the last decades of the nineteenth and early decades of the twentieth centuries. The argumentation presented in these pages has tended to take for granted, as indeed other critics have done, that Sbarbaro, by virtue of his excellent knowledge of French and ample ties with France, even through relatives, had a more direct involvement and familiarity with the French symbolist models discussed here.[1]

An example of how these ascendancies can work is offered in this poem in the third stanza:

---

[1] The volume by Giovanardi, published in the "Bibliotheca biographica" series of the Istituto della Enciclopedia Italiana, Govanni Treccani, Rome, 1982, advances the research by Glauco Viazzi (*Poeti simbolisti e liberty in Italia,* Vanni Scheiwiller, Milan, 1967, 1972 and the more recent *Dal simbolismo al Dèco,* Einaudi, Turin, 1981) and by the poet Mario Luzi who compiled the important anthology *L'Idea simbolista,* Mondadori, Milan, 1959.

senza avere il soffribile sofferto.
La volontà mi prende di gettare
come un ingombro inutile il mio nome.
Con per compagna la Perdizione
a cuor leggero andarmene pel mondo.

> Mi cresce dentro l'ansia di morire
> senza avere il godibile goduto
> senza avere il soffribile sofferto.

The regret for a life not lived was a common lament of the twilight poets. Gozzano affirms in "Cocotte":

> Il mio sogno è nutrito d'abbandono,
> di rimpianto. Non amo che le rose
> che non colsi. Non amo che le cose
> che potevano essere e non sono
> state . . . Vedo la casa, ecco le rose
> del bel giardino di vent'anni or sono![2]

Gozzano was translating literally Georges Rodenbach's

> ce qui pouvait être et n'aura pas été.[3]

Appropriately Gozzano's reference is to a childhood episode in which a lovely (seen through the innocent eyes of the child) lady neighbor reaches over a fence to embrace the child, now poet. In the memory of the poet the lady was defined as "cocotte" by his mother who had just learned of the episode. The whole poem, like so many by Gozzano, is an exploration of what might have been, and represents a calling to the mysterious lady to reenact what could have been, but never was.

Sbarbaro has completely eliminated the playful element and substituted for it the bitter reality of his own sad experience. Nothing could have pleased the *crepuscolari* more.

This poem appeared originally in *Lacerba*, June 15, 1913 with the title of "Torbidità."

---

[2] Guido Gozzano, *op. cit.*, p. 118.

[3] The observation belongs to Gianfranco Contini in *Letteratura dell'Italia Unita, 1861–1968*, Sansoni, Florence, 1968, p. 643.

23

I, who cross the usual shabby
streets like a sleepwalker,
upon seeing you, am startled.

You walk ahead of me, slow like
a queen.
Suddenly awakened from my sleep
I regulate my step
to the sagacious melody of yours.
The chances of love and glory
beckon to my heart.
With the foolish curls of her head
and the wing of her hat I can still
lighten the burden of my sadness.
I am still young, inexperienced,
my heart yet ready for all sorts of follies.

Now a light breaks the drowsiness of my life.
All is suspended as if in wait.
I no longer think. I am content and mute.
My heart beats to the rhythm of your step.

As we hope to have sufficiently demonstrated, the most important task of the critic—reminds us Robert Scholes—is to identify the tradition out of which a poetic text emerges and to compare it to a reasonable number of texts in that tradition. Gérard Genette, quite appropriately, speaks of *architextes,* masterworks out of which others are generated.[1]

For this poem, which Camillo Sbarbaro called "Passante" in the June 1914 issue of *La Riviera Ligure,* a number of such *architextes* are quickly recognizeable: Charles Baudelaire's

---

[1] Robert Scholes, *Semiotics and Interpretation*, Yale University Press, New Haven, 1982, pp. 39–40. Gérard Genette, *Introduction à l'architexte*, Seuil, Paris, 1979.

—23—

Io che come un sonnambulo cammino
per le mie trite vie quotidiane,
vedendoti dinanzi a me trasalgo.

Tu mi cammini innanzi lenta come
una regina.
                    Regolo il mio passo
io subito destato dal mio sonno
sul tuo ch'è come una sapiente musica.
E possibilità d'amore e gloria
mi s'affacciano al cuore e me lo gonfiano.
Pei riccioletti folli d'una nuca
per l'ala d'un cappello io posso ancora
alleggerirmi della mia tristezza.
Io sono ancora giovane, inesperto
col cuore pronto a tutte le follie.

Una luce si fa nel dormiveglia.
Tutto è sospeso come in un'attesa.
Non penso più. Sono contento e muto.
Batte il mio cuore al rimo del tuo passo.

"A une passante" in *Les Fleurs du Mal,* Gabriele D'Annunzio's "La passeggiata" in the *Poema Paradisiaco,* Guido Gozzano's poem "Le non godute," which appeared in *La Riviera Ligure* in April 1911. These texts establish a *topos* which Sbarbaro obviously feels compelled to treat given the themes and situations described in *Pianissimo.*[2]

Unlike its models, this poem tries to capture the sense of expectation and suspense caused by the sudden appearance of the urban goddess of Perdition, who, like a light breaking the

[2] Baudelaire's "A une passante", see *op. cit.,* p. 114. D'Annunzio's "La passeggiata", in *op. cit.,* pp. 29–34. Gozzano's "Le non godute" in *op. cit.,* pp. 226–233.

drowsiness of life, temporarily frees the *persona* from his state of torpor and creates a reasonable expectation, a state of availability and disposition.

By contrast Gozzano's poem seems to us the description of an old print full of charm and mystique, but one that fails to go beyond the expression of common desires, the vague daydreams of an eternal adolescent. The final augury, at the end of the poem, of the appearance of a special "true, eternal lover" (v. 88) results in the disappointment and unfulfillment of a "hunger that does not sleep" (v. 95). The whole experience remains another memory "rising from a useless past" (v. 74). In Gozzano this kind of memory, this image of an old print from the past, has no power to either provide a consolation or elicit a solution. The situation it describes is neither infernal nor purgatorial, that is to say, it provides the poetic *persona* no comfort and no hope.

As proof that the theme was a well worn one, D'Annunzio had shifted the scene from Baudelaire's more typical "rue assourdissante" to a more sensuous, perhaps, more Italian, boardwalk, replacing at least some of the urban crowd with a more naturalistic setting. In that setting "la passeggiata" becomes one long conversation, actual or imagined, and takes inspiration from a verse by A. Mary Robinson ("Love without wings" in *An Italian Garden*, 1886) "I know you love me not . . . I do not love you . . .", with which D'Annunzio begins and ends his poem. Here and there, in what is a very uneven poem, the poet gives vague suggestions of another reality, for example:

> Di profondi invisibili rosai
> giunge tale un divino odore effuso

At times when I look at my life,
all that I did discolors
like embers turning into ashes;
a sudden fear of dying crosses
my body like a cold shudder.

che atterra ogni desío di chi l'aspira.

Non ad altro la nostra anima aspira
che a una tristezza riposata, eguale.
Conosco il vostro portentoso male;
e il dolore ch'è in voi forse m'attira
più de la vostra bocca e dei capelli

vostri, dei grandi medusèi capelli
bruni come le brune foglie morte
ma vivi e fieri come l'angui attorte
de la Górgone, io temo, se ribelli,
e pieni del terrible mistero. (vv. 53–65)
. . . .
. . . . . Voi siete l'Eccelsa.

Voi che passate, voi siete l'Eccelsa.
E passate cosí, per vie terrene! (vv. 75–77)

But the other reality D'Annunzio evokes is the usual mythical one, his mysterious lady another Gorgonean sister, snaky-haired goddess of the depths, reduced to the delineations of the woman/salvation as suggested in so many novels of the decadent nineteenth century.

Sbarbaro's poem becomes a lesson in how poetic myths are developed and revised as the elements of the immediate sources of this poem are carefully selected and refocused in a very compact and personal poem. The central image that is capable of blending the various suggestions, is the "sagacious melody" of the lady's step, to whose rhythm the poet adjusts the beating of his heart, a most emphatic thematic word. The images are not exploited in themselves, but create expectation, suspense, perhaps even fear, an emotion more in tune with modern man's condition.

–24–

A volte quando guardo la mia vita
e, tizzo che di cenere si copre,
ciò che feci ai miei occhi si scolora,
con un brivido freddo mi percorre
l'improvvisa paura di morire.

If I knew that tomorrow I should die,
I would leave my house
and saunter along the streets
to be alone with myself,
above me the vast and empty sky,
under my feet the earth cold and hard;
as if alone I'd face the great void.

Like a tiny breeze upon a weak flame,
no illness will quietly
snuff out my life upon a pillow!

In my pilgrim roving I'd see those places
where I walked as a child with my father;
I'd give
my friends the first and last kiss;
I'd touch the grass
the way one touches a baby's head,
knowing it's the last time;
and then take leave from the sweet earth:
sweet like that she will have never seemed . . .

Then place the seal upon my life.

Sbarbaro originally published this poem in *La Riviera Ligure*, in June 1914 with the title of "Voto." "Ex voto" was also the title of a poem by Gozzano. The Latin phrase expresses a wish, desire or vow, and is normally associated with religious zeal and affirmation of one's determination in carrying out a promise. Sbarbaro uses the same expression in a *truciolo*, "Spotorno" as perhaps an expression of trepidation and commotion in the presence of his mother's town, the one to which he will eventually retire with his sister.

Se domani morissi, se sapessi
di morire, la casa lascerei
ed uscirei a zonzo per le vie
per rimanere solo con me stesso
con sopra il capo il cielo vasto e vuoto
sotto i piedi la terra fredda e dura,
come solo sarei in faccia al nulla.

Tra gli umidi guanciali non mi spenga
senza rumore qualche malattia,
come debole fiamma poco vento!

Pellegrinando andare per quei luoghi
dove passai da piccolo col padre;
dare
il primo bacio e l'ultimo agli amici;
toccare l'erba
come si tocca un capo di bambino
e saper che quell'è l'ultima volta;
prender congedo dalla dolce terra:
dolce così non mi sarà mai parsa . . .

Poi mettere alla vita il mio sigillo.

In this poem the poet seems to empty the expression of any religious connotation by emphasizing the sense of abandonment and the preference for a tragic death without preparation, rather that a death that follows a long illness (which was, of course, his father's). The sense of anticipated drama, the rehearsal of those last minute activities, the implied promise that it will be this way, accentuate the sense of horror that at times crosses the pages of *Pianissimo*.

25

I await you at the turn of every street,
Perdition. I search for you in the eyes
of any passing woman . . .
I stop by the pavillions at the fair
to see the snake woman,
the tiny girl that flies . . .

Oh the joy of giving all for nought!
To hold this life, that is our only wealth,
in the same count as straw!

The one frequented by them all, who laughs
with ease and little understands, the one
who with the shrug of a shoulder, the swing
of a hip can dissolve my own interior
world, the one scorned by all, who ignores
her power,
she, I pray, will cross my path.

Like the beggar come to the shore
of the river, his very last coin
to throw away with a hearty guffaw,
so would I for her laugh away my life.

Originally published in *Quartiere Latino* 28 February 1914, this poem picks up the theme of perdition with the added colors of the circus and the familiar reference to the house of pleasure with its much frequented woman. Baudelaire's *Petits*

–25–

Io t'aspetto allo svolto d'ogni via,
Perdizione. Ti cerco dentro gli occhi
d'ogni donna che passa . . .
Sosto dai baracconi nelle fiere
a vedere la donna del serpente,
la fanciulla che vola . . .

Oh voluttà di dar tutto per nulla!
di tenere nel conto d'una paglia
questa vita ch'è tutto il nostro bene!

Quella che tutti ebbero, che ride
facile e non capisce, quella che
con un crollar di spalle e un muover d'anca
dentro tutto il mio mondo mi dissolva,
quella più disprezzabile che ignora
la sua potenza,
io prego che la strada m'attraversi.

Io, come un mendicante che venuto
sulla sponda del fiume, sghignazzando
l'unico soldo che possiede getta,
per lei la vita getterei ridendo.

Poèmes en Prose and "Le vieux saltinbanque" in *Le spleen de Paris* represent some of the literary allusions of the poem. Allusions to which Sbarbaro will return in his *Trucioli* especially the earlier ones of the period 1914–1920.

26

In my nocturnal roving through the city
I live my deepest life.

Shutters silently lit!
Dark windows open in the night!
In atria of stone the voice of water!
Among slaughtered beef a candle lit
to the Madonna! Shapeless human shadows
behind the steamy windows of cafès!

I turn into the blindman at the crossroad
who plays, his eyes vaguely to the sky.
Oh the pleasure to be alone and listen to myself!
To hear for hours in the night
steps nearing, then fading quickly!
To be the whore who whispers
her word to the man going past!
The old woman at the door
who hangs on to the nauseated soldier,
begging him for one last drink!
And the desire to go even lower!

Skimming along the houses cautiously
I sense behind those hollow walls
generations respiring.
And I know the hostility of certain
tough alleys,
the fright certain city squares can give . . .
Perhaps oblivious of them all I walk
toward my liberation! — Folly.

"Nottambulism," the original title of this poem which appeared in *Quartiere Latino* in December 1913, reveals once more the poet's perspective of the city. Nightwalking gives the elliptical inventory of city images a strange sense of horror and

–26–

Quando traverso la città la notte
io vivo la mia vita più profonda.

Persiane silenziose illuminate!
Finestra buia aperta nella notte!
Negli atrii di pietra voce d'acqua!
Tra le bestie squartate lumicino
alla madonna! Ombre umane informi
dietro i vetri nebbiosi dei caffè!

Mi trasformo nel cieco del crocicchio
che suona ritto gli occhi vaghi al cielo.
Voluttà d'esser solo ad ascoltarmi!
Udire nella mia notte per ore
avvicinarsi e dileguare i passi!
Essere la puttana che sussurra
la parola al passante che va oltre!
la vecchia della porta
che s'attacca pel soldo della grappa
al militare ch'esce nauseato!
E voluttà di scendere più basso!

Rasentando le case cautamente
io sento dietro le pareti sorde
le generazioni respirare.
E so l'ostilità di certe vie
tozze,
la paura di certe piazze vuote . . .
E forse ignaro m'incammino verso
—oh mia liberazione!—la Follia.

mystery. In the vision of the *flâneur* inanimate objects, slaughtered animals, along with saints and a broad array of human shadows are portrayed with uniformity of tone to lead to one inevitable conclusion: to walk further toward folly!

27

At times by the side of the road
overtaken by infinite discouragement,
there I sit; and wonder where I'm going,
why I walk on. And I think of my death
and I see myself an inanimate puppet
laid out in the coffin too small . . .

How many more dawns will the world
bear after we are gone!
                    Of what we suffered,
of all we held so dear in life
not the faintest remembrance will remain.

Generations pass
like the current of the river . . .

A deadly heaviness weighs down
my heart.
          I would like to be turned
into some ancient ruin
and see the hours follow one another
and men change their course, the sky
with each dawn take color, then lose it again
by night . . .

This poem, perhaps the most beautiful of the collection, is closest to our contemporary sensibilities as it translates in lasting visual images the sense of disheartened abandon which brings the poet's *persona* to the contemplation of death.

The metonymic, narrative approach, so typical of all of *Pianissimo*, seems to give the metaphors a fresher and more readily understood inventiveness: the dawns that will follow us, the generations like currents of the river, the ancient ruin, the course of man's journey, the skies at dawn and at night repeating their inevitable change of colors become the only remaining elements of a universe in which history has finally

–27–

A volte sulla sponda della via
preso da un infinito scoramento
mi seggo; e dove vado mi domando,
perché cammino. E penso la mia morte
e mi vedo già steso nella bara
troppo stretta fantoccio inanimato . . .

Quant'albe nasceranno ancora al mondo
dopo di noi!
Di ciò che abbiam sofferto
di tutto ciò che in vita ebbimo a cuore
non rimarrà il più piccolo ricordo.

Le generazioni passan come
onde di fiume . . .

Una mortale pesantezza il cuore
m'opprime.
Inerte vorrei esser fatto
come qualche antichissima rovina
e guardare succedersi le ore,
e gli uomini mutare i passi, i cieli
all'alba colorirsi, scolorirsi
a sera . . .

run its course. Deprived of our histories, our chronologies of human achievements and conquests, man is left to contemplate a very ancient ruin. To it the poet wishes to be made similar, but not to know the ultimate truth of the universe, to discover how it all will end, rather to contemplate the inevitable passing of time.

It is the same solution of Pirandello's *Uno nessuno e centomila*, begun about the same time of *Pianissimo*, but published in 1925–26 in *La Fiera Letteraria*. Like Vitangelo Moscarda, the protagonist of *Uno nessuno e centomila*, the poet realizes what a gulf exists between the appearance of things and reality itself.

Only the complete denial of existence, and the contemplation of time can return the individual to the essential elements of life, emptied of anger and anxiety. Moscarda achieves this through madness, Sbarbaro's *persona* finds tranquillity and peace through resignation.

This poem has some very specific Baudelairean echoes in "Spleen":

> Désormais tu n'es plus, ô matière vivante!
> Qu'un granit entouré d'un vague épouvante,
> Assoupi dans le fond d'un Sahara brumeux;
> Un vieux sphinx ignoré du monde insoucieux,

(continued on next page)

28

Frail, with shining eyes and cheeks
painted red,
my dark soul in search
of its match
finds you at the gate awaiting men.

You are my sister in this hour.

To accompany you to some diner
along the waterfront
and watch you eat voraciously!
And to lie without desire
in your bed!
Cadaver, next to a cadaver,
and drink from the sight of you all
bitterness, like a sponge drinking water!

And then touch your hand, or the hair
that someone must have once combed
in a pony tail upon your head!
And feel myself watched by your hostile

Oublié sur la carte, et dont l'humeur farouche
Ne chante qu'aux rayons du soleil qui se couche.[1]

Appropriately enough, Baudelaire had begun his poem with:

J'ai plus de souvenirs que si j'avais mille ans.

and in the following stanza gives us a sample of those *souvenirs. Le tirois* and *la fosse commune* are combined by Sbarbaro into the image of the *bara troppo stretta* to demonstrate once more the extremely personal, yet always enlightening way in which poets attend to each other's voice, and always derive their own song.

–28–

Magra dagli occhi lustri, dai pomelli
accesi,
la mia anima torbida che cerca
chi le somigli
trova te che sull'uscio aspetti gli uomini.

Tu sei la mia sorella di quest'ora.

Accompagnarti in qualche trattoria
di bassoporto
e guardarti mangiare avidamente!
E coricarmi senza desiderio
nel tuo letto!
Cadavere vicino ad un cadavere
bere dalla tua vista l'amarezza
come la spugna secca beve l'acqua!

Toccare le tue mani i tuoi capelli
che pure a te qualcuno avrà raccolto
in un piccolo ciuffo sulla testa!
E sentirmi guardato dai tuoi occhi

---

[1] *Les Fleurs du Mal, op. cit.* pp. 94–95.

eyes, poor creature, and to torture you
by asking your mother's name . . .

No joy can compare to this bitterness:
to be able to make you cry, and be able
to cry with you.

In a letter to Prezzolini dated January 1913 we learn that Sbarbaro sent this poem, originally entitled "A una puttana" ("To a Prostitute") along with the second poem in *Pianissimo*, "Paura." Prezzolini rejected both poems. "Paura" was eventually published in March 1913 by *La Riviera Ligure*, and "A una puttana" appeared in *Quartiere Latino*, on 14 January 1914 with the revised title "A una donna."[1]

Whether woman or prostitute, the subject has ample confirmation of its appeal and popularity in the literature of the nineteenth century and the early decades of the twentieth. The element of shock is not to be discounted as part of the poet's motivation. The Italian middle class lived with a deplorable double standard, one that had been institutionalized and amply exploited in both literature and opera.

29

At times in the oppressive heat of the city
the singing of cicadas startles me.
And suddenly it brings before me
fields prostrate in the light . . .
I am astonished that water and trees
are still in this world,
all the good things of the earth
that sufficed one day to my forgetting . . .

---

[1] The letter to Giuseppe Prezzolini is now in *Il tempo della Voce*, Longanesi-Vallecchi, Milan-Florence, 1960, p. 581.

ostili, poveretta, e tormentarti
domandandoti il nome di tua madre . . .

Nessuna gioia vale questo amaro:
poterti fare piangere, potere
pianger con te.

(continued from page 166)

The moralistic attitude of the poet is clearly evident in those lines which force the break of the usual client relationship, in order to explore the more personal one (the mother's name, the hair someone must have combed, etc.).

Guglielminetti finds the most immediate antecedent in Baudelaire's "mendiante rousse" and in line 12 of "Un nuit que j'étais près d'une affreuse Juive" in which there is the specific reference to

> comme au long d'un cadavre un cadavre étendu[2]

a verse Sbarbaro translates with particular precision and simplicity, while creating a perfect mirror image (chiasmus) with the word *cadavere*.

–29–

Talora nell'arsura della via
un canto di cicale mi sorprende.
E subito ecco m'empie la visione
di campagne prostrate nella luce . . .
E stupisco che ancora al mondo sian
gli alberi e l'acque,
tutte le cose buone della terra
che bastavano un giorno a smemorarmi . . .

---

[2] Charles Baudelaire, *op. cit.*, "A une mendiante rousse", p. 114, "Une nuit que j'étais près d'une affreuse Juive", p. 60.

In such foolish stupor the drunk
receives the cool night air.

But then as I sense my soul adhering
to every stone of the unresponsive city
like a tree with all its roots,
I smile to myself ineffably and as if
by the force of wings my elbow I raise . . .

May 1913

This closing poem, along with "A volte sulla sponda della via," appears to have been composed especially for the collection and publication of *Pianissimo*. Most of the other poems had appeared in various publications, but these two compositions in particular articulate the ultimate moralistic thesis of the work.

Giorgio Bàrberi Squarotti sees the poem as the admission that even nature is ultimately insufficient to resolve the sense of alienation and solitude of the poetic *persona*.

> The old motif, contrasting city and country, returns in the last composition of *Pianissimo* to express the moral anguish of the soul as it recognizes the useless and illusory hope of a refuge, of salvation in nature from solitude, from the situation of crisis, of interior laceration. The image of the open country, of water, evoked by the song of the cicadas heard in the burning streets of the city, is no longer enough, as it once was to free man from his existential anguish; the stones of the arid, desolate city represent the only landscape capable of matching cruelly and inexorably the state of total interior aridity; the only place in which, impossible any other comfort, man in a state of crisis can live his bitter existence.[1]

The development of the poetic *persona*, from the adolescent restricted to the quiet and subdued paternal house, to the *flâneur*, that modern wanderer of the urban setting, has been

---

[1] Giorgio Bàrberi Squarotti and Stefano Jacomuzzi, *La poesia italiana contemporanea: Dal Carducci ai nostri giorni*, D'Anna, Florence-Messina, 1968, p. 211.

Con questo stupor sciocco l'ubriaco
riceve in viso l'aria della notte.

Ma poi che sento l'anima aderire
ad ogni pietra della città sorda
com'albero con tutte le radici,
sorrido a me indicibilmente e come
per uno sforzo d'ali i gomiti alzo . . .

maggio 1913

completed. The child, once attracted by the song of the inebriated in the street, is now one of those drunks, with only a distant memory of family and nature, that once sufficed to his forgetting. By parallel it is now the singing of cicadas in the distance that startle the *persona*, a complete reversal that marks the final stage of the infernal journey.

This journey from childhood to the infernal city and its myths is also a journey through a kind of literature that either created or alimented those myths. *Pianissimo* challenges not only the ideas, but the rhetoric as well, of a kind of literature that has lost a sense of its mission, that no longer is dedicated to showing reality, rather seeks to distract the reader's commitment to reason and common sense. Like Jules Renard, Sbarbaro wants the reader to confront the phenomenology of things and emotions without the mitigation of any preconceived ideas, nor the "assistance of that seemingly deathless bourgeois myth, inspiration."[2]

That is the reason why *Pianissimo* is not only an important work of poetry but is also a work of civic poetry in the tradition that goes from Dante to Pier Paolo Pasolini, for in challenging the myths of decadent literature, D'Annunzian rhetoric, and futurist visionaries, Sbarbaro challenges as well the political domain which inevitably brought forth fascism.

---

[2] Gilbert Sorrentino, "A Novel as Cold and Brilliant as Ice," a review of Jules Renard's *Poil de carotte, in Washington Post, Book World*, Vol. XIV, no. 25, June 17, 1984, p. 8.

Lettera dall'osteria

"Lettera dall'osteria" appeared in *La Riviera Ligure* with the slightly different title of "Lettera da una taverna," in March 1915. The original date of publication was the summer of 1913, only weeks following the date of completion of *Pianissimo*. The drinking poem was dedicated to Silvio Volta, one of Sbarbaro's dearest friends, and one of the original group that had published at their expense *Resine*.

The "Letter" is still connected to *Pianissimo* for similarity of themes and for the poetic *persona*, which in this poem appears by far more talkative and playful. In very subtle ways what has changed in this poem is the entire linguistic orientation, evident in the tone, in the more descriptive and explicit elaboration of details; even the geography of the setting is virtually extended to the entire world, albeit around the drinking table.

A partial confirmation of this is to be seen in the absence of Leopardian and Petrarchan constructions, in the more resolute and less meditative tone, in the explicit direct address to a very specific person. The vague and surrealistic scenario that has dominated all of Sbarbaro's poetry from "Organetto" all through *Pianissimo*, is replaced by a real locale, a real scene of very characteristic, even if provincial, Italian life.

All this suggests that Sbarbaro is reverting to a plurilinguistic model, away from the monolinguistic poetic structure of Petrarch and Leopardi. Davide Puccini, and Marziano Guglielminetti believe that the "Lettera" is a clear signal that the poet has exhausted the monolinguistic and elegiac tendency of his previous compositions, and moves now into a different linguistic orientation which he carries also into *Rimanenze*, especially the compositions of the early twenties. As we will see, "Versi a Dina" will mark a return to the elegiac tone of *Pianissimo*, something that has authorized Guglielminetti to affirm that the elegiac is the tone most comfortable to Sbarbaro.[1]

[1] Marziano Guglielminetti, *op. cit.*, pp. 35–40; Davide Puccini, "Lettera dall'osteria: verso la *terraferma* del *naufrago* Sbarbaro" in *Sigma*, nos. 33–34, January-June 1973, then in *Lettura di Sbarbaro*, Nuovedizioni Enrico Vallecchi, Florence, 1974. The reference to the language of Dante and Petrarca is of course from Gianfranco Contini's famous essay "La lingua del Petrarca," originally published in the April 1951 issue of *Paragone*. It was later reproduced in the collective volume *Il trecento*, Sansoni, Florence, 1953. I am using the text printed in Francesco Petrarca, *Il Canzoniere*, testo critico e introduzione di Gianfranco Contini, annotazioni di Daniele Ponchiroli, Einaudi, Turin, 1964, fourth ed. 1972, pp. vii–xxxviii.

Letter from a tavern

In a state of grace, at night
I write to you from a tavern, my pal Volta.

In a state of grace, for I know
no better way than through the fog
of wine to contemplate the landscapes
that an inferior artist displays
along the walls, the hairy hostess
or the smiling girl who brings the pitcher.

To strike a conversation with whomever
is near; to smile at one who
smiles; to love everyone;
bypassed by space and time,
to see the world like a God Almighty.

Then leave the pub as light
as a montgolfier in flight;
to feel the pavement of the street
uncertain like velvet under the feet
and a desire to sing out loud.

I pilot myself through this muted world
like a ship that lists to the usual port.
Scampering of cats at the thump of my steps.
The same alluring rectangle of light
in an alley swarming with phantoms.
In corners the bitter smell of chloride.

This is how I get even, my pal Volta.
Since I was destined to love no one,
I cling to things as in a shipwreck.

How many times I looked at the ships
leaving port as an escape!
New York, Calcutta, London: endless names.

Lettera Dall'Osteria

In istato di grazia, amico Volta,
di notte da una bettola ti scrivo.

Stato di grazia: ché non so più grande
bene, di contemplare
tra la nebbia del vino i paesaggi
di cui rozz'arte ornò all'intorno i muri,
e l'ostessa baffuta o la ridente
ragazzotta che reca la terrina.

Attaccare discorso con chi capita
vicino; a chi sorride
sorridere; volere a tutti bene;
scantonato dal Tempo e dallo Spazio,
guardare il mondo come un padreterno.

E uscire dalla bettola leggero
come la mongolfiera che s'invola;
sentir come tappeti di velluto
i lastricati sotto il piede incerto;
e voglia di cantare a squarciagola.

Per il mondo cambiato mi piloto,
nave che sbanda, al consueto porto.
Fuggir di gatti innanzi al passo sordo.
Rettangolo di luce, prepotente,
nel vicolo che fruscia di fantasmi.
Acre odore, allo svolto, di cloruro.

In questo mi rifaccio, amico Volta.
Poi che dato non m'è d'amare alcuno,
m'aggrappo come naufrago alle cose.

Quante volte guardai come uno scampo
i bastimenti ch'escono dal porto!
New York, Calcutta, Londra: nomi immensi.

I used to dream of losing myself, of being
another, able to forget my very name.

Even this illusion is now gone:
my cowardice weighs on my foot
like the lead ball of the convict.

Thus let my life go on, my life
an object of pity to you, of laughter
to others;
and let this consensus suffice,
that of my noblest friends: the inebriated . . .

Till that day comes, I hope, that I may leave
this place and with sure foot start out
to some empty square, to the dark
waters of a river . . .

My friend, I know that now you are
quite at the mercy of Venus.
                                        Lucky you! The blood
flows through your veins more boldly,
your breathing slows at times and your
heart almost pauses as if by death.

But if the day should come—and may it never—
when of the fire only ashes should remain,
and you should come searching for your friend,

you'll find him at the tavern
with the faded red curtains
and with the sign above: AL GOTO GROSSO.

I will not ask of you or her.
But I'll hand you the full glass
that we may reach together in silence
oblivion.

summer 1913

Perdermi là sognavo, essere un altro,
dimenticarmi sino del mio nome.

Anche questa illusione ora è caduta:
la mia vigliaccheria mi pesa al piede
come palla di piombo al galeotto.

E dunque così tragga la mia vita,
oggetto di pietà per voi, di riso
agli altri;
e mi basti riscuotere il consenso
dei magnanimi amici, gli ubriachi . . .

Finché giorno verrà, spero, ch'io esca
di qui con passo fermo e m'incammini
a qualche piazza vuota, a qualche buia
acqua di fiume . . .

Amico, so che Venere ti tiene
ora in balìa.
Felice te! ti corre
il sangue nelle vene più gagliardo,
ti si chiude la gola a volte e sosta
come per morte il battere del cuore.

Ma se tempo verrà—né venga mai—
che del fuoco la cenere sol resti,
e tu allora a cercar vieni l'amico.

Lo troverai nella taverna che ha
ai vetri stinte tendinette rosse
e scritto per insegna: AL GOTO GROSSO.

Io non ti chiederò di te di lei.
Spingerò verso te colmo il bicchiere
perché in silenzio con l'amico beva
l'oblio.

estate 1913

Rimanenze
(Remains)

Introduction

Sbarbaro's *Rimanenze*: Poetry as the art of memory

Rimanenze was published by Vanni Scheiwiller of Milan in 1955. In presenting the poems, poems of his youth and young adulthood (when he was in fact 67 and had already retired to Spotorno in 1951), Sbarbaro credited the preservation of the texts to the literary critic Mario Costanzo, to his lifelong friend and confidant, Angelo Barile, and to Elena De Bosis Vivante.

The volume contained "Lettera dall'osteria" (later separated from the collection), four unpublished poems found by Barile in a small handwritten notebook, dated 1921, three poems from 1922 "Donna sul canto della via," "Liguria" and "Scapitozzano gelsi" originally published in *Primo Tempo*, October 15, 1922. Along with these leftovers the volume collected "Versi a Dina," a love poem in five short movements, and a closing poem, "La bambina che va sotto gli alberi," dated respectively 1931 and 1932. "Versi a Dina" and "La bambina che va sotto gli alberi" appeared in *Circoli*.[1]

---

[1] "Versi a Dina" appeared in the January-February issue of 1931 and "La bambina che va sotto gli alberi" in July-August, 1932.

With the title *Rimanenze*, a word which denotes precisely what the English "remnants" conveys, with its storeroom connotations, suggesting remnants of cloth from various bolts, Sbarbaro meant no denigration of his work. All the titles of his works denote in fact an element of remainder and residue, a metaphor of survival from neglect and oblivion. This sort of metaphor of refuse is quite similar to Montale's *Gli ossi di seppia*.

In *Rimanenze* Sbarbaro brings together not only compositions from two different decades, but poetry that moves across the whole spectrum of Italian linguistic and artistic orientation. *Pianissimo* is basically monolinguistic in its composition and stylistically draws inspiration from the two poets of classical Italian poetry who are normally considered to represent the purist, exclusionist tendencies of Italian literature: Francesco Petrarca and Giacomo Leopardi. *Rimanenze*, instead, represents both monolinguistic and plurilinguistic models. In the first seven poems Sbarbaro follows inclinations already displayed in "Lettera dall'osteria" toward the more descriptive and away from the meditative and elegiac tone of *Pianissimo*. In "Versi a Dina" the poet returns to the meditative and elegiac patterns, to demonstrate that, in the end, they are the most suitable to his poetic voice.[2]

Nonetheless, whatever the linguistic model, there is in all of *Rimanenze* a dimension of permanence and endurance that is absent in *Pianissimo*. As Sergio Solmi clearly stated, as early as 1949, the "danger of *Pianissimo*" was always that "its voice of subdued confession" might "be exhausted in a pure lament," without solution, without hope, and, most of all, without any answer to the internal emotional and psycho-

---

[2] See note to "Letter from a tavern" for the reference to the Contini essay on the language of Petrarca and Dante, as they represent models of poetry and prose throughout the centuries. The critic Franco Croce originally advanced the idea that "Versi a Dina" represents a return to the monolinguistic model in his presentation on Sbarbaro at the Congresso nazionale di studi su Sbarbaro, now in *Atti*, *op. cit.*, pp. 95–116.

logical dilemma which the poet expressed through abandon and resignation.[3]

In *Rimanenze* even nature, seen earlier as a vague refuge from the infernal cityscape, takes on a new consistency, and in the theme of autumn offers a solution of contentment and peace. The poet has learned to be satisfied with a nature still Leopardian in its unpredictability, aridity and meagerness, yet "the only constancy, the only fidelity he knows in the uncertainty of all things."[4]

In *Pianissimo*, Sbarbaro was sensitive to the Baudelairean lesson of depicting all things with "extreme discretion"[5] and distance, qualities that accentuated the meditative and mysterious tone of the compositions while underscoring the personal drama, and the poet's separation from life. In *Rimanenze* the suggestions of nature reach levels of controlled abandon and celebration and offer possibilities of a sentimental realization.

This new attention to the reality around him is evident in a number of obsessive metaphors which Sbarbaro expresses through the functions of the eye and the ear. Eyes are mentioned seven times in the first poem "Occhi nuovi." They are both the subject and the object of the short poem which concludes with the poet's declaration that those "muddy puddles" are his own eyes. The visual preoccupation is indicated in the second poem by words such as "barbaglio" and by the verb "trasalì." In "Voze" the eye, harsh toward others, turned tender (*s'inteneriva*) only on the faces of the earth. And in "Donna ferma sul canto della via" the eyes are blank and pretend not to see. In the next poem "Liguria" the traveller's eye describes a world whose most distant images always recall the poet's native Liguria. In "Scapitozzano gelsi; batton cerchi" the earth looks upon its own fruits like a mother gazes at her offspring.

---

[3] Sergio Solmi, "I *Trucioli* di Sbarbaro," *op. cit.*

[4] *Fuochi Fatui*, *op. cit.*

[5] Walter Benjamin, *op. cit.*, pp. 185–186.

The reason for these obsessive metaphors is to be found in the poet's constant desire to castigate the tone of pathetic eloquence, typical of the *crepuscolari*, which translated into a sense of abandonment and derision in *Pianissimo*. As Franco Fortini has observed, Sbarbaro is working his way up from the pathetic and defeated themes of the *crepuscolari*, while still retaining the deliberate pathos and eloquence that he learned from reading Leopardi.[6]

Thus "Young, astonished eyes" is a composition of exceptional density and structure that draws inspiration from a single thematic intuition, one that is nearly impossible to define, as often happens in the hermetic poetry of the twenties and thirties. Here the poet, through various poetic devices, forces the reader to focus on the total background of the phenomenological world behind the story. The color print of the world, so reminiscent of Gozzano and other twilight poets, the anticipation of the sky, the eyes that dare not look into the eyes of others, the eyes of orphans led by the hand, the street, the room rented for the hour of lust, loathing, pain, shadow, puddles, etc. are all part of the cosmology envisioned by the poet up to this point, and which he can now describe with greater distance, as the metonymic arrangement of objects indicates.

In *Pianissimo* the poet, in essence, refuses to act upon the reality he describes through his own story and suffering. *Rimanenze*, instead, depicts reality with greater poetic sensibility, the result of more elaborate mimetic representations.

But what really sets these poems apart from Sbarbaro's other production, both in verse and prose, is the role that memory plays in them. The theme of memory in these poems makes this hybrid collection a very striking and unusual postscript to *Pianissimo*. If this confirms the importance of *Pianissimo* on the basis of historical and literary reasons, it does not detract from the relevance and significance of the later compositions.

Memory is implied in the first two poems through the

---

[6] Franco Fortini, *op. cit.*, p. 21.

personal recounting of the poet's own dramatic childhood and youth. In "Voze" and "Liguria" past and present intertwine, occasionally reaching levels of ecstatic celebration of nature and its seasons. Against them the poet measures his own life, much the same way as Ungaretti in *Una vita* or Saba in his *Canzoniere*. "Donna ferma sul canto della via" thus represents another moment of the poetic *persona*'s existence, a moment of anti-heroic expression, with which the reader is already well acquainted. In "Scapitozzano gelsi; batton cerchi" the poet elaborates the final stage of his difficult biography, and expresses the hope of a new beginning.

But it is in "Versi a Dina" that the theme of memory is more fully exploited. The love story, a new and unexpected development in the arid existence of the poet, is introduced in the very first lines with the ephemeral plot of fireflies. The image of plot is echoed in words like "weft," "drawing," and "puzzle."

The five movements of "Versi a Dina" and "La bambina che va sotto gli alberi" are filled with reticence and trepidation as they unfold the memory of the plot, with verses that open and close like an accordion. Their story is quite clear. They bring to a close, and perhaps to some sort of dénouement, the human tragedy that Sbarbaro has told in all his works. The first and fifth movements review once more the limits of the story which reverberate the other three movements with greater objectivity and distance. In addition the third movement explores memory as the mediation between past and present, even as we sense the metamorphosis of the tale that creates and recreates the plot.

Sbarbaro, like all true artists, is always conscious of his own craft, and constantly seeks to redimension the total import of his creation with explicit references to the process of metamorphosis of all artistic creations. In *Pianissimo* "the song of the sirens" was the clue to the fine line of discrimination between reality and fiction. In "Versi a Dina" memory itself can play and replay the plot *ad infinitum*, like images on a screen, while the poet is forever conscious of the fact that it was all "a cruel imagining."

Maurice Blanchot has understood perfectly how intimately a part of all fiction, and even poetry, this metamorphic process is:

> The tale is bound up with the metamorphosis alluded to by Ulysses and Ahab. The action that the tale causes to take place in the present is that of metamorphosis on all levels it can attain. If for the sake of convenience—because this statement cannot be exact—we say that what makes the novel move forward is everyday, collective or personal time, or more precisely, the desire to urge time to speak, then the tale moves forward through the *other* time, it makes that other voyage from the real song to the imaginary song, the movement which causes the real song to become imaginary little by little, though all at once (and this 'little by little, though all at once' is the very time of the metamorphosis), to become an enigmatic song always at a distance, designating this distance as a space to be crossed and designating the place to which it leads as the point where all singing will cease to be a lure.[7]

Memory is the designation of distance between the poet's plot and the story itself. Through memory the poet is able to maintain the necessary distance among all the plots, and between past and present. Only art can redeem them from oblivion, that "dreamlike town where I was / yesterday and the heart already can't recall," yet through memory "ooze sweet words" the lover may have never said. That is why memories are "our last surviving good," "secret honey," like the "color of the sea," like a sense of "summer," the outline of "a road along the houses and the orchard wall," or the movement of a lover. They are the things that enable our minds to reenact each time each event "till it consumes our last memory." Once more the poet has managed to make the time of artistic creation coincide perfectly with the time of his own personal experience, this time without a heavy-handed sense of the confessional and the pathetic. For in *Pianissimo* Sbarbaro's voice was one of desperate and pathetic confession and thus his poetry had no time; neither past nor present existed, only a circular inevitability and fatalism, and memory had no

---

[7] Maurice Blanchot, *op. cit.*, p. 111.

resonance, except in a minimal way as it reviewed occasionally the fortuitous microcosm of the family.

In *Rimanenze*, instead, memory dominates and designates each minimal plot—the child playing on the steps, the old woman by the meager fire, the old cobbler by his bench, the aging man weighing a bunch of grapes. Memories are warm to the soul like the fires of past suns are to the tree, so that even fall, our last spring, can perhaps bring on the lips of a man the "trembling flower of a smile."

Yet this interiorization process, through which the poet is able to achieve a sentimental participation with all things, cannot offer any metaphysical and absolute solution to suffering and disappointment. Like the "boats in vain calling to each other," like "mere hands that fail to touch," neither memory, nor the poet's new-found confidence in nature and its seasons can insure a happy ending to the human dilemma. At best they represent a consolation, a tenderness, a momentary pause.

The reason for this is that Sbarbaro is never celebrating the "big" event, the major plot, the saga. His novel is not a "blockbuster," nor will he sing the popular, catchy tune. That is not what poetry is for him. He never addresses mankind, the nation, the civilization, the world at large. That is why he is perfectly happy to let others celebrate commemorative events, he will be satisfied with what others may call insignificant.

Unlike Eliot, for example, who wished to embrace "memory" as "the power of holding at bay primitive impulses always on the doorstep of modern man,"[8] or Pound who saw memory as the "art that kept alive what civilization kept trying to conceal, to cover, to lose, a harmony with nature which was symbolized by the gods and had been the essence of the Eleusinian cults"[9] Sbarbaro saw memory as an extremely precarious thread, a preciously thin line separating what was from what was not.

---

[8] Cairns Craig, *Yeats, Eliot, Pound and the Politics of Poetry*, University of Pittsburgh Press, Pittsburgh, 1982, p. 144.

[9] *Ibidem*.

In these poems Sbarbaro favors neither the primitive impulses nor a harmony with nature, and the objects of man's progress are not raised to symbols, never represent the essence of a cult.

Like Leopardi one century before, Sbarbaro continues to hold to a basically materialistic concept of nature; for him human progress is never to be glorified, for man, in his small, insignificant presence in the universe, is still living a precarious balance between the imperfect reality of things and the distant images of his divine potential.

That is why viewed in their historical perspective, "the boats in vain calling to each other" fail to represent human progress and technology. The boat is a familiar image of the twenties and thirties, one that occasionally rises to the consciousness of a myth (think of how Federico Fellini exploits it in the film *Amarcord:* The Rex becomes an empty and shallow paper-mache prop). But it is not to that kind of boat Sbarbaro can possibly draw our attention. He has in mind the humble craft of fishermen. And the "mere hands that fail to touch" can certainly give us a distant allusion to Michelangelo's Sistine Chapel hands of the Creation, and thus remind us of the mediation of all artistic intervention, but, like the "peacock" of the second poem, and the train that disturbs the quiet village, they are evidence of a presumptiousness from which Sbarbaro wishes to take the necessary distance.

Through this delicate nuance, so similar to Baudelaire's "extreme discretion," Sbarbaro is able to turn something he barely lived through (*Erlebnis*) into something that has the weight of an experience (*Erfahrung*).[10] His memory is neither the *mémoire pure* of Bergson's famous theory of *Matière et mémoire,* nor Proust's *mémoire involontaire*. It instead assumes the same function of *shock* that Walter Benjamin considers so very central to Baudelaire's artistic creations.

> Perhaps the special achievement of shock defense may be seen in its function of assigning to an incident a precise point in time in

[10] Walter Benjamin, *op. cit.* pp. 195–196.

consciousness at the cost of the integrity of its contents. This would be a peak achievement of the intellect; it would turn the incident into a moment that has been lived (*Erlebnis*).[11]

Yet events in Baudelaire's poems are not connected with any specific time, which is always "peculiarly chopped up" (Proust), they stand outside of time, and are defined only by virtue of the notion of the *correspondances*.

> The *correspondances* are the data of remembrance—not the historical data, but data of prehistory. What makes festive days great and significant is the encounter with an earlier life. (As in "La vie antérieure")[12]

In Sbarbaro's poetry time is always just a *prop*, an integral part of the plot itself. All his controlled artistic production confirms this, especially the impressionistic *poèmes en prose* of *Trucioli* from the image of the vine growing accustomed to life in the pavement of the arid city, in the earlier collection, to the closing line of the last collection, *il grido del silenzio* ("the wall of silence").[13] "La vie antérieure" is always the central reference of Sbarbaro's poetry, always plays a central role in every plot.

In "Versi a Dina" the images the poet collects are not symbols of a traditional "love story," but the "data of remembrance." In the first *Rimanenze* the eye alone, like Baudelaire's (remember that of Baudelaire's *eyes* Walter Benjamin has said that "one is inclined to say that they have lost their ability to look"[14]), can never satisfy all the expectations of the poet. Thus they become eyes in which the eyes of others dare not look, and the poet can no longer submit to their sway, except by forsaking all illusion (just like Leopardi).

Like Baudelaire, Sbarbaro too has been "jostled" (Benjamin) by the experiences of the city with its crowds, impersonality and dehumanization. In "Versi a Dina" the presence of the city becomes a blind giant, and the prostitute on the corner of the streets a normal fixture of its socio-economic

---

[11] Walter Benjamin, p. 165.
[12] Walter Benjamin, p. 184.
[13] *Trucioli*, p. 11 and p. 327.
[14] Walter Benjamin, p. 191.

necessity. Only by reducing memory itself to a prop of another life can the poet alleviate the awesome weight of his loneliness, turn the tragic life that fate has willed him into a fleeting meager gift of nature, experience another event, or turn to "real" what may have never been, like the words the lover may have never said.

In the end, by doing so, the poet reaffirms that all true poetry is the event that hides the experience, the experience that highlights the event, the memory that plays and replays it on the indelible screens of the mind, like the plots of fireflies on any summer twilight. When it is true poetry then the art of memory speaks to the reader of his own individual story and that story will always match that of the nation, as well.

At a time of exaggerated nationalism and insipid patriotism during the fascist twenties and thirties, Sbarbaro's poetry offered an unmistakeably discordant voice. For instead of Italy, as a homeland, *Rimanenze* invoked Liguria, symbol of aridity and harshness; instead of the modern metropolis, sang of Voze, instead of affirming the beautiful love story, sought to dwell on the deleterious effect of memory.

Earlier in *Pianissimo*, Sbarbaro attempted to cleanse the poetic language of all its traditional trappings and the most offensive avantgarde extremes and experimental approximations, to offer a new poetics of introspectiveness and autobiographism that were in the air. With *Rimanenze* of the early twenties and thirties, Sbarbaro would expunge from the new fascist memorialism its most fallacious and delusive myth: the glorification of the past and the illusion of human progress. By going against the current the poet was able to give us a work that goes beyond its most immediate accomplishments and suggestions to offer us a poetic consciousness that will not easily be forgotten.

Rimanenze
(Remains)

Young, astonished eyes—
looking at the world
like a colorful print;
eyes clear like air
beckoning to the sky above the earth
—like pain in the shadow of a swallow,
like tears in the showers of springtime—

    eyes into which the eyes of others
    dare not look:

        eyes alone
        like orphans holding hands in the street;
        gloomy like the mirror
        of the room that bore
        the repugnance of infinite faces;
        eyes that crying can no longer wash;
        eyes like puddles, my very own.

1921

The train rolled by in a dazzle
of brass, like a cannon, guides fast
and furious like the waters in the wake of a ship.

Like a lonely beggar by the wall
out to warm himself in the sun,
the village was startled
and lends its deaf ear to that muffled
rumble that suddenly recalls
the world's existence.

1921

Occhi nuovi,
attoniti—che guardano
come una stampa colorata il mondo;
occhi colore d'aria,
anticipi di cielo sulla terra
—il dolore v'è l'ombra d'una rondine,
un'acquata di primavera, il pianto—

occhi cui non ardiscono guardare
altri occhi:

occhi soli
come orfani a mano per la via;
tetri come lo specchio
della camera ad ore che patì
la ripugnanza d'infiniti volti;
occhi che nessun piangere più lava;
occhi come pozzanghere, miei occhi.

1921

Il rapido passò, dentro un barbaglio
d'ottoni, un rombo. Fervono le guide
come dietro la nave l'acqua bolle.

Ne trasalì
destato il borgo che pigliava il poco
sole, mendico abbandonato al muro;
e l'orecchio di sordo porge al rombo
affievolito, che di soprassalto
l'esistenza del mondo gli ricorda.

1921

He knows not who or what it was that went by . . .

Walking along the usual street
brooding over some common words,
something glorious appeared
and filled his eyes with wonder.

Was it a peacock showing off its colors?
or a purple cloud, suspended alone
in the air, suffocating the world?
or was it a ship that sailed full speed
along the morning sea
toward uncharted land?
He doesn't know.
Afterwards it was
as if he had lost all memory of himself;
water in the cup of one's hands
those poor words were lost.

Forgetful, he smiled within himself,
like a man deep in thought
along a country path
in winter; if the scent of a violet
reaches him, he knows not whence it comes.

1921

Voze, you wash in the sun the misery
of the few roofs, bunched together
like sheep against the downpour;
like linen closets, you smell
of lavender, and are like your nets
that taste of salt;

—in the shadow of your alleys, the rooster
totters along in conceit; in the open doorway
a child plays; behind him the dark and cold
kitchen where an old woman

Non sa che fu—qualcuno che passò . . .

A lui che andava per la trita via
rimuginando povere parole,
qualche cosa apparì di glorioso
che di stupore gli occhi gli riempì.

Fu un pavone che si sventagliò?
una nube di porpora, sospesa
sola nell'aria, che affocava il mondo?
o nave che solcava a piene vele
verso una terra sconosciuta un mare
mattutino?
                    Non sa.
                              Dopo, fu come
se svuotato l'avessero di sè;
acqua colta nel cavo della mano,
si persero le povere parole.

Dismemorato, nel nascosto volto
egli sorrise, come uom che va
assorto per sentiero di campagna
d'inverno, se lo sfiora
alito, non sa donde, di viole . . .

1921

Voze, che sciacqui al sole la miseria
delle tue poche case, ammonticchiate
come pecore contro l'acquazzone;
e come stipo di riposti lini
sai di spigo, di sale come rete;

—nell'ombra dei tuoi vichi zampa il gallo
presuntuoso; gioca sulla soglia
il piccolo, con dietro il buio e il freddo
della cucina dove su ramaglie

bends to kindle the last pitchpine;
on the terraces the corn shines tall
and the sorb apple turns red; what growth
one wrings from the avaricious hills,
strains the slender walls, the sod
turns to dust, the fig tree dwarfs crooked—

in you, Voze, I run into the child
I once was, the sad infant searching
the ground for bad apples thrown
to the birds, attracted only by the obscure
desire to taste the dregs;
the naughty child hidden behind the door
enjoying his name called through the house
by one who raised him lovingly
and now wrung her hands
imploring that they go
to fish him out of the pond . . .

Once he has drunk at every rotten
well,
and no one will be left to look for him
in the empty house,
may he find refuge in you as in a mother.

If the eye is still harsh toward others
and tender only to the faces of the earth,
in the house of old that bears still
upon the threshold the horseshoe
to bring it luck,
save him the attic window
that faces a sea of lapis lazuli
down there, and quenches its thirst
at the perennial spring by the olive tree,

Voze, sweet name that melts
in the mouth . . .

1921

una vecchia si china ad attizzare;
sulle terrazze splende il granoturco
o rosseggia la sorba; nei coltivi
strappati all'avarizia della roccia
i muretti s'ingobbano, si sbriciola
la zolla, cresce storto e nano il fico—

in te, Voze, m'imbatto nel bambino
che fui, nel triste bimbo che cercava
in terra mele mézze per becchime
buttate, tratto dall'oscuro sangue
a mordere ai rifiuti;
nel cattivo celato dietro l'uscio
che godeva d'udirsi per la casa
chiamare da colei che lo crebbe
—e si torceva presso lui non visto,
la povera, le mani e supplicava
che s'andasse con pertiche alla gora.

Quando bevuto egli abbia ad ogni pozza
guasta,
più nessuno lo cerchi per la casa
vuota,
come in madre in te possa rifugiarsi.

Se l'occhio che restò duro per l'uomo
s'inteneriva ai volti della terra,
nella casa di allora che inchiodato
reca sull'uscio il ferro di cavallo
portafortuna,
sérbagli sopra i tetti la finestra
che beve al lapislazzulo laggiù
del mare, si disseta
alla polla perenne dell'ulivo,

Voze, soave nome che si scioglie
in bocca . . .

1921

Woman standing at the corner of the street,
eyes blank as if not to see,
neither with your voice do you nag, you are
rather in the golden road like a dull
stone;

You are perhaps the marionette that flops
along the wall, expressionless,
arms dangling!
                                        and if you are alive,
may you stand before everyone silent,
finger pointing dark the hole
of your mouth . . .

I look at you but not without fear, so much
you resemble me; neither alive nor dead;
woman standing at the corner of the street.

1922

Meager sliver of land framed by the sea,
marked by the arid ridges of your hills;
worn down by sudden rivers; corroded
by salt like the ring of a mooring;
scourged by the noon-day heat; beaten
by the winds that sweep ashore
the algae with the petrel
—a stone altar raised between sky
and sea where the canicular heat
burns the wild aroma of herbs,
that's what you are.
                                        Liguria,
my land, I'll always carry
in my heart the image of you
like a traveler wears the simple
cross hung there by a mother crying.
                                                        Wherever I have been
—in rich pastures where the grass

Donna ferma sul canto della via,
che dagli occhi non mostri di vedere,
non importuni con la voce, stai
nella strada dorata come pietra
sorda;

fossi la marionetta che s'affloscia
al muro, l'occhio vacuo, le braccia
penzoloni!
                    e se viva
sei, t'impuntassi innanzi a ognuno, muta
che indica col dito nero il buco
della bocca . . .

Senza paura non ti guardo, tanto
mi rassomigli; non viva, non morta;
donna ferma sul canto della via.

1922

Scarsa lingua di terra che orla il mare,
chiude la schiena arida dei monti;
scavata da improvvisi fiumi; morsa
dal sale come anello d'ancoraggio;
percossa dalla fersa; combattuta
dai venti che ti recano dal largo
l'alghe e le procellarie
—ara di pietra sei, tra cielo e mare
levata, dove brucia la canicola
aromi di selvagge erbe.
                                        Liguria,
l'immagine di te sempre nel cuore,
mia terra, porterò, come chi parte
il rozzo scapolare che gli appese
lagrimando la madre.
                                        Ovunque fui
nelle contrade grasse dove l'erba

simulates the sea; in sweet lands
where the sky melts in tenderness
before astonished eyes along canals,
where women gently balance
golden pails on their hips—everywhere,
the mere recollection of your image
pierced me with joy.

How I walked you in my youth! At every
turn the discovery of new sights
stirred my heart like Cabot's
the day that from his wavering bark
he first glanced the rising Cape
in a sea filled with wonder.
Headlong I threw myself at your fountains
soul and knees prostrate to drink.
I partook of you in the flour
of the wheat that rises from your hills,
kneaded and shaped in bread,
seasoned by slow flowing oils,
flavored by the potted basil
that perfumes your houses.
In the ports of your cities,
in the swarm of your homes, in the narrow
cracks of your alleys, I searched for love.
I drank your biting wine
by the shady roadside where drivers
pause, and in musty taverns, from heavy
mugs as from fine crystals
of the credenza,
—to eat and drink of you,
to mix my fleeting life
with yours.

A token of love in the flesh, I got
my varied soul from you,
Oh Liguria whose skies are as tender
in winter as in springtime.

simula il mare; nelle dolci terre
dove si sfa di tenerezza il cielo
su gli attoniti occhi dei canali
e van femmine molli bilanciando
secchi d'oro sull'omero—dovunque,
mi trapassò di gioia il tuo pensato
aspetto.

Quanto ti camminai ragazzo! Ad ogni
svolto che mi scopriva nuova terra,
in me balzava il cuore di Caboto
il dì che dal malcerto legno scorse
sul mare pieno di meraviglioso
nascere il Capo.
Bocconi mi buttai sui tuoi fonti,
con l'anima e i ginocchi proni, a bere.
Comunicai di te con la farina
della spiga che ti inazzurra i colli,
dimenata e stampata sulla madia,
condita dall'olivo lento, fatta
sapida dal basilico che cresce
nella tegghia e profuma le tue case.
Nei porti delle tue città cercai,
nei fungai delle tue case, l'amore,
nelle fessure dei tuoi vichi.
                                        Bevvi
alla frasca ove sosta il carrettiere,
nella cantina mucida, dal gotto
massiccio, nel cristallo
tolto dalla credenza, il tuo vin aspro
—per mangiare di te, bere di te,
mescolare alla tua vita la mia
caduca.

Marchio d'amore nella carne, varia
come il tuo cielo ebbi da te l'anima,
Liguria, che hai d'inverno
cieli teneri come a primavera.

Your sun shines even through
fine threads of rain,
beauty that smiles
then turns suddenly to tears.
Along the road deceived by tepid pauses
the hasty violets
rush to blossom, only to fail to scent.

The windy ridges of your mountains,
backbone of your pebbly river-beds;
your sea, whether the sun transforms it
into a train that dazzles, or lights
reflect in it like a handful of fine gold
the nights when boats call to each other;
your docile slopes shaded by the pale
olive tree, like canescence
come to bless this arid land:
—bitter or sweet, ephemeral or eternal,
it is you, land and sea, the only faces
that speak to the desert of my heart.

A pagan, if I lived by the net,
I'd sacrifice to your deity, oh Liguria,
red mullets gaping on a bed of algae;
armfuls of lemons in the sun,
if I had an orchard; a pot of carnations,
at very least, if nothing else I owned:
what you generously give I gladly offer.
My last oar, old sailor,
I'd dedicate to you.

But words are of no avail to speak of you:
the moan of a sea gull in the sky,
the fury of the sea breaking against the rocks;
these are the only songs to match with you.

Were I the very soil
where the blade of grass finds roots,
or the pine stubbornly anchored to your tuft,

Brilla tra i fili della pioggia il sole,
bella che ridi
e d'improvviso in lagrime ti sciogli.
Da pause di tepido ingannate,
s'aprono violette frettolose
sulle prode che non profumeranno.

Le petraie ventose dei tuoi monti,
l'ossame dei tuoi greti;
il tuo mare se vi trascina il sole
lo strascico che abbaglia o vi saltella
una manciata fredda di zecchini
le notti che si chiamano le barche;
i tuoi docili clivi, tocchi d'ombra
dall'oliveto pallido, canizie
benedicente a questa atroce terra:
—aspri o soavi, effimeri od eterni,
sei tu, terra, e il tuo mare, i soli volti
che s'affacciano al mio cuore deserto.

Io pagano al tuo nume sacrerei,
Liguria, se campassi della rete,
rosse triglie nell'alga boccheggianti;
o la spalliera di limoni al sole.
avessi l'orto; il testo di garofani,
non altro avessi:
i beni che tu doni ti offrirei.
L'ultimo remo, vecchio marinaio
t'appenderei.

Ché non giovano, a dir di te, parole:
il grido del gabbiano nella schiuma
la collera del mare sugli scogli
è il solo canto che s'accorda a te.

Fossi al tuo sole zolla che germoglia
il filuzzo dell'erba. Fossi pino
abbrancato al tuo tufo, cui nel crine

crest combed by the northern wind;
were I a grape cooking in the heat of your gravel . . .

1922

Mulberry pruning; barrel hoops in place.
Winter wood dumped on the pavements
and sounds of axes
echo in every yard.

The chestnut tree slings its fruits in the woods;
free them from their husks, chestnut man! Hurry!
Fill the sacks; in the cities they're already
rushing the street vendors for the fresh hot ones,
hands in their pockets, and red noses,
the children at the end of the school day.
And we too at night chatting
over some wine with our friends, will peel
some roasted ones; nothing could be more wise.

The earth looks upon its fruits
like an exhausted mother between the smile
and the trembling tears, looks upon the new born
that just made her scream . . .

The soul swaddles an intimate peace;
and holds to spy beyond the window panes,
in that dark hole the black hands of the cobbler,
as if it were in that circle of light
the ultimate felicity.
The cobbler dares not ask
much more than the hissing pot
give odor of legumes
and dawn see him at his bench again,
so that then at night, in the deep mug of wine,
he may see come true the shallow hopes
that even in his poor childhood
must have made his heart tremble.

passa la mano ruvida aquilone.
Grappolo mi cocessi sui tuoi sassi.

1922

Scapitozzano gelsi; batton cerchi
a botti. Si rovescia sui selciati
la legna per l'inverno e suona d'ascia
ogni corte.

La castagna che sfrombola sei boschi
liberala dal riccio, castagnaio!
insaccala; ché già in città fan ressa
alla padella delle caldarroste,
con le mani intascate e i nasi rossi,
i ragazzi all'uscita della scuola.
E pure noi la sera, chiacchierando
tra il vino con gli amici, sgusceremo
bruciate; ché non è più saggia cosa.

Guarda la terra la sua genitura,
affaticata madre che, tra il pianto
tremolandole un riso, il nato guarda
che la fece gridare . . .

L'anima fascia una raccolta pace;
e la tiene a spiar, di là dei vetri.
lo stambugio, le nere
mani del ciabattino, come fosse
in quel cerchio di luce la pensata
felicità.
Che il borbottar della pignatta esali
un odor di legumi, altro non chiede,
e al suo deschetto lo ritrovi l'alba.
E la sera nel gotto denso vede
avverate le povere speranze
che pure a lui fanciullo
avranno fatto palpitare il cuore.

Autumn, primavera of the earth;
the trees remember still the fires of suns
past,
like the soul the warmth of its memories.
Autumn, my own late spring:
time when on the bitter
mouth of man
breaks the trembling flower of a smile.

1922

Autunno, primavera della terra:
serba l'albero il fuoco dei passati
soli,
come l'anima il caldo dei ricordi.
Autunno, tarda nostra primavera:
tempo che sull'amara
bocca dell'uomo
spunta il fiore tremante del sorriso.

1922

Versi a Dina

—1—

The weft of fireflies, remember
on the sea at Nervi, my very first delight?
(Dreamlike town where I was
yesterday and the heart already can't recall.)

Perhaps I don't recall the gesture that engraved
you within, yet in me ooze sweet words
that you don't know you ever said.

Ultimate delusion of all lovers!
In vain they must have tangled lives
if even memories, our last surviving good,
are mere hands that fail to touch.

Each is left with his own lost
felicity, a bit dazzled and alone,
in the world empty of significance.
Secret honey of which it feeds;
till it consumes its last memory
and all is as if it had never been.

Oh how little divides what was
from what was not!
                    Less
than the wake of a ship water from water.

It must have been
the fireflies of Nervi, the cicadas

Versi a Dina

—1—

La trama delle lucciole ricordi
sul mar di Nervi, mia dolcezza prima?
(trasognato paese dove fui
ieri che già non riconosce il cuore).

Forse. Ma il gesto che ti incise dentro,
io non ricordo; e stillano in me dolce
parole che non sai d'aver dette.

Estrema delusione degli amanti!
invano mescolarono le vite
s'anche il bene superstite, i ricordi,
son mani che non giungono a toccarsi.

Ognuno resta con la sua perduta
felicità, un po' stupito e solo,
pel mondo vuoto di significato.
Miele segreto di che s'alimenta;
fin che sino il ricordo ne consuma
e tutto è come se non fosse stato.

Oh come poca cosa quel che fu
da quello che non fu divide!
                                        Meno
che la scia della nave acqua da acqua.

Saranno state
le lucciole di Nervi, le cicale

and the house on the sea at Loano,
and all my smallest joy—and you—
as long as it can torture me to remember.

—2—

Now that you have come,
now that you have danced
into my life
like a breath of air in a closed room—
words and voice fail me
to celebrate you, my long awaited love
and to tacitly sit by your side is quite enough.

The chirping that nearly deafens the woods
will hush at dawn
when the sun jumps over the horizon.

But in my disquietude I searched for you
when as a boy
on summer nights I took
to the window as if stifled:
I did not know, my heart was panting.
All yours are the words
that came to my mouth all alone
like waters flowing over the edge,
the deserted hours, when my manly lips
childishly went forth all alone
for the sheer desire to kiss . . .

—3—

It was the color of the sea and summer
the road along the houses and the orchard walls
where for the first time I looked for you.
At my incredulous glance you left,
uncertain, the sidewalk on the other side.
You did not even look at me. You squeezed
my wrist with the strength of one who clings.

e la casa sul mare di Loano,
e tutta la mia poca gioia—e tu—
fin che mi strazi questo ricordare.

—2—

Ora che sei venuta,
che con passo di danza sei entrata
nella mia vita
quasi folata in una stanza chiusa—
a festeggiarti, bene tanto atteso,
le parole mi mancano e la voce
e tacerti vicino già mi basta.

Il pigolìo così che assorda il bosco
al nascere dell'alba, ammutolisce
quando sull'orizzonte balza il sole.

Ma te la mia inquietudine cercava
quando ragazzo
nella notte d'estate mi facevo
alla finestra come soffocato:
che non sapevo, m'affannava il cuore.
E tutte tue sono le parole
che, come l'acqua all'orlo che trabocca,
alla bocca venivano da sole,
l'ore deserte, quando s'avanzavan
puerilmente le mie labbra d'uomo
da sé, per desiderio di baciare . . .

—3—

Era color del mare e dell'estate
la strada tra le case e i muri d'orto
dove la prima volta ti cercai.
All'incredulo sguardo ti staccasti
un po' incerta dall'altro marciapiede.
Nemmeno mi guardasti. Mi stringesti,
con la forza di chi s'attacca, il polso.

Then side by side we proceeded silently for a while.

Now a car, barely conquered calamity,
has brought me
toward the place of our first encounter.

My heart already recognizes the turn
when the car like a burst enters the street,
and there you are "you left
uncertain the sidewalk on the other side"
(it was only a cruel imagining:
in vain he tries with this anxiety
the role, if evil already overtook it.)

The time to think of you; but in the instant
what delightful thorn pierced me!
No other joy you gave me was as intense
as this, it could not be.
I loved you. I loved. I too had someone
in this world.

Oh blessed road among the houses,
where for the first time in my life
my heart felt pity for someone other than myself.

—4—

And . . . oh what life was to me,
my love, before I met you . . .

A desert the earth: at times the world
an image that trembles out of focus.
My day from night not much different:
the usual faces seen in dreams
like phantoms; so as to not discern
whether my life were wake or sleep.
Like the man frightened by the market place,
stands back before that vacuity,
how many times I loathed the day
that forced my eyes to morning!

A fianco procedemmo un tratto zitti.

Una macchina adesso mi portava,
procella appena dominata, verso
il luogo di quel primo appuntamento.

Già la svolta il mio cuore riconosce
e, raffica, la macchina la imbocca,
ed ecco *tu ti stacchi*
un po'incerta dall'altro marciapiede.
(Non era che un crudele immaginare:
paralitico tenta con quest'ansia
la parte, se già il male la guadagni.)

Il tempo di pensarti; ma nell'attimo
che dolcissima spina mi trafisse!
Acuta come questa non mi desti
altra gioia, non mi potevi dare.
T'amavo. Amavo. Anche per me nel mondo
c'era qualcuno.

O strada tra le case, benedetta,
dove la prima volta nella vita
pietà d'altri che me mi strinse il cuore.

— 4 —

E la vita sapessi a me che fu,
Amore, prima che ti conoscessi . . .

Un deserto la terra; a volte, il mondo
una sfocata immagine che trema.
I volti consueti dai fantasmi
visti in sogno, il mio giorno dalla notte
poco diverso; sì da dubitare
se veglia o sonno fosse la mia vita.
Uomo che s'atterrisce della piazza,
arretra innanzi a quella vacuità,
quante volte dal sonno ripugnai
al giorno che le palpebre forzava!

One day in the tumultuous city
where flights of roads open
infinite prospects to the naked eye,
in me instead stupor brought discomfort.
The city tired me with its
panting
like the flowing of a river that can't find
its outlet; it frightened me with its size
like a colossus that lacks the light
of gaze . . .

When suddenly like the obscure
drawing that a child attempts with blocks
lights up with the missing one
the tumult subsided, my rage
calmed down, river that appeases in the sea,
like two embracing in the dark.

—5—

Come fall it happens that searching
with a ladder the naked vine, a man

—old is the man and autumn colors
his soul inside with melancholy;
for with the year it seems to him his life
also may end;
what little he got from life
brings to his throat a dryness, he swallows—

may find among the reddish leaves
one left over bunch of grapes.
He fills
his hand, filled by a childlike joy;
he weighs it with his eyes in disbelief.

Un dì nella città tumultuosa
dove fughe di strade a vista d'occhio
aprono prospettive d'infinito,
disagio da stupore in me nasceva.
M'affaticava la città col suo
ànsito
quale andare di fiume che non trovi
foce; m'impauriva con la mole
quasi colosso che non abbia luce
di sguardo . . .

Quando, improvvisamente come oscuro
disegno che coi dadi bimbo tenta
s'illumina del dado che mancava,
si compose il tumulto, si placò
l'ànsito, fiume che si placa in mare,
in due che s'abbracciavano nell'ombra.

—5—

Càpita all'uomo che d'autunno spoglia
la vite, sulla scala che ne fruscia

—vecchio è l'uomo ed autunno gli colora
l'anima dentro di malinconia;
chè con l'anno gli pare la sua vita
anche finisca;
il poco che da essa ebbe gli mette
in strozza come una secchezza e inghiotte—

tra i pampini arrossati di scoprire
un superstite grappolo.
Ne colma
la mano, preso d'infantile gioia;
soppesa quasi non credesse agli occhi.

For his thirst the year's crop saved
that fruit; summer matured it,
the autumn sun turned it to gold,
the plant gave it its last juices.

The grape he hulls in his mouth
not to lose a single drop, drips with sugar;
each grape graces him with a silent
delight . . .

Happy and resigned eyes gaze
with each missing grape
the passing of its first, perhaps last, sweetness.

1931

The girl that runs under the trees
has no burden but that of her tresses
and a tiny song in her voice.
She sings alone
and jumps along the way; for she does not
know that greater joy she'll never have
than that bit of lively gold on her back
and that joy in her throat.

We who hold
no other happiness except of words,
and no bright colored bow upon our nape nor the vast
hope that fills her heart to overflowing,
if it's not too much to ask, take first
our life then that lonely joy.

1932

Alla sua sete riserbò l'annata
quel frutto; glielo maturò l'estate,
glielo dorò il sole dell'autunno,
la pianta vi spremè l'ultimo succo.

Cola zucchero l'acino che sguscia
in bocca per non perdere una goccia;
ogni acino lo riga di delizia
silenziosa . . .

Guardan gli occhi felici e rassegnati
col grappolo scemare
la sua prima, fors'ultima, dolcezza.

1931

La bambina che va sotto gli alberi
non ha che il peso della sua treccia,
un fil di canto in gola.
Canta sola
e salta per la strada; ché non sa
che mai bene più grande non avrà
di quel po' d'oro vivo per le spalle,
di quella gioia in gola.

A noi che non abbiamo
altra felicità che di parole,
e non l'acceso fiocco e non la molta
speranza che fa grosso a quella il cuore,
se non è troppo chiedere, sia tolta
prima la vita di quel solo bene.

1932

Selections from *Shavings**

I

By now I resemble the vine I once saw in astonishment. It climbed a house wall out of the cobblestone. Transplanted it would have died.
My soul has put its roots in the stones of the city, elsewhere it would not know how to live. And if by chance I look up to the distant mountains for some relief, they really no longer speak to me.
The atrocious lights at the end of a blind alley excite me instead.
My heart still hangs in *ex voto* in some dark, desolate street.
The aspects of things touch me the way no human gesture could.
Like the vine I feed on aridity. More than a woman I am deluded by silks and artifices. Mere flashings in a mirror appease me.
At times, to disturb the inertia in which I lull myself, a one-dimensional world, from who knows that recesses of my being, appears before me, and lost in it, my own infancy.
At this calling I raise myself, and trembling I lean to listen . . .
Ah, it was but a memory of a previous existence!

Perhaps I am petrifying.
My eyes already seem made of glass, that's how long I do not cry; and the heart seems but a heavy pebble.

---

*The numbering of the selections follows the 1963 printing of the 1948 Mondadori edition.

From *Trucioli*

I

Ormai somiglio a una vite che vidi un dì con stupore. Cresceva su un muro di casa nascendo da un lastrico. Trapiantata, sarebbe intristita. Cosí l'anima ha messo radice nella pietra della città e altrove non saprebbe piú vivere. E se ancora m'avviene di guardar come a scampo ai monti lontani, in realtà essi non mi parlano piú.
Mi esalta il fanale atroce a capo del vicolo chiuso. Il cuore resta appeso in ex voto *a chiassuoli a crocicchi. Aspetti di cose mi toccano come nessun gesto umano potrebbe.*
Come la vite mi cibo di aridità. Piú della femmina, m'illudono le sete e gli artifizi. Il lampeggiar degli specchi m'appaga.
A volte, a disturbare l'inerzia in cui mi compiaccio, affiora, chi sa da che piega di me, un mondo a una sola dimensione e, smarrita per esso, l'infanzia. Al richiamo mi tendo, trepidante mi chino in ascolto . . . Ah non era che il ricordo d'un'esistenza anteriore!

Forse mi vado mineralizzando.
Già il mio occhio è di vetro, da tanto non piango; e il cuore, un ciottolo pesante.

2

Ventisettembre St. in the first rosy morning sun. Mostly in the shade: grey and monumental; but all pink up there, in the square like a flower atop the stem. Some needless lamps. The trolleys, like buzzing wasps, are already shuttling back and forth: dark down here, up there they sparkle. Windows acquire in the sun a touch of fire. In the square a fine mist of gold dust turns everything dark. Shadows of buildings steaming. In the end the guides of the trolley shine like tracks overrun by water.

3

One livid dawn in the city when the trolleys loaded with commuters poured toward factories and the store shutters rolling up screamed in the stillness, I felt a sense of anguish. In the woman who slowly crossed the street I saw the dankish larva that will shrivel up the plant. The mouth of another disgusted me like the sight of a leech. In the slender figure that crossed the exit of the post-office I recognized an atrocious locust.

4

The downpour like a brush has given the landscape a quick touch up: it has washed the façades of the houses, revived the fading hills. The air too is clean.
Every shade of green is now more appreciable.
Like small town girls dressed in their Sunday best, the houses form prints of checks and plaids of all colors. Look at that yellow; oh, the naiveté of that light blue!
Eastward a light of magnesium makes the scene livid.
Roofs sparkle.
Where the mountain was furrowed before, now shines a vein of silver.

2

Via Ventisettembre al primo sole, rossiccio. Per la maggior parte, in ombra: grigia e ímonumentale; ma rosea lassú la piazza—fiore in cima al gambo.
Dei lumi inutili. I tram, vespe ronzanti, fanno già la spola: bruni qui, lassú sfavillano. Una vetrata mette nel roseo un tocco di fuoco.
A volgersi dalla piazza, invece, un pulviscolo d'oro annebbia tutto. Sagome di palazzi, fumanti. In fondo, le guide del tram, lucenti come carraie colme d'acqua.

3

Una livida alba cittadina che i tram carichi s'avventavano verso le officine e le saracinesche sollevate gridavano, provai un senso d'angoscia. In una femmina lenta che traversava la strada scorsi la larva molliccia che fa intristire la pianta. La bocca d'un'altra mi ripugnò come la vista d'una mignatta. Nella magra che incrociava sprezzante l'uscita dei portalettere riconobbi un'atroce cavalletta.

4

La spazzola dell'acquazzone ha dato alla lesta una ripulita al paesaggio: lavato la faccia alle case, avvivato i monti sbiaditi.
Anche l'aria è netta. Ora si apprezza ogni gradazione di verde.
Villanelle vestite a festa, le case fanno insieme una stoffa a quadratini, a rettangolini di tutti i colori. Quel giallo! l'ingenuità di quel celeste!
A levante, illividisce la scena una luce di magnesio.
I tetti specchiano.
Dov'era una ruga, la montagna fa mostra d'un filone d'argento.

II

Ever since I have been able to talk, my life has been struck by immobility. Of the most desirable good, like a fruit, if a word touches it, there will be nothing left but the peel. And when I was able to pray "Father who held us on your knees . . ." in that moment my father died (his natural death was a regrettable and unnecessary repetition).
Thus I immure myself and words are the rocks. My life is marked like the trolley by the tracks without any possible switch. For if anxieties seize me, and certain alarms sound, the recluse inside myself, he too, lifts up his eyes to that tiny patch of blue in the sky.
Needlessly the night train must have left me sleepless as a child; and I will die in my bed having sung Perdition.

Perhaps at the end of this road is silence. Already every word is too much for me. Soon I will fill the page with a mere interjection.

At the end of this road is silence, I hope. To have no face among men, but to see dawn rising on the other parts of the world! A shiphand, to throw away this insipid European soul and return from countries where one can kill with thick vulgar rings upon one's fingers . . .

May I turn mute, and the words not uttered remain like stones on my heart, as long as I may depart one day for the world and forget my very name.

7

Always ready to break away, when the fever of the city seizes me, the more to life I radicate myself. Only possible gesture of love: to take my mute wandering for a walk. (Little do the coachmen know, in offering me their services, that motionless at the corner of the street I am consumating my wedding night with the city.)

II

Da quando posso parlare, la mia vita è colpita d'immobilità.
Del piú desiderabile bene, se la parola lo tocca, rimane la buccia. E quando potei pregare: Padre, che ci hai tenuto sui ginocchi . . ., *in quel punto mio padre morì (la sua morte naturale fu un bis increscioso).*
Cosí da me mi muro e pietre sono le parole. La mia vita è segnata come il tram dalla rotaia senza possibili scarti. Perché se delle ansie mi prendono, se squillano allarmi, il recluso anche lui alza gli occhi al pezzetto di cielo.
Inutilmente il direttissimo della notte m'avrà lasciato insonne, fanciullo; e mi spegnerò nel mio letto avendo cantato la Perdizione.

Ma forse in fondo a questa strada è il silenzio. Già ogni parola m'è di troppo. Presto riempirò la pagina con una interiezione.

In fondo a questa strada è il silenzio, io spero. Non aver volto fra gli uomini, ma vedere l'alba nascere sulle altre parti del mondo!
Mozzo, rigettare questa frolla anima europea e tornare dai paesi dove si può uccidere con grossi anelli volgari al dito . . .

Diventi muto e le parole non dette mi restino pietre sul cuore, purché parta un giorno pel mondo a scordarmi anche il nome.

7

Io, sempre pronto a staccarmi, quando la febbre della città mi prende, alla vita mi radico. Solo gesto d'amore possibile: condurre a spasso la mia muta meraviglia. (Non sanno i cocchieri, offrendomi i lor servigi, che fermo alla cantonata sto consumando le mie nozze con la città.)

There are streets that open up like questions to which there are no answers; others that fill us with daring like sudden fanfares; others that appease us like a breath of sea . . .
But the least notable aspects are those that grip me. Thus to penetrate the secret of the stuffy little square, I'd gladly switch place with the notary's clerk who has no clients; to live the life of that branch of the street, I'd gladly switch roles with the accountant buried in that dark underground warehouse. . . .
And in the presence of others the wrinkle that marks my face like the effort of a mute to express himself! And, coming back, the regret, that still crosses me like a sword, of not knowing how the sun lights a certain street at a certain hour!

Desire in the end to be a common man in order that my passion without voice would make me only suffer and nothing more.

III

Crossing a deserted street between the dark shadows of two mountains, I hoped my life would disappear, like a creek in the sand. Through the stone countryside I hoped to scream in terror without voice as in nightmares.
Then returning home the hour when the intoxication is nothing more than bitterness, I expected that the shadowy and reproaching face of my father would come toward me.
And embracing an unknown female in the bed possessed by all, I prayed that rubber doll would fall off in my hands, the foulness of the anatomic piece . . .

Dressing and undressing; opening and closing; through the city I drag myself, and its din fills me like an echo chamber; when I barricade myself in the smoke of my cigarette as in a world all mine, I hide the light by which my sister, now employed, toils all night; in the dead hours, in the greatest silence the expectation of something stops my heart.

Ci sono vie che s'aprono come domande che non han risposta; altre, che riempiono d'ardimenti come fanfare improvvise; altre, che pacificano come il respiro del mare . . .
Ma gli aspetti meno notevoli sono quelli che m'impugnano. Allora, per penetrare il segreto della piazzetta muffita, mi cambierei col commesso del notaio senza pratiche; per vivere la vita di quel braccio di strada, col contabile seppellito nel buio del fondaco . . .
E ruga, davanti ad altri, che mi segna la faccia come al muto lo sforzo di esprimersi! E, al ritorno, rimpianto che mi attraversa ancora come una spada, di non sapere in che modo il sole illumina a cert'ora certa via!

Desiderio, alla fine, d'essere un uomo qualunque perché la mia passione senza voce mi facesse solo soffrire.

III

Percorrendo una via deserta fra buie forme di monti, sperai che la via si perdesse, rivo nella sabbia. Per il paese impietrato, di terrore io gridassi senza voce come nei sogni.
Rifacendo la strada di casa all'ora che l'ebbrezza non è piú che amaro, m'attesi che a paro mi venisse il viso d'ombra e di rimprovero di mio padre.
Abbracciando un'ignota su un letto di tutti, pregai mi restasse tra mano il bambolotto di gomma, la laidezza del pezzo anatomico . . .

Vestendomi e svestendomi; aprendo e chiudendo la porta; mentre per città mi trascino e del suo frastuono mi riempio come la caverna dell'eco; quando, a nascondermi il lume che fila, la sorella che s'impiega, nel fumo della sigaretta mi asserraglio come in un mondo a me;
nell'ore morte, nel piú grande silenzio
m'arresta il cuore l'aspettativa di qualche cosa.

Thus from aridity springs forth the desperate invocation of the supernatural.

13

In an artificial spring landscape made of canvas and cardboard, moves the dancer—monstrous flower of flesh and silk. Certainly she moves along an harmonic plot that her winged feet touch and leave, taking from it the companion sound of its gesture.
I like this town: old boats with their golden bellies, monocled by an occasional flower, a fox, a voracious mouth; the drinking glass across the way to deceive one's eye . . . I like this town where all is false and brilliant, this rainbow-like veil hiding putrefaction . . .
His eyes fixed on the one who sways her hips and uncovers her shoulder, the merchant all flushed can barely breathe in search as he is of women, mere toys in his thick hands; the artificial old man; one eyed Alphonse, like a dog that won't let go his bone . . .
But the dancer is the mirror, I hope, that any breath can mist, the rose that smelling alone will cause to shed its petals.
Touch it and it will wither—like an old woman that, outraged, rounds the corner.

15

Spotorno, avaricious land. The olive blanches in the sun, and the sorb tree lades hard bunches of fruits.
You sit tacitly on a grassy beach, staring at a pale sea, trembling at times like a handful of sequins; offshore the orange shell of an oil tanker.
The gravel bed is blinding. The mountain displays its white wounds.
In the orchards the peeling pink houses are startled by the passing of the train. News of a choppy sea floods the village.
Sportorno, landscape of the soul; sky one drinks by just looking.

Cosí dalla mia aridità scaturisce la disperata invocazione del soprannaturale.

13

In una primavera posticcia di tela e cartoni, la ballerina si muove—fiore mostruoso di carne e di seta.
Certo si muove su una trama armonica, che i suoi piedi alati toccano e lasciano, traendone il suono compagno del gesto.
Mi piace questo paese: le barcacce dal ventre dorato fiorite di radi monocoli, di volpi, di bocche voraci; il bicchiere di contro dove lo sguardo s'inganna . . . Mi piace questo paese dove tutto è falso e brillante, questo velo iridato sulla putrefazione . . .
Con gli occhi in lei che molleggia l'anca e scopre l'ascella, fiata a stento il mercante congestionato, in cerca di donne, balocchi per le sue grosse mani; il vecchio artificiale; l'alfonso guercio, cane su un osso . . .
Ma la ballerina è lo specchio, io spero, che un alito appanna, la rosa che si sfoglia a odorarla.
Toccata, avvizzirebbe—vecchia che, piena d'onta, scantona.

15

Spotorno, terra avara. Vi imbianca l'olivo, il sorbo vi si carica di mazzetti duri.
Ti siedi e taci sulla spiaggia sterposa di contro a un pallido mare. Vi tremola a volte una manciata di zecchini; al largo passa il guscio rossastro della petroliera.
Il greto abbacina. La montagna mostra bianche ferite. Negli orti le casette screpolate rosee trasaliscono al passaggio del direttissimo. Allaga l'abitato la voce della maretta. Spotorno, paesaggio dell'anima; cielo che a guardarlo si beve.

I live *ex voto* each time I see how ingenously the waterfront behaves before this rising sun. The hills are like sheep following the shearing. The promontory facing Bergeggi is nothing but the curls of its pinetops.
And the sea! I know a sea seething with gold where sails flash like slender flames; a sea so impalpable as to think it a trick of one's eyes; a sea that's all liquid sapphire in which one would like to dissolve.
And another that's but a grey slate, barely turning to silver in the orient.
Of all the seas I know, this is the one I love: it awakens in me the spirit of adventure.
When suddenly, a fiery ball leaps in the appropriate scenario, trailing at its feet a pattern all orange, flapping like a rug hung to dry.

IV. Geography

As a child I envied the wooden lady at the stern:
carried along the waters she sees capes vanishing in the distance tumultuous cities rising in their places.

Condemned to the chair, I hated the dear paternal walls. I became like a paraplegic who sees the world outside as all beauty.

Philadelphia became thus where cars in flight reach the third floor, the Fiji Islands where women wear laced sponge and Portugal where wrought iron red lights denote brothels.

That's how the sedentary soul constructed to its comfort a child's map made of hearsays just thrown together.

Sadder still, I indulged also in landscapes seen in dreams: a metropolis of white stone, uninhabited and lunatic, the cistern where among green jewels lived a snake-like water faucet.

To-day, pacified I smile.

One takes the most wonderful trips from the table of a pub.

Vivo in un *ex voto* a vedere come la marina si comporta ingenuamente davanti a questa levata di sole. Le colline paion pecore dopo la tosatura. Il promontorio in faccia all'isolotto di Bergeggi è appena ricciuto di pinastri.
E il mare!—Conosco un mare brulicante d'oro dove le vele sono fiamme esili; uno, impalpabile da credere ad un inganno degli occhi; un mare che è tutto uno zaffiro liquefatto, in cui si vorrebbe stemperarsi.
Questo, è una grigia lavagna, appena argentata a levante. Piú di tutti i mari che so, è questo che amo: esso risveglia in me l'anima avventurosa.
Quand'ecco, nell'appropriato scenario, il sole balza, bolla infocata, sciorinandosi ai piedi un tremolante tappeto arancione.

IV Geografia

Fanciullo invidiai nel porto la donna di legno popputa: portata sull'acque vede i capi svanire in lontananza, nascere le città tumultuose.

Condannato alla sedia, poi, odiai le care pareti. Divenni nella stanza il paralitico che vede il mondo tutto bello fuori di lí.

Filadelfia fu allora dove l'auto in volata sale al terzo ordine di palchi
dove le femmine portano collane di spugne, le isole Figi
il Portogallo, dove lampioncini rossi a bracci di ferro indicano i postriboli.

Cosí l'anima sedentaria si fabbricava a conforto con dei sentito dire *affastellati insieme un'infantile carta geografica.*

Piú triste, di paesaggi visti in sonno mi compiacqui: una metropoli di bianca pietra disabitata e lunatica, la cisterna dove verde monile viveva una serpe acquaiola.

Oggi pacificato sorrido.

Si fanno a un tavolo d'osteria i piú meravigliosi viaggi.

17

From the night dampness that stagnates over the gulf in steam, Rapallo emerges at dawn a lustruous archipelago of rooftops.
The last festoons of wisteria collapse under the downpours of May. In the air already the acidulous odor of new hay.
The olive trees climb along the hillsides like sheep ready to be shorn.
By night the dark and warm farmland spurts myriads of fireflies.

V

In the grey cinematographic world women pass like exclamations of color.

They walk like haughty doves. The ticking of their heels is my reawakening.

There are women that fashion makes into curious animals; others into greenhouse flowers.
There is the child with worn-out heels who still looks unshakably straight ahead
the bride that the glitter of the store windows enchants like the eye of a snake.

I am startled by the young girl that goes past me dancing on the rhythm of her hips; the star of the nearby musical café walks her heels deep into my heart. It is I that at the foot of the trolley await the stabbing of some fleeting ankle.

Yet there is a country where I can never go. With my most anxious silence I question those who have been there.

And not because of the kisses that send you walking down the streets like gods, the dimples, the blushes, the snatching of a body still fresh;

17

Dall'umido della notte che stagna sul golfo in vapore, Rapallo
all'alba emerge, lustro arcipelago di tetti.
Si sfanno sotto le acquate di maggio gli ultimi festoni di glicine.
Si respira nell'aria, acidetto, l'odore del fieno novello.
Gli uliveti salgono i colli, simili a greggi da tondere.
A notte, la campagna bruna e calda sprizza lucciole.

V

Nel mondo cinematografico grigio esclamazioni di colore passano le donne.

Camminano come colombe altezzose. Il ticchettio dei passi è il mio risveglio.

Ci sono donne che la Moda fa somigliare a curiosi animali; altre, a fiori di serra.
C'è la creatura che ha i tacchi consunti ma guarda incrollabilmente innanzi a sé
la sposa che il barbaglio della vetrina incanta come l'occhio del serpente.

Mi fa trasalire la fanciulla che m'oltrepassa sul ritmo dei fianchi; mi passeggia con gli stivaletti sul cuore la stella di caffè concerto.
Io sono che a piedi del tram aspetto la pugnalata della fugace caviglia.

Ma c'è un paese dove non potrò andar mai. Interrogo quelli che vi furono col mio piú anscioso silenzio.

E non per i baci che fanno per strada camminare come iddii, le pozzette, i rossori, il fresco corpo ghermito;

I long for love for its sadness, I sought its passion to lose me through its ashes.

Oh, to know the cruelty of a wait, the return along the walls! The pangs of love in front of a door! Life inside of a room, filled only with a ghost!

In the daily's short story, the intrigue of passion, hinting the well worn plot,

> "Oh flower of my life they whisper after me,
> and something gets me in my throat."

Were I, at least, able to cry like an old spinster reading her sentimental novel!

Regret grips me and nearly breaks my heart.

VI

As a child, what wonderful lovers I had.
They came out of magazines bought secretly, looked at by light of candle.
Oh the libertine images seen through the eyes of an adolescent!

The squeaking of the door, behind which spied a familiar eye, nearly froze me. Still in every female that toured my room, my desire discovered a mythical bacchante
while even now I am excited by the mere rectangle of light in the alley where I cannot enter without a thump in my heart.

And if the regret of my first lovers awakens in me the will to cry, afterwards I can still recognize them, starry-eyed, coming out of a theatre, at the passing of a carriage.

But when a woman sits on the street car next to me, something awakens me like a nudge.
I see that I will never walk down a side street with a woman at my arm.

per la sua tristezza amo l'amore, cercai per la sua cenere la passione che mi perdesse.

Oh conoscere la crudeltà dell'attesa, il ritorno lungo i muri! Spasimo davanti a una porta! Vita nella stanza, piena solo d'un fantasma!

Nella novella del quotidiano, l'intreccio di passione s'accenni, abusato,

o fior di mia vita *mi zufolino dappresso*
qualcosa alla gola mi prende.

Potessi almeno piangere come la zitella sul romanzo sentimentale!

Un rimpianto m'attanaglia che pare il cuore mi voglia scoppiare.

VI

Fanciullo, ebbi delle meravigliose amanti.
Uscivano da giornali comprati di soppiatto, scorsi a lume di candela.
Oh le immagini libertine viste coi miei occhi di adolescente!

Poi mi gelò il diruggìnio dell porta dietro cui un occhio spia. Ma in ogni femminella che faceva il giro della stanza il mio desiderio scorgeva una ménade
e ancora m'esalta il rettangolo di luce nel vicolo dove non entro senza un tuffo al cuore.

E se, dopo, il rimpianto delle prime amanti mi dilata il petto come una voglia di pianto
all'uscita d'un teatro, al passare d'una carrozza gli occhi stupefatti le riconoscono ancora.

Ma quando una ragazza sale sul tram accanto a me, qualche cosa come un urto mi desta.
Capisco che non camminerò mai per una strada fuorimano tenendo una donna allacciata.

And it would be so sweet to kiss this one next to me who seems to wait that I speak to her.
I see her so distant, as someone that to me cannot possibly matter.
And since I lived my love affairs only in my fantasy, and since neither the others were made of flesh, but were mere phantasms I embraced, and nothing real, I sense suddenly that I have never really kissed a woman, and with a sudden chill I see myself crossing the world like a priest all in black.

18

She sang with her throaty voice, her eyes still.
I looked astonished at her arms so real. Through the bed I felt the warmth of the rest of her body permeating as good as fresh bread at home.
And in my heart I thought:
—How did you ever end up in this public room? Perhaps like the swallow that came in through the window blinded by the sun, and collapsed after hitting the walls in an attempt to escape. —I can feel your heart beating in my hand. —What disruption your arrival must have brought among those automatic dolls! Men too will be perturbed. Here the air used to be artificial like the orange on the dresser; but convenient to those who could breath no other. You opened a window.
She spoke of a little niece, Pepíca. She told the names, the places. Perhaps she thought it necessary to open a bit of her soul to justify herself.
—I have never fallen in love with anyone—I went on telling her in silence. —You are the first woman that I see so close. The others walk past me closed in themselves, or merely exchange words of convention. Not one of them has made me feel more than a burning desire or a sense of failure for my useless life. But as I want a flower at my modest table to fool the eye, in life I need to hope that love will come, oh, any kind of love. If only I could love just once, even the most ill-fated love. I look forward to it. It's my only regret. At times my lips reach out by themselves for the sheer desire to kiss.

E costei che è vicina e pare aspetti le parli e sarebbe tanto dolce baciare la vedo lontana, cosa che non mi riguarda.
E poiché i miei amori li consumai nella fantasia e neppure gli altri furono corpi, ma fantasmi abbracciati, nulla di saldo,
sento improvvisamente che non ho mai baciato una donna e con un leggero freddo mi vedo nero prete traversare il mondo.

18

Trillava a gola piena, occhi fermi.
Guardavo con stupore le sue braccia vere. Per la coltre sentivo il tepore del suo corpo propagarsi buono come per casa quello del pane. E in cuore le dicevo:
—Come sei capitata in questa stanza di tutti? Forse al modo della rondine che, accecata dal sole, infila la finestra e, dopo molto urtare nelle pareti, stramazza. —Sento il tuo cuore sbattere nella mano. —Che scompiglio, il tuo arrivo, tra le bambole automatiche! Anche gli uomini ne saranno disturbati. L'aria qui era finta come l'arancia del comò; ma a chi sempre la respira, conveniva. Tu hai aperto una finestra.
Discorreva d'una nipotina, Pepìca. Diceva i nomi, i luoghi. Forse le pareva necessario schiudermi, per giutificarsi, un po' della sua anima.
—Io non ho mai amato—seguitavo a dirle in silenzio. —Sei la prima donna tu che vedo da vicino. Le altre m'oltrepassano in sé chiuse o scambiano parole di convenienza. Ché nessuna m'ha mai dato piú d'un desiderio scottante o d'un senso di mancamento per l'inutile vita. Ma come alla mia mensa povera voglio il fiore per illudervi gli occhi, nella vita ho bisogno di sperare che un amore verrà. Oh qualunque. Potessi una volta amare e fosse il piú sciagurato amore. Lo aspetto. È il solo rimpianto. A certe ore s'allungano le mie labbra d'uomo, da sé, per una voglia di baciare.

That's what I thought; but to her I said instead: "You are Pepíca. Sing!"

Later I saw her in the street. Other women slipped past me whose make up and lightness of step made them look false. She, instead, made real gestures, her face lit up with happiness. A man who turned to her in a smile escorted her. And by the way she moved her feet, I don't know, or from the roundness of the wrist she uncovered at every gesture, she confirmed my very first impression of her: a human being alive among shadows.

That's why when Madam told me that Nuccia had been taken away, I was not surprised but lit a cigarette. "So" I said "there is always love in this world." For Madam it was not a question of love but "of too much money in circulation."

—Inside this place it's best to think love doesn't exist—I thought. In that moment Ginetta walked in and promptly jumped on my lap. With that movement her breast, a bit tired but still sweet, bounced out of her dress, an homage to my lips, while she caressed my face with hers, small and dark in the shadow of the tresses she shook without pause.

And I was about to think that I must be satisfied and that adult dolls have soft skin, and wise lips, when suddenly she uttered that laughter I knew, that she accompanied with the crinkling of her nose. At that moment I could not keep myself from feeling it was the pressing of my hand in pulling her to me that had brought about that outburst; that's how I recalled entire women made to order in inflatable rubber. So, without impatience, but firmly, I got her off of me.

Alone again, Madam said: "Ginetta is leaving too". I looked at her teased hair, the composed face of a madam. What in her was vaguely repugnant seemed to show up in me also, in some way.

And I said with a smile: "It's just you and me, Madam".

Questo pensai; ma le dissi: "Pepíca sei tu. Canta!".

In seguito la vidi per via. Donne mi scivolavano accanto che le ciprie e la levità del passo faceva parere fallaci. Lei gestiva un po', accaldata di lietezza in volto. Un uomo l'accompagnava che le si volgeva sorridente. E pel modo di posare i piedi, non so, o per il polso rotondo che nel gesto scopriva, mi confermò nell'impressione che di sé m'aveva dato la prima volta: d'un essere vivo tra larve.

Per cui quando la padrona m'annunciò che Nuccia se l'eran portata via, non stupii ma accesi una sigaretta.
"Sicché" feci "c'è sempre amore pel mondo."
Per madama non si trattava d'amore ma "del troppo danaro in giro".
—Qui dentro è buono credere che amore non esiste—pensai.
In quella entrò Ginetta che mi venne cavalcioni sui ginocchi. Nell'atto le sgorgarono dalle scollatura, s'offrirono alle labbra, i seni un po' stanchi ma dolci ancora, mentr'ella andava strofinando sul mio il viso minuto e buio nell'ombra delle trecciole che senza tregua scoteva.
E io già pensavo che a ciò dovevo star pago e che le bambole per adulti han pur morbida pelle e labbra sapienti, quando quella fece sentire un risetto che le conoscevo e che accompagnava con l'arricciare del naso.
Non potei lí per lí difendermi dal senso che il premere della mia mano nel recarmela contro avesse fatto traboccare per le nari quel soffio; per cui mi tornò il ricordo delle donne intere che si fabbricano in gomma su commissione. Onde, senza impazienza ma con fermezza, me la tolsi d'addosso.
Tornati soli, disse Madama: "Anche Ginetta se ne va".
Guardai i suoi capelli gonfi, il viso composto di padrona. Ciò che in lei vagamente ripugnava, mi parve dovesse scorgersi su me pure, in qualche modo.
E dissi in un sorriso: "Restiamo noi, madama.".

20

In that thick cluster of houses in Old Ventimiglia there is an ancient little church. One night in my roving I turned upon a square; it appeared to me as if detached in a sky more azure than by day, and a great moon turned into mother-of-pearl a flock of little light clouds clustered together.
There was nothing more than this; but the moon gave that place an aspect so astonishing that it seemed to live in an old print.

A passing child held by a woman's hand jibbed at the sight of the sky, longing for the moon as for a new toy; and both stopped in the middle of the square in exclamations of wonder.

A man, skimming the wall so as not to disturb the two, chose to say only:

'Clouds like sheep
If not today, it will rain tomorrow'

Then, taking two steps, he too stopped to look up, captured by the same wonder.
This remembrance will have the power to make me smile, who knows how many more years.

21

Noli comes to my heart. Disdainful of the earth, she looks to the sea like a wounded gull. The forbidding mountains won't have in spring the whiteness of a single apple blossom. Only the olive tree makes roots. The sea is a cold, infinite slate crossed by the shivering wind. Here came Dante, and here Bruno taught grammar to the *putti*. From here set sail the navigators out to round the Cape of Good Hope, when the sea was still full of wonder.

Women there are without mercy.

20

C'è nel fungaio di case di Ventimiglia vecchia un'antica chiesetta. Una notte che vagando sbucai su una piazza, essa m'apparí, staccata su un cielo più celeste che di giorno dove una grande luna faceva di madreperla un gregge di nuvolette ammonticchiate e leggere.
Non c'era che questo: ma la luna dava al luogo un aspetto cosí stupito che pareva di vivere in un'antica stampa.

Un bambino, che passava a mano d'una donna, alla vista del cielo s'impuntò, smaniando alla luna come verso un giocattolo nuovo; e i due si fermarono in mezzo alla piazza con esclamazioni di meraviglia.

Uno, rasentando il gruppo di premura, volle dir solo:

Cielo a pani
Se non piove oggi piove domani

ma, fatti altri due passi, anche lui s'arrestò a viso in su, colto da stupore.
Questo ricordo avrà virtú di farmi sorridere chi sa fra quanti anni ancora.

21

Mi cade in cuore Noli. Sdegnosa della terra, guarda il mare come un gabbiano ferito. La montagna arcigna non ha a primavera il biancore d'un melo. Solo l'ulivo vi attecchisce. Anche il mare è una fredda lavagna infinita, percorsa da brividi di vento.
Qui Dante discese e Bruno insegnò *a'putti la gramatica*. Di qui i navigatori partirono a doppiare il capo di Buona Speranza, quando il mare era pieno di meraviglioso.

Le donne vi sono senza grazia.

The sea breeze corrodes the red lookout towers, smooths over the pavement of the rough, dark porticoes.

I remember the low wall above Noli where I paused one afternoon to catch some sun. Too far to hear the sea. On shore the fishermen mended their nets. It seemed sweet to retire in one of those little houses crazed by the sun. From a tiny orchard down below rose the sweet odor of bitter oranges in bloom.

VII

In the landscape of the pub I am satisfied to be the chocolate tanned hunter.

But I prefer to live in *affiches*.

I am the man who brags portentously like an idol of VOULEZ-VOUS UN PEU D'OR MAXIMA VOUS EN DONNERA
I inhabit the most hallucinating milieu—pavements that reflect strange hanging pommels—of MURATTI'S AFTER LUNCH CIGARETTES

With the mineral water lady I dissolve like a butterfly in the shimmer of the crystals.

I make myself again the perfect NAUTILUS. Detached from the continent, I discover the new living styles just out of some diabolic forge.
Abysmal dawns refresh my eyes.

I witness the silent fights of sharks.
In the darkness lined by slow phosphoric shapes I hear my human heart beating.

> I live the stupefied life of the medusa
> the millenarian one of banks of coral
> the twilight one of beings that are neither beast nor plant
> . . .

Il marino morde le torri rosse a vedetta, lustra l'acciottolato dei portici tozzi e bui.

Mi sovviene il muretto sopra Noli dove indugiai un pomeriggio a prendere il sole. Il mare non s'udiva. Sulla spiaggia i pescatori rammendavano le reti. Mi pareva dolce finire la vita in una di quelle casette screpolate. Da un orticello lì sotto saliva l'odorino dei chinotti in fiore.

VII

Mi basta di solito nel paesaggio dell'osteria essere il cacciatore cioccolata.

Ma di preferenza vivo nelle affiches.

Sono l'uomo dallo sparato portentoso simile a un idolo di VOULEZ' VOUS UN PEU D'OR MAXIMA VOUS EN DONNERA
Abito l'ambiente allucinato—pavimento che specchia, strani pomi penduli—di MURATTI'S AFTER LUNCH CIGARETTES

Con la dama dell'acqua minerale mi dissolvo farfalla nel fuoco dei cristallami.

Mi fabbrico altre volte il NAUTILUS *perfezionato. Staccato dal continente, scopro le nuove fogge viventi uscite da una fucina diabolica.*
Mi rinfrescano gli occhi le aurore abissali.

Assisto alle mute lotte degli squali.
Nelle tenebre rigate da lente forme fosforiche odo battere il mio cuore d'uomo.

> *Vivo la vita stupefatta della medusa*
> *quella millenaria del banco di corallo*
> *la crepuscolare degli esseri né bestia né pianta . . .*

Remembrance of humanity, my collision with a ship down.

That's how the bloated opium smoker eludes the desolation of his room.
That's how the soul fiddles, sick child with soap bubbles.

25

A little boy came forward toddling on his crooked little legs catching with every step a bit of mud as if it were a flower.

He didn't notice my caress.

His eyes were filled with such clear wonder that, afterwards, I thought I had caressed a daisy.

26

In my mind I see pine trees projecting clearly like silhouettes above the dazzling light of the sea, down there; woods of umbrella-like pines, laden with cones hanging like bats; dusty hedges, bogs, junipers lit-up with berries.
We were not turbulent. We walked, my sister and I, the road between Varazze and Invrea, between us the dark and silent shadow of our father.
There were in the woods curious flowers, never seen again: blue corollas atop a straw-like stem that we used to chew.

37

At the end of supper three of us were left to look at each other, a bit disillusioned. Of Christmas nothing but some mistletoe I cut from a tree, and it's already withering.
When all of a sudden we hear quite an uproar and a child with two others behind pushes open the door and wanders in.
They wear little hats shaped like mushrooms and short little suits with tiny pockets bulging with food. They carry triumphantly a manger of colored cardboard that all three must have thought wonderful.

Ricordo dell'umanità, mi scontro nella nave coricata.

Cosí il gonfio fumator d'oppio elude la desolazione della sua stanza.
Cosí l'anima si gingilla, bambino malato con bolle di sapone.

25

Un bambino veniva avanti traballando sulle gambine discoste e cogliendo ad ogni passo un po' di fango come un fiore.

Non s'accorse della mia carezza.

Aveva gli occhi pieni di sí chiaro stupore che, dopo, credevo d'aver accarezzato una margherita.

26

Mi viene in mente i pini stagliati netti sul barbaglio del mare, laggiú; il bosco di pini parasole, gremito di pigne appese come pipistrelli; le siepi polverose, gli acquitrini, i ginepri accesi di coccole.
Non eravamo turbolenti. Camminavamo, mia sorella e io, lo stradale tra Varazze e Invrea, con in mezzo l'ombra zitta e nera di nostro padre.
C'erano nei boschi dei curiosi fiori non piú rivisti; corolle azzurre in cima a paglie, che noi mangiavamo.

37

A fine cena restiamo in tre a guardarci; un po' delusi. Di natalizio non c'è che il fascio di vischio da me spiccato a un pino e che già si accartoccia.
Quando s'ode gazzarra e spinge l'uscio un bambino dietro a cui altri due s'azzardano. Hanno dei cappellucci a fungo e degli abitucci sommari dai taschini che rigurgitano di cibarie.
Recano trionfalmente un presepe di cartone colorato che tutti e tre devono considerare meraviglioso.

Suddenly the biggest one, in a very sharp voice, breaks into a song that tells in verse of the birth of baby Jesus. He mimes. The other two listen with conviction. All three appear to wear some rouge: it's the cold and perhaps a bit the wine received from homes along the way.

Finally the singer drops his arms and the playing voice that has run down. One of us, more caring, rewards them with left-overs from a plate and sends them out; but not so fast as to miss the "hurray" and a "boo", a malice, they tell me, so typical of soldiers: the only sad thing and they had to learn it from the men. With great clamour they swarm to knock at another door.

That's how on Christmas night children go from house to house behind the littlest one who lights the way with his wide, cow-like eyes through streets hazardous with ice.

Thank you, children. Because of you this one too has been a little bit like Christmas.

Terres, 1918

38

There are still the animals to make me smile: light grey or yellow locks of wool the tiny chicks with little winking eyes. Baby ducks fluttering in the puddles: zig zagging all over; and noisily fighting with their wooden beaks over the least little thing, perhaps a piece of paper.

And the frog! All palpitations: its throat of white satin, cold, flaccid lower belly, tiny nostrils. The only still things the tiny black pearls of its eyes.

In search of new acquaintances I visit the public gardens. I recall a palmiped, the size of a pigeon, looking like a brightly colored tin toy. It moved among its smaller colleagues as cocky as a mother-in-law.

Di colpo il piú grandicello rompe in una voce acutissima che descrive in versi la nascita del Bambin Gesú. Gestisce. Gli altri lo ascoltano con convinzione. Tutti e tre paiono imbellettati: è il freddo e un po', forse, il vino avuto nelle case.

Finché il cantore lascia cadere le braccia e la voce-giocattolo che ha consumato la carica. Uno di noi, sollecito, li ricompensa da un piatto e li caccia; non cosí presto che non si oda un *evviva* e un *abbasso*: malizia, mi dicono, che usano coi soldati: l'unica cosa trista e l'hanno appresa dagli uomini.
Con baccano sciamano a bussare a un'altra porta.

Cosí nella notte di Natale vanno di casa in casa dietro il piú piccolo che fa luce con un occhio di bue per le vie rischiose di gelo.

Grazie, bambini. Per voi anche questo è stato un poco Natale.

Térres, 1918

38

Ci sono ancora gli animali che mi fanno sorridere; i batuffoli di lana bigia o giallina dei pulcini dagli occhietti palpebranti. Gli anitraccoli che starnazzano nella pozzanghera: bordeggiano; si disputano clamorosamente coi becchi di legno magari il pezzo di carta.

E la rana! Palpita tutta: il gorgozzule di raso bianco, la pancetta fredda, i forellini delle nari. Di fermo non ha che le perline nere degli occhi.

In cerca di conoscenze, visito i pubblici giardini. Ricordo un palmipede, grosso come un piccione, che pareva un giocattolo di latta chiassosamente colorato. Tra i minori colleghi procedeva presuntuoso come una suocera.

I smile.
From contemplating animals I emerge like a plant after a downpour. Refreshed.

And yet it happens, despite what you might expect, that for some animals you feel no sympathy. These are the animals who look like humans. By a strange contagion each got his disposition from the quarrelsome master, or the tight-fisted one, or the peevish old maid with whom they live.
I remember the entrance in to the courtyard of a donkey all beaten, tied up to the carriage of a street vendor. I went up to him in welcome, but the irritated beast attacked me, and in its rage fell to his knees, showing me the full yellowish keyboard of his teeth. He brayed. The poor animal was so unaware of caresses as to mistake mine for harrassment.
I remember another one tied to the wagon of the Royal Mail. What good were the blinders to that poor beast out of whom no other abuse could have drawn a protest and whose legs wore down the same cobble-stones day after day? His eyes lacked all expression, it seemed as though he was totally sexless. He oozed humanity. Beneath the equine features one could easily distinguish the physiognomy of the clerk.

This is how the commerce with humans alters the divine nature of animals, like the awl the cobbler's thumb.

But, by now, if I envy anyone, it's the tree.

Freshness and innocence of the tree! It grows as it pleases. Sound, serene. The sun, the rain touch its every leaf. Forever fanned.
Trembling, shining of leaves like a language subdued and persuasive!

Rather than that of men, I hold dear the physiognomy of trees.
There are trees all disheveled and trees composed like two hands in prayer.
Trees that are delicate lace hanging free; others like paschal candles.

Sorrido.
Dalla contemplazione degli animali esco come la pianta dall'acquazzone. Rinfrescato.

Eppure avviene che vicino a una bestia non provi, contro l'aspettativa, alcuna simpatia.
Sono le bestie che hanno lo sguardo degli uomini. Per contagio passò in essi l'anima rissosa del padrone o quella tirchia o bisbetica della zitella con cui vivono.
Ricordo l'entrata in un cortile d'un somarello malconcio, attaccato al carretto di un rivendugliolo. A me accorso a festeggiarlo, la bestia irritata s'avventò, cadendo nell'ira in ginocchio e spalancandomi addosso la tastiera giallognola dei denti. Ragliava. L'animale era cosí ignaro di carezze da scambiarle per angherie.
Ricordo un altro animale attaccato ad un furgone delle Regie Poste. A che servivano i paraocchi a quella bestia cui nessun sopruso avrebbe cavato una protesta e le cui zampe consumavano quotidianamente i medesimi ciottoli? I suoi occhi mancavano di espressione, come lui, pareva, di sesso. Trasudava umanità. Sotto i tratti equini si distingueva senza fatica la fisonomia dell'impiegato.

A questo modo il commercio con gli uomini snatura la divina indole degli animali, come la lesina il pollice del ciabattino.

Ma, ormai,se qualcuno invidio, è l'albero.

Freschezza e innocenza dell'albero! Cresce a suo modo. Schietto, sereno. Il sole, l'acqua lo toccano in ogni foglia. Perennemente ventilato.
Tremolio, brillare del fogliame come un linguaggio sommesso e persuasivo!

Piú che d'uomini, ho in cuore fisonomie d'alberi.
Ci sono alberi scapigliati ed alberi raccolti come mani che pregano. Alberi che sono delicate trine sciorinate; altri, come

Patriarchal trees, as big as houses, broken by the hard work of squeezing for generations the sweetness of their fruits. There is the city tree, a shout of green, only real thing in the atrocious desert. But more than anything, I remember two trees, growing from the bed of a creek, side by side, like two slender brothers . . .

To be a tree, just a common tree.

39

Like blessings fallen from the sky, or graces not deserved, insignificant remembrances happen at times upon my soul.
Aspects, mostly detached seem suspended in mid-air of my Liguria: the one I love: where the backbone is made of stone and the earth is red and scarce and the grass sparse and strong; and all is rough and dry as if any superfluity were devoured by an interior ardor.
For example, a small apple tree met during my wanderings above Spotorno. It squeezed for me alone its green little apples that never quite ripen.
A place discovered by our father behind a country wall: brimming so with violets that I still see their dazzling light in my eyes.
The days of skipping school, days full of flowers, of birds in flight: in March the song of the cuckoo and springs in damp woods. Upon returning I always felt stunned.
Grapes looted by night in grandfather's orchard.
Still hanging on the vine, without stirring I'd let the sweetness of the grapes fill me under a sky full of stars.
A swell place full of purple shadows, sopping wet: one of those days that seduce me but that I do not love. A pregnant woman went by with her little ones and a basket; she offered me some of the green grapes that avarice squeezed from the uncultivated sites.
These remembrances surface without reason, so sweet they almost seem untrue—in my burned out life, like grass obstinately growing in the pavement of the city.

ceri pasquali. Alberi patriarcali, vasti come case, rotti dalla fatica di spremere per generazioni la dolcezza dei frutti.
C'è l'albero di città, grido del verde, unica cosa ingenua nel deserto atroce.
Ma piú di ogni altro, due alberi ricordo. che crescevano da un greto di torrente, allato, come svelti fratelli . . .

Essere un albero, un comune albero . . .

39

Benedizioni piovute dal cielo, grazie non meritate, mi cadono talvolta nell'anima dei ricordi insignificanti.
Aspetti, per lo piú staccati e come sospesi a mezz'aria della mia Liguria: quella che amo: dove l'ossatura è pietra e la terra rossa e poca e l'erba rada e forte; e tutto scabro e asciutto come se ogni superfluità fosse divorata da un ardore interno.
Ad esempio, un meletto, conosciuto nei miei vagabondaggi sopra Spotorno. Spremeva per me solo le sue meluzze verdoline mai mature.
Un luogo scoperto da nostro padre dietro un muretto di campagna: zeppo cosí di viole che ne ho ancora negli occhi il barbaglio.
Le scuole marinate, piene di fiori, di voli di uccelli: con a marzo il canto del cuculo e le primavere nei boschi umidi. Ne tornavo stordito.
L'uva saccheggiata nottetempo nell'orto del nonno. Arrampicato alla vite, chiotto, mi lasciavo inondare dalla soavità del grappolo sotto lo stellato fitto.
Un luogo sgargiante, pieno d'ombre violacee, zuppo d'acqua: di quelli che mi seducono ma non amo. Una donna gravida passò coi suoi marmocchi e un cavagno; e m'offrí di quella uvetta verde che l'avarizia spreme dai luoghi incolti.

S'affacciano questi ricordi, senza ragione, dolci cosí che non paiono veri—nella mia vita arsa, erba che si ostina nel lastricato della città.

Vico Crema

At first it existed only in my imagination, a red façade in an alley one always avoided. To the few men who ventured in along the walls with their head looking up, the most brazen hussies uttered obscene propositions from behind their shutters.

Then it took on a name—Vico Crema—and it was located just below the belfry of a Cathedral. Going by with my father I used to stare. In every woman with a dress hanging loose around the waist I discovered a mysterious priestess.

My first time was with a woman who fanned herself at the door.

My evil companion brought me there. I was left with the impression she had eyes of glass.

Sin still existed then. One walked sort of absent-mindedly; then quickly turned the corner.

In the alley an archway and an acrid stench were all you could expect. The corner tavern with heavy curtains at the windows made me wish I were a big merchant to dawdle in there and drink "trani" out of thick mugs; then inebriated come out through the back door and into the alley for an orgy. (I could see the wallet thick with notes worn by too much fingering).

This was one of the most tenacious dreams of my adolescence.

The bordello, that kept its iron gate half-closed during the day, opened at rush hour a window, like those at the cinemas, to hand back the I.D.'s; and a woman with a cigar in her mouth manned the entrance to the hallway on the street floor, where the girls waited in the crude light of an acytelene lamp.

On the walls, the color of freshly-slaughtered meat, was written: *Maison de Société*—1 Franc.

(There was also a private entrance: a steep staircase where through the grill you could see the robes flapping on the legs of the girls as they climbed briskly to their room, followed by the stumbling men).

Vico Crema

Dapprima fu, nell'immaginazione, una facciata rossa in un vicolo evitato. Ai radi uomini che accostavano il muro a viso in su, delle svergognate di sotto le persiane tenevano proposte oscene.
Poi prese un nome—Vico Crema—e si situò sotto il campanone d'un Duomo. Passando col padre, vi ficcavo gli occhi. In ogni donna sciolta in vita scoprivo una delle misteriose sacerdotesse.

La prima volta fu con una che si sventagliava sulla soglia. Mi conduceva il *cattivo compagno*. Mi restò l'impressione che avesse gli occhi di vetro.
Allora esisteva il Peccato.Si camminava distrattamente; poi si scantonava di colpo.
Accoglieva all'entrare un archivolto e l'acre odore.
L'osteria d'angolo che aveva sulla strada delle tendine fitte, mi dava voglia d'essere un grosso mercante per indugiarmi là dentro a bere il *trani* dal gotto massiccio; poi ebbro per l'altra porta uscire nel vicolo all'orgia. (Vedevo il portafoglio gonfio di biglietti segnati dal sudicio delle ditate.)
Fu questo uno dei sogni piú tenaci della mia adolescenza.

Il bordello che teneva socchiuso lungo il giorno il cancello ferrato, apriva nelle ore di ressa uno sportello donde si ritirava la tessera come nei cinema usa; e una donna alla porta, con un *toscano* in bocca, contendeva l'ingresso alla stanzetta a pianterreno, dove in una cruda luce di acetilene le ragazze aspettavano. Sulla parete color carne macellata si leggeva: *Maison de Société—1 Franc*.
(C'era anche un ingresso riservato: ripida scaletta donde, per la griglia, si vedevano le vestaglie sventolare sulle cosce delle ragazze che salivano leste alle stanze, seguíte dall'uomo incespicante.)

I always used to take the first one, strangled by desire and shame. When I left I was unable to utter even the simplest parting. My eyes saw burning flesh where there was nothing but the most wretched nudity, and mistook for gorgeous clothes, the poorest rags in garish colors.
Still, the first words they uttered, their eyes, the way they embraced were a silent blanket that suffocated the flames. Some even showed maternal concern. Poor things, innocent like candle vendors in the streets.

What does remain of that crowd? Remembrances of them are like a peeling fresco. Nearly all their faces are missing. A hairdo, the way they turned, a word one may not have known how to pronounce, is all that remains. (Of the greatest loves, who knows if much more remains).
They are the lovers of widowers, of the poor, of those who afterwards pause to clean their glasses. One I remember for a small bouquet of wildflowers left by a customs guard.
They too have their platonic lovers. One night I noticed in the alley a little boy singing up to the windows, with all his passion; the woman at the door denied him entrance on account of his age.
Like recluses they cultivate small plants in their rooms. They wish to get out just like girls in boarding schools and they bring back the programs for the cinema. On their dressers they keep dolls for which they care as if they were children to raise.

If I had mistaken my sex, I would have been one of them; with this thirst of mine for a bit of daily joy, I would have surely lost myself; over a ribbon, a tiny mirror, perhaps for even less.

Oh the creatures who open their eyes wide in the icy mirrors of a café! In place of hearts they have soap bubbles, light and just as colorful. Their love is their body which they swaddle with wrappings delicate like the skin of an egg and fragrant like the peel of a tangerine. Expert hands construct their hairdos in their varied tints. On the glass shelf above the wash basin, they have, sealed in vials, April breeze, the scent of gardens

Prendevo sempre la prima, strangolato di desiderio e di vergogna.
Il piú delle volte non mi riusciva che di spiccicare un saluto andandomene.
I miei occhi vedevano carni brucianti dove non erano che povere nudità e scambiavano dei cencetti colorati per gonne fastose.
Ma la prima parola, gli occhi, il modo che abbracciavano erano la coltre silenziosa che soffoca la fiamma. Alcune mostravano persino delle preoccupazioni materne. Le poverette erano innocenti come venditrici di candele.

Che resta ora di quella folla? Il loro ricordo è un affresco che si scrosta. A quasi tutte manca la faccia. Rimane un'acconciatura, un modo di volgersi, una parola che non seppero di dire. (Dei grandi amori chi sa se resta di piú.)
Sono le amanti dei vedovi, dei diseredati; di quello che, dopo, s'indugia a pulire le lenti. Ricordo, da una, un mazzetto di fiori campestri lasciato da una guardia di finanza.
Hanno anch'esse i loro amori bianchi. Una notte rasentai nel vicolo un ragazzetto che cantava a viso in su, appassionato: la donna alla porta gli negava l'ingresso per l'età.
Recluse, coltivano in camera il vasetto. Desiderano uscire come educande e dal cinematografo riportano il programma. Tengono sul comò delle bambole che riguardano come bambini da crescere.

Se mi fossi sbagliato di sesso, io sarei stata una di loro; con questa sete d'un po' di gioia quotidiana mi sarei perduta; per un nastro, per uno specchietto; per meno.

Oh le creature che aprono gli occhi di bistro nella ghiacciaia di specchi del caffè!
Al posto del cuore hanno una bolla di sapone lieve e variopinta. Il loro amore è il loro corpo, che fasciano d'invogli delicati come la pelle dell'uovo e fragranti come la buccia del mandarino. Mani esperte architettano i loro capelli dalle tinte piú vaghe. Sul vetro del lavabo tengono, sigillate in fiale, la

after rainfall. They are little convinced by the greed of men: sweeter than the most devoted lips is to them the puff with which they powder.

Now I admire them; then I could not have. My face would have fallen.

Vico Crema holds in my life the place that for others is the memory of their first love.
One day I saw a flyer with which an owner advertised to the crews the new address of his bordello.
Anyway when I find myself in the little city by the sea, I never fail to walk as far as that infamous alley; which I then cross in a hurry, a guilty man, the desolate soul of a widower.

In memory of Carlo Tomba*

If I think of my youth—so short-lived and artificial—I see his pale and long face in front of me in the dim false light of a tavern. Between us was always the half-liter, centerpiece of the world. Glass after glass we drank till one reached for the other's hand. The ice had been broken and we could finally touch like ghosts. Then we went out arm in arm into a world thus transfigured.
In the square the story-teller was widening circles of enchantment that one could hardly feign to cross. We looked for a tavern as if it were an Eldorado; the one most simple and out of the way always stood the chance that it might reveal to us some new aspect of the city—a city we constantly despaired of capturing in our embrace. The poorest neighborhoods were our favorite. Sizing them up lovingly with our eyes, we scouted alleys, tiny squares . . .

*Close friend of the poet and prominent photographer of Savona.

brezza d'aprile, l'olezzo del giardino dopo la pioggia. Si lasciano manomettere poco dall'ingordigia degli uomini: piú soave delle labbra piú devote è la peluria di cigno con cui si incipriano.

Le ammiro ma non avrei potuto. La mia faccia sarebbe caduta.

Vico Crema tiene nella mia vita il posto che, per altri, il ricordo del primo amore.
Un giorno mi venne sottocchio un foglietto volante con cui il tenutario comunicava alle ciurme il nuovo indirizzo del postribolo.
Tuttavia, quando capito nella piccola città di mare, non manco di allungare i passi sino all'antico vicolo infame; che percorro in fretta, uomo in fallo, con l'animo desolato del vedovo.

A Carlo Tomba

Se penso la mia gioventú—poca e artefatta—, vedo il bianco affilato viso di lui che mi sedeva in faccia nella luce falsa delle taverne. Tra noi era il mezzolitro, centro di un mondo. Bicchiere su bicchiere, si beveva finché la mano dell'uno cercava quella dell'altro. Il gelo era rotto per cui ci toccavamo come spettri. E s'usciva a braccetto per il mondo trasfigurato.
Nella piazza il cantastorie allargava cerchi di incanto che si stentava a varcare. Come d'un eldorado, andavamo in cerca d'una locanda: quasiché la piú meschina e fuori mano fosse per rivelarci un nuovo aspetto della città—che disperavamo di abbracciar tutta. I quartieri poveri erano i preferiti. Facendone degli occhi l'amoroso inventario, perlustravamo i vicoli, le piazzette . . .

Oh the lives we lived! We were for one moment the very serious girl employed at the bank; the clerk up to clean his glasses in the doorway of his basement shop; the old woman collecting a coin in the public place, a dark, mean man one is bound to run into; the little girl that skips across the street, swallowed by some doorway . . . .

Lives lasting an instant; yet they were lives more intense than ours vacuous . . .

Within the hour all things took on ambiguity. Some things existed only for us. Every street had a meaning, every attic closet aroused suspicion. Worn out faces and anxious, people gagging, foreheads dripping with sweat, put us in a state of anguish. They fixed themselves in our minds with the intensity of hallucinations, such as one experiences when, upon leaving, one tries to fix in one's mind the image of the face one does not wish to forget. And there were hours when the character of a mere mezzanine window was more than we needed.

What was my youth if not this disorganized vagabonding? Alienated from humanity I lost myself in a listless love of things. Tragicomic marionette, only protagonist in an inhuman adventure. Dark sponge that imbues all sensations.

Now, but since when? The most vulgar crossroads and alleys no longer speak to me the lacerating language of then. And there are the trees to console me, and the animals that make me smile again. From that day the inebriated and tragic puppet, you knew, is dead. Suicide, precisely as he wished, he lies facedown in some little square where no one goes. Now in lonely hours his survivor relives that ancient bit of joy, melancholic digger roaming in the ruins of his edifice.

And heading, he knows not where—like a child taken by hand against his will—he now turns his desperate face to you and to that larva of youth he once was.

Oh le vite che abbiamo vissuto! Eravamo, per momenti, la ragazza seria al banco; il contabile che viene a forbire le lenti sulla soglia del fondaco; la vecchia che ritira il soldo nel luogo pubblico; l'uomo buio che si scontra; la bambina che traversa a salti la strada e che un portico ingoia . . .
Vite d'un attimo; piú intense della nostra, vacua . . .
Nell'ora tutto si vestiva di ambiguo. Delle cose esistettero solo per noi. Ogni via aveva un significato, ogni sottoscala destava sospetto. Ci angosciavano certi aspetti consunti come visi in pena, bocche col bavaglio, fronti madide. Si fissavano allucinatamente come chi parte il viso che non vuol scordare. E c'erano ore che una finestra di mezzanino ci soverchiava con la sua personalità.
Che fu la mia gioventú se non questo disancorato vagabondare? Sradicato dall'umanità, mi disperdevo in un supino amore delle cose. Marionetta tragicomica, unico protagonista d'un'avventura disumana. Spugna tetra che s'imbeveva di sensazioni.

Adesso, da quando? i trivii e i chiassuoli non mi parlano piú il linguaggio d'una volta lacerante. E ci sono gli alberi che mi consolano e gli animali che mi fanno di nuovo sorridere. Da quel giorno il fantoccio ebbro e tragico che conosci è morto. Suicida, come a lui piaceva, giace di traverso in qualche piazzetta dove non passa nessuno.
Ma rimastica il superstite nelle ore deserte l'antico tozzo di gioia, malinconico scavatore che rovista nella macerie della sua casa.
E incamminato verso dove non sa—fanciullo tratto a mano controvoglia—a te e a quella larva di gioventú con disperata faccia si volge.

From *Shavings* 1920–1928

From *Sprologuio d'estate*

I looked for him where he was sure to be. Around the Antica Piazza dei Tornei I spotted his stocky red frame. We sat at a table of the osteria just like so many years before.

He was still the same road wanderer I had seen that winter of 1914 at Paszkowski's, printing muddy footprints everywhere. He laughed and moved about awkwardly. He made people around him uneasy as if he could at any moment extract from his pocket something covered with blood. That time he pulled from his breast pocket for me the *Canti orfici* which he carried on his person like a certificate of birth.

Later he came looking for me in Genoa; he did not shake my hand; with a reticence in his face flushed with redness . . .

My family barely tolerated him because he had lice. At night a virginal modesty seized him and he slept in his clothes . . . .

The hospitality soon became unbearable to him and by the third day there was no convincing him to stay. I watched him stubbornly depart with the stride of one out to tour the world, heading toward the tracks along the waterfront. For his only *viaticum* he had in his pocket *The Leaves of Grass*.—He disappeared with the same fateful wind that had carried him through the world.

We sat at a table of the osteria just like so many years before.

I did not ask for words: my only comfort was to be with him, I needed no more. But Dino had always been excessive.

"You used to be Sbarbaro . . . " He observed ironically. When my eyes moved toward him with supplication, he answered by laughing out loud. "And now, who are you?"

"I know . . . hush . . . " I wanted to say to him.

"So, you still dance on a tightrope! Lipstick, black pencil . . . "

Da *Trucioli* 1920–1928

Da: *Sprologuio d'estate*

Lo cercai dov'era certamente. Per l'*antica piazza dei tornei* scorsi la sua figura rossa e tozza. Sedemmo a un tavolo d'osteria come tanti anni prima.
Egli era ancora il grassatore di strada che nell'inverno del quattordici avevo visto al Paszkowski stampare orme terrose. Sghignazzava; moveva le membra disordinatamente. Un disagio nasceva intorno a lui come potesse di punto in bianco, sventatamente, cavar di tasca qualche cosa d'insanguinato.
Quella volta s'era tolto di seno per me i *Canti orfici*, che si portava addosso come un certificato di nascita.
Piú tardi, m'era venuto incontro a Genova; senza darmi la mano; con una reticenza nel volto soffuso di rossore . . .
I miei lo sopportavano appena, per via dei pidocchi. La sera, un virgineo pudore lo pigliava dei suoi indumenti . . . L'ospitalità gli fu subito di peso. Al terzo giorno non volle piú saperne. Testardo, lo guardai allontanarsi col suo passo di giramondo verso i *carrugi* di Sottoripa. Per tutto viatico aveva in tasca *Le foglie d'erba*.—Se lo riprese il malo vento che lo cacciava pel mondo.

Sedemmo a un tavolo d'osteria come tanti anni prima. Io non gli chiedevo parole: mi bastava, a conforto, stare con lui. Ma Dino era sempre stato eccessivo.
"Tu *eri* Sbarbaro . . ." m'osservò ironico. Alla supplica che i miei occhi gli mossero, sghignazzò. "E ora chi sei?"
"So . . . Taci . . . " volevo dirgli.
"Allora balli ancora sulla corda! Rossetto, lapis di nero . . . "

"I have nothing else" I wanted to say.
Dino stuck his fingers in his mouth and started to whistle, staring at me. "Waiter!" he concluded.
Waiter! and my wine was too little and failed to inebriate.
But I had not asked him for words; it would have been quite enough just to be with him . . .
To avoid the mockery of his look, I turned my eyes around Piazza Sarzano. That's when to my mouth, or was it to his?, quite spontaneously came the words:

> "All'antica Piazza dei Tornei salgono strade e
> strade e nell'aria si prevede sotto il cielo il mare . . ."

Dino shrugged his shoulders: "Saunterers! That's what we were."

> 'L'aria è appena segnata di nubi leggere.
> L'aria è rosa. Un antico crepuscolo ha tinto la
> piazza e le sue mura. E dura sotto il cielo che
> dura, estate rosea di più rosea estate . . ."

The music made his eyes appear ill. And, like water overflowing:

> "Io vidi dal ponte della nave
> i colli di Spagna
> svanire, nel verde
> dentro il crepuscolo d'oro la bruna terra celando
> come una melodia . . ."

I should have preferred to end it right there.
"Let's go" I said without reflection.
Dino's shoulders danced from the laughter.
"You are not Regolo" he laughed "and I have *arrived*."

Indeed! Insane Asylum of Castelpulci, incurable ward.*

---

*Dino Campana (1885–1932) was hospitalized in 1918.

"Non ho altro" volevo dirgli.
Dino cacciò il pollice in bocca e si mise a fischiare: guardandomi.
"Oste!" concluse.
Oste! E il mio vino era poco e non ubbriacava.
Ma io non gli avevo chiesto parole; mi sarebbe bastato, a conforto, stare con lui . . .
Per non scorgere la beffa del suo viso, mandai gli occhi per piazza Sarzano. Allora alla bocca, naturalmente, a me? a lui? vennero le sue parole:
"A l'antica piazza dei tornei salgono strade e strade e nell'aria pura si prevede sotto il cielo il mare . . ."
Dino spallucciò: "Girandole! Delle girandole, fummo".
"L'aria pura è appena segnata di nubi leggere. L'aria è rosa. Un antico crepuscolo ha tinto la piazza e le sue mura. E dura sotto il cielo che dura, estate rosea di piú rosea estate . . ."
Nella musica i suoi occhi si ammalavano. E, com'acqua che trabocca: *"Io vidi dal ponte della nave—i colli di Spagna—svanire, nel verde—dentro il crepuscolo d'oro la bruna terra celando—come una melodia . . ."*
Io non volevo sopravvivermi.
"Partiamo" dissi insensatamente.
Le spalle di Dino ballarono nell'urto del riso.
"Tu non sei Regolo" sghignazzò "e io sono *giunto*."

"Infatti! Manicomio di Castelpulci, reparto Incurabili."

Farewell to Pierangelo*

He had the habit of disappearing just like that, so as not to upset with his departure our gaiety which we dragged on from one locale to another till very early dawn. In desperation we would come out to try and find some trace of him. Returning at once strangers to one another, the rest of us would hurriedly go our separate ways reluctant to touch hands, or to look and fail to recognize the other's eyes before whom one had earlier removed the most jealously guarded mask . . . And, outside what bothered us, more than the cold of the white night and the discomfort of the hour, was the apprehension that the reality of the day about to resume implacable as ever would dissipate the nocturnal phantasm, and we would never see him again.

This time too he has disappeared just like then: through another doorway without saying goodbye. But back then we knew the hour and the place where we would have punctually met him again.

It is of him in those hours and in those places, alone with his long cigarette holder and the usual glass of soda, that even those who ignored his name hold clearly the memory; for Pierangelo was one of those figures who once seen, are no longer separated from us and besiege us with their anonimity; one of those who in a most varied crowd remain always alone and apart.

In those hours—the last of anybody else's day, the very first of his—this man who seemed so totally unapproachable could listen with equal urbanity to the intentions of a dynamiter and to the young woman who would tell him of her needle work; but one who was like him would sit next to him without needing words.

---

*Pierangelo Baratono, considered by Montale a highly *maudit* Ligurian artist, wrote impeccable Parnassian sonnets and extraordinary stories. His brother Adelchi (1875–1947) was a prominent philosopher.

Addio a Pierangelo

Egli aveva l'abitudine di dileguarsi cosí, per non turbare con la sua partenza la nostra allegria che si trascinava ancora di locale in locale ad alba già alta. Disperati uscivamo a rintracciarlo con gli occhi. Tornati di botto estranei, i superstiti si separavano; con una specie di fretta; ognuno ripugnando a toccare la mano dell'altro, a incontrare senza riconoscere degli occhi davanti a cui s'era pure tolto la maschera piú gelosa . . . E, fuori, piú del freddo della notte in bianco e dell'uggia dell'ora, ci penetrava un disagio, come la realtà del giorno che ricominciava implacabile avesse dissipato il suo fantasma notturno e non dovessimo vederlo piú.

Anche questa volta si è dileguato cosí: per l'uscita che non si sospettava, senza salutare. Ma allora sapevamo l'ora e il luogo dove l'avremmo ritrovato puntualmente.

È di lui in quelle ore e in quei luoghi, a tu per tu col lungo bocchino e il bicchiere di soda, che serbano negli occhi l'immagine pur quelli che ne ignorarono sino il nome; perché Pierangelo era di quelle figure che, vedute una volta, non si scompagnano piú da noi e ci assediano col loro anonimo; di quelle che in mezzo alla folla piú varia restano sempre sole e in disparte.

In quelle ore—le ultime dell'altrui giornata, le prime della sua—quest'uomo che pareva inaccostabile poteva con la stessa urbanità ascoltare i propositi d'un dinamitardo e la signorina che gli discorresse dei suoi lavori d'ago; ma chi era come lui gli stava seduto accanto senza rumor di parole.

The two of them, apparently strangers, despite their aversion would meet each other's glance, and their eyes would light up with the same light like resonators vibrating to the same note. What greater intimacy can friendship give than this subterrenean discovery and recognition of one's own similar blood? Because Pierangelo in those hours was neither engrossed nor unattentive; but rather one traversed by all sounds and images who yet did not appear the least touched by them, like the tree by the changing of the sky and the chirping of the birds.
Truth is that a wall separated him from humanity: the wall of a disgust that with every attempt of evasion sent him back into the prison of his own personality.
From other men he was separated by their making a great to-do over things of no value, by the obedience of machines to necessity and by bull-headed stupidity; but above all by the mask that living together imposes on us all and that alters the naïveté of our natures in the same way that the dirt in which the larva rolls makes it unrecognizeable.

To come out of his role of spectator, he recurred to wine; he figured in fact among those wretched people who pray "give us this day our daily intoxication." But those who shared with him a life of the commonest hours know what price he paid to reach it. The disgust that this drinker felt when facing the first glasses of wine would decompose my face as when I think of a full, slow glass of castor oil.
Our friendship had reched the point where it could, from a gesture of the arm like a person about to free himself, from a word out of context among the others, distinguish the precise moment in which his feet left the ground. From that moment on to keep up with him became risky. Pierangelo threw himself headlong into a metaphysical adventure of which he was by far the leading actor; disturbing marionette of a world made in his own image, where all proportions were altered, all relationships capsized; and in which some nights, to my eyes at least, he had no other companion outside of his own creation, the man in a top hat with his collar turned up, taller than the column of Vendôme where Baudelaire, exalted by hashish, was sketched.

I due allora, estranei in apparenza, avveniva che per la stessa causa, con loro contrarietà, s'incontrassero con gli occhi, negli occhi si illuminassero della stessa luce, risuonatori che vibrano alla stessa nota. Che può dare l'amicizia di piú intimo di questo sotterraneo scoprirsi e riconoscersi del medesimo sangue?
Perché Pierangelo non era in quelle ore né assorto né disattento; ma, traversato da tutti i suoni e le immagini, da essi non pareva tocco piú che l'albero dal variare del cielo e dal pettegolío degli uccelli.
La verità è che un muro lo separava dal prossimo: il muro d'un disgusto che ad ogni tentativo di evasione lo ricacciava nella prigione del suo individuo.
Dagli uomini lo divideva il loro darsi daffare per cose di niun conto, l'obbedienza di macchine alla necessità, la stupidità dalla fronte di toro; ma sopratutto la maschera che la convivenzà impone loro e che snatura l'ingenuità della loro indole al modo che la sporcizia in cui si rivolta rende irriconoscibile la larva.

Per uscire dalla parte di spettatore, egli ricorreva al vino; era anzi di quei sciagurati che pregano "dacci oggi la nostra ebrezza quotidiana." Ma chi divise con lui una vita di tutte le ore sa a che prezzo gli capitava di raggiungerla. Il disgusto che, affrontando i primi bicchieri, questo bevitore non riusciva a celare, decompone a me la faccia se penso a un colmo e lento bicchiere di ricino.
La nostra amicizia era giunta a distinguere, da certo gesto del braccio come di persona che si disimpaccia, da una parola spaesata fra le altre, il punto preciso ch'egli staccava piede da terra. Da quel momento stargli insieme diventava rischioso. Pierangelo si buttava a capofitto in un'avventura metafisica di cui egli era di gran lunga il primo attore; marionetta inquietante d'un mondo fatto a sua immagine, dove le proporzioni erano alterate e i rapporti capovolti; e dove qualche notte egli non ebbe, ai miei occhi, altro compagno che l'uomo in cilindro, a bavero alzato, alto piú della colonna di Vendôme, nel quale Baudelaire schizzò se stesso esaltato dall'hachisch.

The wine that "turns to gold the vile metal of life" was not his. Wine diminished his stature, enabled him to communicate with his kind, to take an interest in the things in which others are interested, to participate in the lives of everyone.

This was certainly a necessity of his nature, for in the last years, his stomach no longer able to withstand alcohol, we saw him guzzling mugs and mugs of beer to barely touch a dissipated happiness always just envisioned; to it he sacrificed all, even to the point of worrying that in the locale where he consumed his melancholic orgy, he would have an exit, once the door was down, with his loaf of bread.

And certainly if he has any regrets, they are directed toward that fictitious life in contrast to the only true one to which he looks now, he who used to repeat in comfort "earthly things barely exist, reality is only in one's dreams."

Of humanity Pierangelo was a contradiction endured over a whole lifetime. Living, which wears us down like usage a coin, till it erases in us our very faces, was powerless over him, more like a downpour on window panes. Of this one man it can be truly said that he lived each day as if it were his last. If he lived his life recklessly, that life hurt no one but himself and he paid for it to the very last.

Valiant knight of friendship, he searched all the time for one who resembled him. To a friend he committed himself whole, without reserve. He gave to all his brotherly embrace and from all he pulled back in the end with more bitterness in his mouth. And perhaps—though it's hard to admit it—he departed from us with a frown, from us who were always a bit alarmed at his persistent youthfulness.

If youth is the age when one is right, Pierangelo was right till the very end: till the very end his ship, among others so much younger in years, and yet already in dry dock either for repairs or to be altogether demolished, took off along a keel that the bite of the sea seemed never to have touched. As if life had barely taught him a thing, he took off while he was preparing himself for yet another celebration. "I finally have my transfer! I am leaving this village forever! I don't know how I can hold

Il vino che "muta in oro lo spregevole metallo della vita" non era il suo. A lui il vino scorciava la statura, gli dava modo di comunicare col suo simile, di interessarsi a ciò cui esso si interessa, di partecipare alla vita di tutti.
Certo fu questa una necessità della sua natura, se negli ultimi anni, rifiutandosi lo stomaco all'alcole, gli vedemmo d'inverno trangugiare gotto su gotto di birra, per toccare una felicità dileguata appena balenata; se ad essa sacrificò tutto, sino a preoccuparsi, nel locale dove consumava la malinconica orgia, che gli restasse da uscirne, a bandoni calati, con un involto di pane.
E certo è a quella vita fittizia come alla sola vera, che, se gli è dato rimpiangere, guarda ora, egli che si ripeteva a conforto "le cose terrene esistono appena, la realtà è nei sogni".

Dell'umanità Pierangelo fu la contraddizione durata una vita. La convivenza che ci consuma come l'uso la moneta sino ad abolire in noi la fisonomia, non poté su lui piú che sui vetri l'acquazzone. Di quest'uomo si può dire davvero che visse ogni suo giorno come fosse l'estremo. Se visse allo sbaraglio, quella vita non fece male che a lui e la scontò puntualmente.
Cavaliere dell'amicizia, cercò tutto il tempo uno che gli somigliasse. All'amico si consegnava intero, inerme. Con tanti scambiò l'abbraccio fraterno e da tutti si ritrasse alla fine con la bocca piú amara. E forse—sebbene dirlo pesa—pure con noi se ne andò imbronciato, che quella persistente gioventú cominciava ad allarmare.
Se la giovinezza è l'età che ha ragione, Pierangelo ebbe ragione sino all'ultimo: sino all'ultimo, fra quelle di noi, tanto piú giovani d'anni, già in bacino per avaria o addirittura in demolizione, la sua imbarcazione spiccò per la chiglia che il dente del salino non pareva avesse mai morso.
Se ne andò mentre, invano ammaestrato dalla vita, s'apparecchiava ancora una volta a chi sa quale festa. "Sono finalmente trasferito! lascio questo borgo per sempre! Non so come mi tengo da abbracciare la gente composta che passa per strada."

back from embracing even the most proper people who pass me in the streets."

I see him on that last day of his life as we saw him that time in Merano; when going toward the evening full of promises in the new city, he felt a moment of dance in the boldness of his step, and it wrung my heart, for he was forty-six.

This time his delusion was spared. In closing his account he found he was in the black with life and he died joyful like one who is innocent. We could not wish a better passing: more than crying for him, we ought to envy him.

They found him with a colored album of botany he had leafed through till very late as if to make up for the terrestrial things he was about to give up. That's how he refreshed his eyes, those eyes that as a boy, locking himself away, had sparkled on books that others read instead in the twilight of their lives. Having lived between cafés and night clubs, the first time that he was brought face to face with nature his naive Satanism collapsed. I see him in the tiny square of a village never tiring of watching, without batting a lash, two goats locking horn. The first woods we showed him he sat dumbfounded. And the last time he was in Genoa he showed us a tiny house on Boccadasse, sprayed by the sea, where he said he would not have regretted the coming of the end. His destiny did not grant him to live this other side of his existence; but along that road providence was reconciling him with humanity.

This new development made him fear for his art: if this form of piety was opening a wedge into his heart, he might not be able to conclude his work on satire: the one passion that kept him going while all else failed him.
Now instead I hear that what remains of him is in the realm of children's fables which he drew from that miraculous, intimate freshness of his. Left aside, like its author, and unappreciated, his other work is instead destined, I hope, to be in time enthusiastically discovered, like that of other solitary and irregular artists with whom Pierangelo boasted blood ties.

Lo vedo in quell'ultimo giorno della sua vita come lo vedemmo la volta di Merano; che, nel muovere verso la serata piena di promesse nella città nuova, ebbe, un attimo, nella baldanza del passo un accenno di danza che mi strinse il cuore in quell' uomo di quarantasei anni.

Questa volta la delusione gli fu risparmiata. Al chiudere dei conti egli era in credito con la vita e morí in gioia come un innocente. Trapasso migliore non sappiamo augurarci: piú che piangerlo, a noi tocca invidiarlo.

Come per un compenso delle cose di quaggiú, a tiro di mano gli trovarono un albo di botanica a colori che aveva sfogliato sin tardi. Cosí, avanti di chiudersi, si rinfrescarono gli occhi che, da ragazzo, avevano luccicato sui libri che, serrandosi a chiave, leggono gli uomini sul calar dell'età.
Vissuto tra caffé e ritrovi notturni la volta che il caso lo mise in faccia alla natura, il suo ingenuo satanismo cadde. Lo vedo su una piazzetta di borgo non saziarsi di contemplare a ciglio fermo due capre che cozzavano. Il primo bosco che gli mostrammo lo pose a sedere in un canto senza parole. E l'ultima volta che fu a Genova ci accennò con pudore a una casupola a Boccadasse, spruzzata dal mare, dove non gli sarebbe spiaciuto finire. Il suo destino non gli consentí di vivere l'altra parte di tale esistenza a rovescio; ma per questa strada la provvidenza lo stava riconciliando con l'umanità.

Egli ne temette per la sua arte: se la pietà si apriva il varco nel suo cuore, egli non avrebbe potuto condurre a termine la sua opera di satira: quella che lo tenne in piedi quando tutto l'altro gli mancò.
Ora sento dire che di lui resta, al contrario, il mondo fiabesco per bambini ch'egli attingeva appunto da quella sua miracolosa freschezza intima.
Rimasta come il suo autore in disparte e ingrata per natura, l'altra sua opera è invece destinata, io spero, ad essere nel tempo entusiasticamente scoperta, come quella di altri solitari e irregolari coi quali Pierangelo vantava legami di sangue.

The embraces of those brothers, ignored throughout time, Pierangelo would ask no more than that.

To life so sparing of kept promises, we owed our public thanks to have let us know this man. For me this is the greatest gift I have had from life after that of expression.
In closing, I ask only the felicity of letting him come alive in some of his pages such as he was, to reveal to others both the extraordinary man and the friend that he was.
For us of course, in the end—today no less than when he was merely absent from us and not only the places that his presence made dear to us—he sits next to us every time a glimmer of our former youth, which we owed to him, comes to brighten our day.
And as long as one of us will live, there will always be the possiblity that Pierangelo may apper at the turn of a street coming toward us full of that light that always came from his inner joy to shake our hands; those hands, Piero, enthusiastic and cordial whose handshake we never received without a touch of remorse stirring us, so unworthy we felt of your joy.

VIII

This year the agave along the waterfront have flowers:
a candelabra of light panicles that fill with wasps.
on the naked road, on the bald, limed mountains a severe July rages.
Greatly diminished, the town opens up like a dry jaw bone upon the sea,
which eludes its thirst with the fine mist of its bitter foam.

I can still see myself in this countryside as if in a mirror;
this aridity sustains me. I still recognize myself in the olive tree packed against the wall, and in the thorn that still manages to live in the burning sand.
But—to lose myself—once it was enough to just look: as if I too were a blade of grass, a lizard resting on a rock. Only through my eyes could I lighten my burden.

Di questi abbracci d'ignorati fratelli attraverso il tempo, Pierangelo non chiedeva di piú.

Alla vita cosí scarsa nel mantenere dovevamo pubblico ringraziamento d'averci fatto imbattere in quest'uomo. Per me è questo il dono maggiore che dalla vita ebbi dopo quello di esprimermi.
Al tempo che mi resta io chiedo ancora tanto di felicità da poterlo far rivivere in qualche pagina quale era, per mostrare agli altri l'uomo straordinario e l'amico ch'egli fu.
Agli altri. Per noi, a buon conto—oggi non meno di quando era solo assente né soltanto nei luoghi che il suo passaggio ci rese cari—egli ci siede naturalmente vicino, ogni volta che un barlume dell'antica gioventú, che a lui dobbiamo, illumina la nostra giornata.
E finché uno di noi vivrà, ci sarà sempre per Pierangelo la possibilità di apparirgli a uno svolto di strada e di venirgli incontro, illuminato da quella sua gioia tutta interiore, a dargli le mani; quelle mani, Piero, entusiaste e cordiali la cui stretta non ricevemmo mai senza che ci nascesse dentro una punta di rimorso, tanto indegni ci sentivamo della tua gioia.

VIII

Quest'anno le agavi del litorale han messo il fiore: un'alberella di pannocchie bionde, alloggio alle vespe.
Sulla vertebra nuda della strada, sui monti calvi e calcinati luglio si accanisce. Scarnito all'osso, il paese s'apre secca fauce sul mare; che ne elude la sete spruzzandolo di schiume amare.

Mi specchio ancora in questo paesaggio; questa aridità mi sostenta. Nell'ulivo incassato nel muro mi riconosco, nello sterpo che vive nella rena ardente.
Ma—per dissolvermi—guardare una volta bastava: filo d'erba anch'io, lucertola su sasso. Per gli occhi mi alleggerivo di me.

At all hours now this other self of mine continues to exist. As if grown beyond expectation it interposes itself cumbersome and stubborn.

If one could only placate him, make him rest in peace till the reawakening, if it should ever come! Like nothing more than a mere slough, stubbornly living out a disproportionate life!

At some dawns the sense of being is so filiform that just moving one's head would be all that is needed, it seems, to fall clean into the void.

Instead, oh the tenacity of life! How many times before we die do we come practically to death as to the only logical conclusion!

My life is now like that of the shingle. Oh the drop that falls in the ferocious aridity! That's how my soul invokes a breath of poetry.

Vagabond cloud, rare drop and warm like blood. You restore the uproar to the banks of the river turning green; seen from a distance even the new shoots, appear already a worm-eaten cabinet.

River bed in time of drought.

All that of me which still moves among the flaming white of the olive trees is but a sinister marionette.

A tutte l'ore addesso il mio individuo persiste. Come troppo cresciuto s'inframmette, ingombrante e caparbio.

Placarlo si potesse, comporlo in pace sino al nuovo risveglio, se giunga! Nient'altro che spoglia, che sproporzionata vita vive ancora!

Certe albe il senso di essere è cosí filiforme, che distogliere il capo basterebbe, pare, per calare senza strappo nel nulla.

Invece, tenacia dell'esistenza! Quante volte innanzi di morire veniamo logicamente a morte!

La mia, è ora la vita del greto. Oh una goccia che cada nella feroce secchezza! Cosı l'anima invoca un soffio di poesia.

Nuvola vagabonda, goccia rada e calda come sangue. Che ristrepiti la piena tra le rive inverdite, remoto pare quanto che butti e fogli uno stipo tarlato.

Alveo in tempo di magra.

Di me tra le fiamme bianche degli olivi non si muove che la marionetta sinistra.

From *Shavings* 1930–1940

Lichens

1. An herbarium of lichens clutters my whole room, fills it with the smell of underbrush. In forms of chips of wood and shreds of rocks, the collection contains, even within each specimen, nothing short of the whole world.
Because to make a collection of plants is to make a collection of places. Nothing better than a plant holds traces of the place where it was born; intrinsic to it, like the one that portrays nature and feels its every characteristic, a plant represents that place in the most concrete way. With the voice of the creek or the breathing of the sea, with city or mountain air, a plant evokes even the season and the hour of when it was picked. Even dried it still holds signs of where the sun touched it.

2. As a boy, questioned in front of the whole class about *orobanche*, I had to peek, raising myself on the tips of my toes, in the book open before the teacher to see if I should start to speak of roots or claws. That's why perhaps, as soon as the study of botany ceased to be an obligation, I started an herbarium. It was in those years that I made the wonderful encounter with the *Carlina Vulgaris*, that radial wheel of silver that opens up flush with the soil; that tassle of silk that is the *Eriophorum*; the *Anagallis Tenella* which "with hands made of leaves anchors itself to clay, and rings loudly in its humble pink colors".
Encounters/epiphanies. I received the image of every plant the way the stratum—that holds it forever—receives the imprint of a leaf or a shard. In the loving inventory of the smallest corner of the world, the one most congenial to me, I was fulfilling, without knowing it, my "listless love of things".

Trucioli 1930–1940

Licheni

1. Mi ingombra la stanza, la impregna di sottobosco un erbario di licheni. Sotto specie di schegge di legno, di scaglie di pietra contiene pocomeno un Campionario del Mondo.
Perché far raccolta di piante è farla di luoghi. Nulla come la pianta che da sé vi è nata ritiene d'un sito; intrinseca ad esso, come quella che ne ritrae la natura e si risente d'ogni sua circostanza, lo ripropone nel modo piú concreto. Con la voce del torrente o il respiro del mare, con l'aria di città o di altura, evoca in chi la colse l'ora e la stagione. Disseccata, serba ancora notizia di come il sole la toccava.

2. Ragazzo, interrogato alla cattedra sull'*Orobanche*, m'alzai in punta di piedi per vedere dal libro che il maestro teneva aperto davanti, se dovevo rifarmi a parlare da radici o da zampe. Per ciò forse, appena lo studio della botanica cessò d'essere un obbligo, iniziai un erbario. È di quegli anni l'incontro esclamativo con la raggiera d'argento, che s'apre raso terra, della *Carlina*; col fiocco di seta dell'*Erioforo*; con l'*Anagallis tenella* "per manine di foglie aggrappata all'argilla, scampanellante d'un'umile rosa".
Incontri-apparizione. Di ogni pianta in me ricevevo l'aspetto come lo strato—che la serba per sempre—l'impronta d'una foglia, d'un'elitra. Nell'amoroso inventario d'una minima parte del mondo, quella a me congeniale, appagavo senza saperlo il "supino amore delle cose".

Later, encouraged by my predilection for the most unpretentious forms of existence, I turned to the most neglected and discarded forms of life. The musci which I picked on patrol on Mount Asolone, Mount Lémerle and Mount Assa are now in Falköping, Sweden and in Berkeley, California.
In the end I arrived at the lichens: a port to which I was already assigned by a verse in my first little book:

La dorata parmelia il muro incrosta

(The golden Parmelia on walls and bark of trees is the most obvious and brightest of lichens.)
Now in my memory—where of the whole history of the world, two or three precise facts barely survive.—of lichens I recall instead with their physiognomy, infinite names and surnames; something that does not happen with anything else. With trees, for example, it is already enough if I can distinguish by the name the magnolia from the pine. The fact is that trees live a life so much fuller and more harmonious than ours, that to give them a name is equivalent to limiting them; whereas with the inconspicuous and neglected lichens, when you see them and greet them by name, you help them, it seems to me, to exist.

3. The lichen thrives from the region just below the clouds to the rocks sprayed by the sea. They climb up to summits where no other plant life takes root. It is not discouraged by the desert; glaciers will not scare it away; neither will the tropics nor the arctic pole. It challenges the darkness of the darkest caves, and it ventures into the craters of volcanoes.
It fears only the nearness of man.
Because of this misanthropy, the city is the only barrier capable of stopping it. If it should cross over, either it seeks refuge atop the tallest bell towers, or it sacrifices its own personal characteristics along with its well-being.
City lichens are sterile, dismal, asphyxiated. Human breath pollutes them. In Rome to find a lichen still recognizeable for itself, one must climb atop the dome of Saint Peter.

Piú tardi, preso a mano dalla mia predilezione per le esistenze in sordina, mi volsi a forme piú scartate di vita. A Falköping in Svezia, a Berkeley in California si conservano muschi che colsi di pattuglia sull'Asolone, sul Lémerle, sull'Assa.
Finché approdai ai licheni: porto che già m'assegnava un verso del mio primo libretto: "la dorata parmelia il muro incrosta". (La "dorata parmelia" è, su muri e cortecce il piú ovvio e festoso dei licheni.)
Ora nella memoria—dove di tutta la Storia Mondiale, situati nel tempo, sí e no due o tre fatti galleggiano—di licheni ho, con la fisonomia, infiniti nomi e cognomi. Ció che non m'accade per altro. Di alberi, ad esempio, è molto se, per nome, distinguo la magnolia dal pino.
Gli è che l'albero vive d'una vita tanto piú piena e armoniosa della nostra, che dargli un nome è limitarlo; mentre gli incospicui e negletti licheni, a salutarli a vista per nome, pare di aiutarli ad esistere.

3. Il lichene prospera dalla regione delle nubi agli scogli spruzzati dal mare. Scala le verte dove nessun altro vegetale attecchisce. Non lo scoraggia il deserto; non lo sfratta il ghiacciaio; non i tropici o il circolo polare. Sfida il buio della caverna e s'arrischia nel cratere del vulcano.
Teme solo la vicinanza dell'uomo.
Per questa sua misantropia, la città è la sola barriera che lo arresta. Se la varca, o va a respirare in cima ai campanili o, con la salute, ci rimette i connotati.
Il lichene urbano è sterile, tetro, asfittico. Il fiato umano lo inquina. A Roma, per trovare un lichene riconoscibile, bisogna salire sulla cupola di San Pietro.

4. It can set up house anywhere; but, in choosing its domicile, every species has its preferences. Most lichens live in wood or rock. But of the former there are those that choose the olive tree, others cherry, others pine. Others with more difficult tastes, won't settle anywhere except in their very special tree: the jujube, the elder.

On the same tree, there are those that live in leaves, those which live in the bark, and others in the wood; and of these latter some live in live wood, some only in dry wood, and some only in rotting wood. There are some that will dwell only on charred wood. Neither is there a shortage of fence lichens, beam post lichens, telephone pole lichens; lichens on culm stalks; on hedges, on musci . . .

The same for stone-dwelling lichens. Some choose limestone, and others flee from it to the extent of not being able to tolerate even the least amount in the composition of the rock. Some choose sandstone and pudding-stone; some gypsum, and some trachyte and basalt.

You see, the lichen attaches itself to the hardest rock; with acids of its own it breaks down the rock, it punctures it in order to protect its own seeds from the winds. You can find in the Alps huge slabs drilled right through like sieves by the passage of a *Verrucaria*.

Others live on the naked earth. I save in tiny boxes, protected in cotton, some lichens so delicate that the least bump could dissolve them into dust: I gathered them off the crags of Volterra, and the clay of Asciano. Others live in sand. In that case, in the impossibility of affixing themselves to one single element of foundation that is not constantly shifting, these lichens rolled about and, at times raised by the wind, reached by the sun on every side, learn to be self-sufficient. They roll up and gather into balls. Among lichens they are the déracinés, those that lack a fixed abode; like the *Parmelia Vagans* of the Kirghiz steppe, and the *Aspicial Mangereccia* of the deserts (the one in which some irreverent scientist recognized the manna from heaven sent down to feed the people elect). The ones among these lichens that are totally inept by constitution to lead a nomadic life settle themselves as best they can on whatever the sand offers that is more stationary. In the dunes of Dunkerque I collected some on bones, on china, on leather.

4. Mette casa dovunque; ma, nella scelta del domicilio, ogni specie ha le sue preferenze. I piú dei licheni abitano il legno o il sasso. Ma, tra i primi, chi elegge l'ulivo, chi il cipresso, chi il pino. Alcuni, di gusto piú difficile, s'insedian solo su un albero loro proprio: sul giuggiolo, sul sambuco.

Dello stesso albero, poi, chi abita le foglie, chi la corteccia, chi il legno; e, tra gli ultimi, chi il legno quando è vivo, chi quando è secco, chi quando è marcescente. Ve ne sono che si accasano solo sul legno carbonizzato. Né mancano i licheni delle staccionate, dei travi, dei pali telegrafici; dei culmi; delle siepi, dei muschi . . .

Lo stesso, per i licheni sassicoli. Quale sceglie a domicilio il calcare e quale lo fugge al punto da non tollerarne la presenza nella composizione della pietra. Quale, l'arenaria e la puddinga; quale il gesso e quale i trachiti ed il basalto.

Perché il lichene attacca le pietre piú dure; con acidi di sua privativa, le disgrega, le buca per mettere i suoi semi a riparo dei venti. Si incontrano sulle Alpi lastroni, dal passaggio d'una *Verrucaria* bucherellati come crivelli.

Altri, vivono sulla nuda terra. Ne serbo in scatolette, messi in scampo nella bambagia, di così delicati che il menomo urto li risolverebbe in polvere: raccolti sulle balze a Volterra, sulle "crete" ad Asciano.

Altri campano sulla sabbia. Allora, nella impossibilità di fissarsi su un elemento che manca loro continuamente di sotto, voltolati e talora sollevati dal vento, raggiunti in ogni parte dal sole, imparano a bastare a se stessi. Si arrotolano, si appallottolano. Sono i *déracinés* dei licheni, i licheni senza fissa dimora; come la *Parmelia Vagante* delle steppe chirghise, come l'*Aspicilia Mangereccia* dei deserti (nella quale una scienza irreverente ravvisa la Manna mandata dal Cielo a sfamare il popolo eletto). Quelli di essi, inetti per costituzione a far vita da nomadi, si sistemano alla meglio su ciò che nella sabbia offre presa. Sulle dune di Dunkerque ne raccolsi alloggiati sull'osso, sulla porcellana, sul cuoio.

And there are vitreous lichens. Rumor had it that at one time a stain threatened the destruction of the stained glass of the cathedral of Reims. A perforating kind of lichen had chosen that sumptuous place for its abode. No less demanding, another one has rented the tomb of Cecilia Metella along the Appian Way. And there lives in Chile a lichen, the shape of a lump of sulphur, that holds out for its defence the hook part of the awn in the pricks of opuntia on which alone it installs itself: it is the *Chrysothrix* also known as the Golden Curl, for which it was baptized "touch me not".
Finally—to give an indication of its own and all its colleagues' repugnance of man—there is a bookish *Anthracothecium*; it is a *Gylecta* and—it hurts me to say it—it is a coprophiliac.
Other lichens, what ever their habitat, need water as their accomplice; or the wind. And of the former some chose stillicide, some lake water and some running water; while others will deal only with sea water.

5. As for dimensions: there are lichens as big as plaques that a man could not embrace; threadlike ones that unraveled could measure a kilometer; others like trees reaching one's hip.
And there are miniscule ones: the *Virgule* lichen, the *Period*, the *Asterisk*. And there are some so tiny that only a magnifying glass will reveal them.

6. The lichen is the most varied of all plant life. Koerber was wong when he thought he could group them all under the categories of crusty, leafy and arborescent. How many meanings would each one of these adjectives have to entail in order to embrace, as well as it can, the polymorphism of the lichens! Many lichens resemble roof-tiles; many others recall the design of pavements: triangular, pentagonal, polygonal blocks. Others are shaped like tiny milky ways, stellar systems. Others, like some hanging from branches, form all sorts of beards, manes, and Absalom style hairdos.
One whole tribe, the *Grafidee*, covers its supporting host with a tapestry of indecipherable writing: in both upper and lower case characters, both raised and indented: linear, forked,

E vi sono licheni vitricoli. Corse anzi a suo tempo i giornali l'allarme per una macchia che minacciava di distruzione i vetri istoriati della cattedrale di Reims. S'era scelto quell'alloggio sontuoso un lichene dell stirpe dei perforatori.
Non meno esigente, un altro ha tolto a pigione sull'Appia la tomba di Cecilia Metella. E vive nel Cile un grumo di zolfo che protende a difesa la lancia in resta della spina di opunzia sulla quale unicamente si insedia: è la *Chrysothrix* o Ricciolo d'oro, battezzata per questo "non mi toccare".
Infine—a scontare per tutti i colleghi la ripugnanza per l'uomo—c'è un *Anthracothecium* libricolo; e una *Gyalecta*—duolmi dirlo—coprofila.
Altri licheni, qualunque sia l'*habitat*, esigono l'acqua per complice; o il vento. E, dei primi, chi acqua di stillicidio, chi acqua di lago, chi acqua corrente; e chi se la fa solo con l'acqua di mare.

5. Per dimensioni: ci sono licheni come placche—che un uomo non abbraccia; come refe—che, dipanati, raggiungerebbero il chilometro; come alberi—che arrivano all'anca.
E ne abbondano di minuscoli: c'è il lichene Virgola, il lichene Puntofermo, il lichene Asterisco. E ne esistono di cosí esigui che solo la lente li rivela.

6. Il lichene è il piú multiforme dei vegetali. Koerber si illuse di irreggimentarli tutti sotto le denominazioni di crostosi, fogliosi e arborescenti. Ognuno di questi aggettivi quanti significati deve accogliere per abbracciare alla meglio il polimorfismo dei licheni!
Molti formano tetti d'embrici; molti, pavimenti: a tasselli triangolari, pentagonali, poligonali. Altri Vie lattee, sistemi stellari. Altri, penduli dai rami, barbe, criniere equine, capigliature assalonniche.
Un'intera tribú, le Grafidee, tappezza il sostegno di scritture indecifrabili: a caratteri minuscoli o maiuscoli, immersi o in rilievo: lineari, forcuti, cinesi, cuneiformi.

Chinese and cuneiform characters. Others, the *Caliciee*, barely visible to the naked eye, reveal under magnification apocalyptic landscapes as if fulminated by lightning; landscapes in which upright hooded cobras sit on their tails smoking like tripods from the funnels that cover them.

All sorts of manufactured things simulate the lichens: encaustic painting, inlays, perforations, mosaics; byssy and felts; coblets, claves, needles, buckles, helmets, shields, nails; matches; ribbons, nets, flabella; inlaid leather; velvets and laces on a cushion. Lichens seem to be made on whole or in part, of the most disparate substances: of starch and of flour; of wool and of purple dye; of gold, sulphur, sealing wax; of sponge, cork, anthracite; of sheepskin, of Gutta-percha.

There is the beehive lichen; the labyrinth, the madrepore; lichens like oyster banks, and others like coral banks. Fern-like lichens and polyp-like ones, complete with suckers. In shapes of spheres, trapezoid, like berries, like a brigand's gun.

The *Encephalographa Cerebrina*, the name alone will tell you, seems like a small brain.

7. The lichen is the most polychromatic of plants. Its range goes from milk-white to Stygian black, it draws from the greatest intensity through an orchestration of tones and shades as to give way to the richest repertory of colors.

Not to shoot off astonishing, if gratuitous, pyrotechnics, I'll limit myself to the chastest, the most honest of all colors: the color which is the absence of colors.

Its principal stages are median grey, brown, dark brown and pitch black; the first stage is in turn divided into pearl-grey, steel-grey, lead-grey, ash-grey, etc.; and so on for all other stages; to specify the gradation of brilliance, hue and saturation in each lichen, the nomenclature turns to the comparative and superlative forms; to the dimunitives likes *fusculus, furvellus, nigritus*; to intensifiers like *tenebricosus*; to participles like *nigricans, fuscenscens* to indicate the tendency toward a color not yet reached; it turns to adjectives like *nigratus, obscuratus* to designate a tint that does not appear proper to the lichen but seems superimposed . . .

Altri, le Caliciee, visibili a stento ad occhio nudo, si rivelano sotto la lente paesaggi fulminati, apocalittici; dove cobra eretti sulla coda fumano come tripodi dall'imbuto che han per capo.
Simula il lichene ogni sorta di manufatti: encausti, intarsi, trafori, mosaici; bissi e feltri; coppe, clave, aghi, fibbie, caschi, scudi, chiodi; fiammiferi; nastri, reti, flabelli; cuoi impressi; velluti e pizzi al tombolo.
Pare fatto, in tutto o in parte, delle sostanze piú disparate: d'amido e di farina; di lana e di porpora; d'oro, zolfo, ceralacca; di spugna, sughero, antracite; di pergamena, di guttaperca.
C'è il lichene arnia; il lichene laberinto, madrepora; il lichene banco d'ostriche, banco di coralli. Licheni felciformi, polipiformi, con tanto di ventose. A sfera, a trapezio, a frutto di mora, a trombone da briganti.
L'*Encephalographa cerebrina*, lo dice il nome, pare un piccolo cervello.

7. Il lichene è il piú policromo dei vegetali.
La sua gamma che va dal bianco latte al buio stigio, attinge tutti gli acuti, attraverso una orchestrazione di toni e di sfumature da dar fondo al piú ricco repertorio coloristico.
Per non accendere girandole sbalorditive quanto gratuite, mi attengo al piú casto, al piú probo dei colori: il colore che è assenza di colori.
Distinte le sue tappe principali in grigio, bruno, fosco ed atro; il primo a sua volta in grigio perla, grigio acciaio, grigio piombo, grigio cenere eccetera; e cosí via per gli altri; a precisare di ciascuno la gradazione, la nomenclatura dei licheni ricorre ai loro comparativi e superlativi; a diminutivi come fusculus, furvellus, nigritulus; ad intensivi come tenebricosus; a participi come nigricans, fuscescens per indicare la tendenza ad un colore non raggiunto; ad aggettivi come nigratus, obscuratus per designare una tinta che non par propria al lichene ma gli sembra sovrapposta . . .

Unhappy with its own imprecision, whenever it can it does like the fashion industry when it speaks of citrus-green, of coral-red: it draws upon the name of the tint adding to it a precise reference. Thus, always in the realm of the black shades, it distinguishes yet an African-black (*maurus*), a mourning-black (*pallatus*), a tower-black (*turridus*), a burned-black (*deustus*), a coal-black (*anthracinus*), soot-black (*fuligineus*), a midnight-black (*tenebricus*), and an infernal-black (*stygius*) . . .

Such gloom of tints mortifies, after all, more than one family: the *Collemacee*. In most lichens, along with the most haunted colors (vermillion, cochineal, oozing blood, blood clot) figure also the most delicate tinges: caesius, amethyst, orange, apricot, crocus; the least definable: *badious, gilvus, galbulus, carfinius* . . neither is there a shortage of two-colored, tri-colored lichens; variagated lichens, spotted lichens like a panther's skin, patchwork ones like a harlequin costume, freely mixed ones like a painter's palette; brilliant lichens, rutilant ones, and even versicolored ones . . . . others, shabby-looking at first sight, reveal their margin, the apothecium or hypotallus to be most colorful; others grey on the outside, inside are white as snow, golden, cochineal. Others it takes no more than a touch of humidity in the air to light them up. Finally even among the funereal *Moerri* of the *Collemacee,* there are those that reach their peak only in the presence of an agent; like the *Thyrea jodopulchra*: that is to say beautiful thanks to the iodine.

8. The lichen is an enigma. Once we have said that it belongs to the kingdom of plants, we have said about all we can be certain of knowing. Even the use of the word "entity" to indicate it is imprudent, if there are those who consider the lichen mothing more than a phenomenon.

Empirically lichens are all the stains we see on rocks and trunks of trees, stains that become more frequent the further we get from the ever-present toll-gates of civilization. This assumption can be confirmed if, scratching that stain, the incision turns green. But from there to total certainty the journey is long. How many of these forms of life were first

Scontenta della sua imprecisione, ogni volta che può fa come la Moda quando parla di verde cedro, di rosso corallo: implica nel nome della tinta o gli accoppia un preciso riferimento. E cosí, sempre nel limbo dei neri, distingue ancora un nero Africano (maurus), un nero Pipistrello (Vespertilio), un nero Corvo (coracinus), un nero Fumo (infumatus), un nero Lutto (pullatus), un nero Torrefatto (torridus), un nero Bruciato (deustus), un nero Antracite (anthracinus), un nero Fuliggine (fuligineus), un nero Tenebra (tenebricus), un nero Inferno (stygius) . . .

Questa tetraggine di tinte mortifica, del resto, poco piú d'una famiglia: le Collemacee. Nella maggior parte dei licheni, accanto a colori ossessi (cinabro, cocciniglia, sangue che spiccia, sangue aggrumato) figurano le mezzetinte piú delicate: il cesio, l'ametista, l'arancio, l'albicocca, il croco; le meno definibili: il badio, il gilvo, il galbulo, il carfinio . . .

Né mancano licheni bicolori, tricolori; licheni variegati, pelle di pantera, veste d'Arlecchino, tavolozza di pittore; licheni fulgenti, rutilanti e persino versicolori . . .

Altri, dimessi a prima vista, han poi il margine o l'apotecio o l'ipotallo colorato; oppure, grigi di fuori, dentro son nivei, aurei, coccinei. Altri, basta ad accenderli un po' d'umido nell'aria.

Infine, anche tra i funebri moerri delle Collemacee, ve ne sono che acquistan spicco toccati da un reagente; come la *Thyrea jodopulchra*: bella, cioè, mercé lo jodio.

8. Il lichene è un enimma. Quando di lui si è detto che appartiene al regno vegetale, si è detto tuttociò che di certo sul suo conto si sa. Persino la parola "entità", adoperata per indicarlo è imprudente, se c'è chi considera il lichene null'altro che un fenomeno.

Empiricamente, sono licheni tutte le macchie che si notano su pietre e tronchi e che si fanno piú frequenti piú ci si allontana dalla cinta daziaria. La presunzione ha una prima conferma se, scalfita la macchia, l'incisione verdeggia. Ma di lì alla certezza è lungo il cammino. Quante di queste forme di vita vennero dapprima accolte fra i licheni, respinte poi nel gregge delle

accepted among the lichens, then discarded into the flock of algae and of fungi, then readmitted among lichens; each time according to the judgement of the observer!

9. An herbarium is a specimen of the world. A great resource in the hours of boredom, I open a package at random. In every one there is the world. When I like a place too much to be appeased by merely seeing it with my eyes, I am aided by an almost scientific fantasy to fool my impossible wish of a greater communion with it: an aerostat instead of wings makes up for the weight of my body; to make myself weightless through it, as, they say, we will be in the atmosphere of the moon. Following my yearning and caprice, I fly over that place; I gently brush with my hand the olive tree as if it were the back of a sheep; I dive into a green, I descend into waters that enchant; resurface at once in that rocky bank; and become curious of that whiteness that trembles on that precipice; I go and I come back, I am here and I am there: I pick that place as I would pick a grape, vying with the butterfly that savours her fields of flowers. With the herbarium the dream comes true; and not just for one place; but the entire world! I open a package at random: I am in San Cristobal, in the Galapagos; I am in India: the Palivi hills; at 4000 ft. above Mount Ndaza (China); among herds of reindeer, on the shores of Ladoga; in Quitalito, in the Andes of Chile; overlooking the Brenva, in Portud; in Batavia in the Botanical Gardens; in an ancient granary in Antwerp; in the Dawson Island on the Tierra del Fuego; in Arcangelo; in Rockland, Maine; in Zacualpan, Mexico:
"Collected by P. A. Purpus on the Yucca Elephantipes . . . . "
And every plant I see and touch, every tiniest frustule documents a point of the globe; it is of it a part. It was born there, at its own pace it grew there. It is to that place totally intrinsic; of it it is a firm token.
In visiting an herbarium what inroads through the world! What leaps in space!
I was just now among the footprints of the Gods on Olympus in Greece, and here I am now on top of Mount Amiata: You are there too, it is an overcast autumn day, among large chestnut trees . . .

alghe e dei funghi, riammesse fra i licheni; a volta a volta, a seconda dell'osservatore!

9. L'erbario è un campionario del mondo. Risorsa delle ore di tedio, a caso apro un pacco. In ogni pacco c'è il mondo.

Quando un luogo mi piace troppo perché vagheggiarlo con gli occhi mi appaghi, a illudere l'impossibile voglia d'una maggiore comunione con esso, mi soccorre una fantasia quasi scientifica: un aerostato in cambio di ali, che compensi il peso del corpo; farmi lieve per esso, come si dice saremmo nell'atmosfera della luna. Dietro la voglia e il capriccio, sorvolare quel luogo; della mano sfiorare l'oliveto quasi dorso di gregge; tuffarmi in un verde, calarmi dove un'acqua canta; aggallare d'un balzo a quel greppo; incuriosirmi del bianco che trema su quel precipizio; andare e tornare, esser qui ed esser là: piluccare quel luogo come un grappolo d'uva, a gara con la farfalla che deliba il suo prato di fiori.

Con l'erbario il sogno si avvera; e non per un luogo; pel mondo!

A caso apro un pacco: sono a San Cristobal, nelle Galapagos; sono in India: colline Palivi; a quattromila piedi sul monte Ndaza (Cina); tra branchi di renne, in riva al Ladoga; a Quitalito, Cordigliera delle Ande, nel Cile; in vista della Brenva, a Portud; a Batavia, nell'Orto Botanico; in un antico granaio ad Anversa; nell'isola Dawson in Terra do Fuego; ad Arcangelo; a Rokland, nel Maine; a Zacualpan, nel Messico: "Raccolse P. A. Purpus sulla Yucca elephantipes . . ."

E ogni pianta che vedo, che tocco, ogni minimo frustolo documenta un punto del globo; di esso è qualcosa. Vi nacque, a suo agio vi crebbe. È intrinseca a quello; ne è pegno.

A visitare un erbario, che scorribanda pel mondo! che sbalzi attraverso lo spazio!

Ero adesso tra orme di Iddii sull'Olimpo di Grecia ed eccomi in vetta all'Amiata: ci sei tu, è un giorno d'autunno coperto, fra grandi castagni . . .

From: *Will-o'-the-wisp*

*

That palm tree, moved by the breeze in the early morning sun, crackles with sparks. At dusk in mid-air all along the way, blink tiny green bits of tin, the gregarious fireflies come to give some appearance of urbanity.

*

If what you read pleases you, it is a sure sign you are empty; if it eludes you instead, there may be hope yet.

*

The power of the aphorism is in its peremptoriness, such as the power of the cut-throat is in his face—force—abuse.

*

I too have read some detective stories, and at the front Fantomas was a great help to me. But as soon as the mystery begins to unfold, I close the book; after dinner why stick my nose in the kitchen?

*

If the blindness, from which we benefit through the process of familiarization since birth, should suddenly fall like a blindfold, our looks, which we find worthy of attributing to God, would please us a lot less.

*

If one tries to embrace all things, he only thinks he is doing so, for in fact he embraces nothing. Life exists in black and white; without the black, there is no white either.

da: *Fuochi Fatui**

*

La palma laggiù, mossa dalla brezza, è, al primo sole, un crepitar di faville. All'imbrunire ammiccano a mezz'aria per l'abitato minuzzoli di stagnola verdolina, lucciole che si inurbano.

*

Se quel che leggi di tuo ti appaga, segno che sei vuoto; spera se ti delude.

*

La forza dell'aforisma è nella sua perentorietà, come quella dello sgherro nel ceffo. Forza—sopruso.

*

Ho letto anch'io dei romanzi gialli e in trincea Fantomas mi fu di grande soccorso. Ma appena il mistero accenna a chiarirsi, chiudo il libro: a fine pranzo non vado a mettere il naso in cucina.

*

Se la cecità di cui beneficiamo per assuefazione dalla nascita cadesse come una benda, ci lusingherebbe forse meno il nostro aspetto che troviamo così bello da attribuirlo anche a Dio.

*

Chi abbraccia tutti, crede ma non abbraccia nessuno. La vita è in bianco e in nero; senza il nero, neppure il bianco.

---

*Still unknown as to its origin in Medieval Latin, *ignis fatuus* (pl. *ignes fatui*) is a phosphorescent light that hovers or flits over swampy grounds at night, possibly caused by spontaneous combustion of gases emitted by rotting organic matter. Also called "friar's lantern," "will-o'-the-whisp." By extension, something that misleads or deludes; a deception.

As an indication of how much age changes us, consider how transitory our sensations and opinions are: not many years ago, the scent of rue offended me like that of cimex of the fields; today I rub its leaves over my fingers.

*

It happens at times that what I write runs away with me, acquires, despite myself, the movement of a song. The word lodges itself in the scheme of a verse; impossible to dislodge it, to break the gratuitous rhythm. It's my alarm bell: nothing else to do but get up and go out.

*

If your duty by chance coincides with your pleasure, what other happiness can you want on this earth?

*

When he met me Rafaello Franchi said that he expected me to be more bitter. Bitter? At the very root, perhaps: the root which, all contorted, allows the tree to rise in the air like a bouquet of flowers.

*

Prodigality, resource of the poor: the only way they know not to feel poor.

*

When I look at what I have just written, I am always disappointed to have not said precisely what it mattered to me to say. What if I have nothing to say? Or perhaps I already said what mattered when arriving out of breath at the end of the race? Or even with my very first cry?

*

Even of my own language I have only an approximative knowledge. So many words I avoid, uncertain as to their meanings; and if I don't look them up in dictionaries, it isn't only because I distrust dictionaries, but because a word not assimilated as flesh and blood over many years would always seem borrowed.

Una spia di quanto l'età ci muta, della provvisorietà delle nostre sensazioni (e opinioni): non è molti anni, l'odore della ruta mi offendeva come quello della cimice dei campi; oggi ne stropiccio le foglie tra le dita.

*

Capita che quello che scrivo mi prenda la mano, acquisti mio malgrado un'andatura cantante. La parola s'insedia da sé nello schema d'un verso; impossibile sloggiarla, spezzare quel ritmo gratuito. È il campanello d'allarme: non c'è che alzarsi e uscire.

*

Se il tuo dovere è in una il tuo piacere, quale altra felicità cerchi su questa terra?

*

Raffaello Franchi quando mi conobbe ebbe a dire che mi prevedeva più amaro. Amaro? nella radice, se mai: la radice contorta che permette all'albero di essere all'aria un mazzo di fiori.

*

Prodigalità, risorsa del povero: il modo che ha di non sentirsi povero.

*

Quando m'accade di metter gli occhi su quello che ho scritto, la delusione ognivolta di non aver detto ciò che unicamente m'importava. Che cosa, se da dire non ho nulla? O forse ciò che importava l'ho detto arrivando con l'affanno in gola della corsa? o già tutto col primo vagito?

*

Anche della mia lingua ho una conoscenza approssimativa. Tante parole le evito, malsicuro del loro significato; e se non le cerco nei dizionari, non è solo che dei dizionari diffido, ma che una parola non assimilata in tanti anni, non divenuta carne e sangue, mi saprebbe sempre di accatto.

*

If thanking the sun is already a form of prayer, then I too pray like a very short-sighted person: without asking.

*

I read that in my youth I lost my way as in a labyrinth and in vain for years looked for a way out. Quite so. An adventure, and not one of the happiest, of which I was obviously not even aware.

*

I feel no affinity with those who when on a train, instead of keeping their eyes on the countryside, no matter how many times they may have seen it before, keep themselves glued to a book, even though it be the *Divine Comedy*.

*

How many letters written and never mailed! Held back not by convenience or generosity, but simply because having exhausted one's resentment, and regained control of oneself, to mail them appears superfluous.

*

The critic who dismissed my first collection of *Trucioli* with the image of the "old lady who continues to mumble some prayers in an empty church, without realizing that the service is over (just like Fragmentism is over)" later published, they tell me, an excellent vocabulary. This rather balances things off.

*

He who praises you adulates himself.

*

Mathematics: a world man invented to be able at least there to breathe certainty: his very own *terra firma*, no matter how illusory.

*

Se ringraziare il sole è già pregare, anch'io prego—da miope; senza chiedere.

*

Leggo che in gioventù mi smarrii in un labirinto e invano per anni cercai un'uscita. Documentato. Un'avventura e non delle più liete di cui a suo tempo non m'accorsi, si vede.

*

Non avverto nessuna parentela con chi in treno, invece d'aver l'occhio al paesaggio, non importa se visto le mille volte, lo tiene su un libro, sia pure la Commedia.

*

Quante lettere scritte e non spedite; trattenute non per convenienza o per generosità; ma perché, una volta smaltito il risentimento e ricuperato il possesso di sé, spedirle si scopre superfluo.

*

Il critico che liquidò il mio primo *Trucioli* con una immagine: "la vecchietta che a chiesa vuota seguita a borbottar preghiere, senza accorgersi che la funzione (il *frammentismo*) è finita" pubblicò in seguito, mi dicono, un eccellente vocabolario. Fatti di assestamento.

*

Chi ti loda si incensa.

*

Matematica: un mondo che l'uomo s'è fabbricato per respirare almeno lì certezza: la sua terraferma, non importa se anch'essa illusoria.

To procrastinate, no matter how little, is a game of chance.

*

Only that for which one does not pay costs.

*

He too, the cypress, gives in to the frivolity of putting out flowers; but who sees them. Like some incumbrance, he hides them in his ascetic compact aspect. Unchanged in the changing of the seasons, unharmed by the weather, he rises unshakably erect, above the insignificant growth that frolics all around him; from the height of his stature I rebuke his rejoicing; and when the coming of winter brings the inevitable clean sweep, he, that Lent preacher, only survivor of the desolate earth, decries with impassive demeanor the caducity, the vanity of all things. Ah, the hypocrite, he does appear at a distance, yes, to be fused in bronze; but seen up close, scrutinized inside . . . rats, wasps, scorpions, cobwebs, debris . . . what does he not hide in that thoroughly buttoned-up priest's cassock of his, that moralist with a dirty conscience.

*

1940–1945

June '40. On display in the window, pig snouts, empty eye-sockets, tracheas, rubber hands: man of the future, free of his fingerprints. By night the light appears to coagulate into purple icicles; all around phantasms denounced by trembling reflections; here and there the face of one who drowned. And in the squares couples take advantage of the circumstances. Trolleys march slowly like funerals

October. Out to supper when the alarm sounded. I did not reach the shelter (a portico protected as best it could against sharpnel) before the lights went out. Here we go again; this time they are not fooling. In the dark women's voices break into familiar litanies. With every explosion loose rubble rains from above into our collars. A man, in shock, attempts some puns; someone else lights one cigarette after another, oblivi-

Rimandare, di poco che sia, è giocare d'azzardo.

*

Solo ciò che non si paga costa.

*

Cede anche lui, il cipresso, alla frivolezza di metter fiori, ma chi li vede? Come una sconvenienza, li dissimula nell'asciutto aspetto di asceta. Immutato nel mutar delle stagioni, illeso dal tempo, s'erge, incrollabilmente ritto, sulla minutaglia che folleggia intorno; dall'alto della statura le rimprovero il breve tripudio; e quando il sopravvenir dell'inverno avvera il previsto repulisti, superstite sulla terra desolata, predica con l'impassibile contegno la caducità la vanità di tutto—il quaresimalista. Ah ipocrita! Par sì, a distanza, fuso in bronzo; ma accostato, scrutato dentro . . . ratti, vespe, scorpioni, ragnatele, detriti . . . Che cosa non nasconde nell'abbottonatissimo abito di prete, il moralista dalla coscienza sporca.

*

1940–1945

giugno '40. Esibiti in vetrina musi di porco, vuote occhiaie, trachee, mani di gomma: l'uomo dell'avvenire, depurato di impronte digitali. Alla notte la luce si rapprende in ghiaccioli violetti; in giro, fantasmi denunciati da vacillanti riflessi; facce qua e là di annegati. Anche in piazza le coppie approfittano. I tram, mortori al passo.

ottobre. A cena fuori quando fischia l'allarme. Non raggiungo il ricovero (un portico armato al più contro le schegge) che la luce vien meno. Si entra in ballo; questa volta fanno sul serio. Nel buio voci femminili intonano litanie. A ogni scrollo piove dall'alto terriccio nel collo. Uno, zittito, tenta freddure; un altro accende sigaretta da sigaretta, sordo alle proteste che si le-

ous to the protests of others. Squashed up against me a woman is shaking terribly from fear; to give her courage I grab her tightly by one arm: "Who's grabbing me?" she screams: sex is always the last to die.

Coming out at the end of the alarm, our street, all streets are covered with rubble and broken glass. Toward Piazza Deferrari the flames are very tall; beyond there the sky is lit up by the fire raging at the port as if it were daytime. In the fear, later to prove unfounded, that some law enforcement officer would prevent me from walking to my house, I take a short cut through Via Foscolo; the romantic street where couples like to walk, now in total disarray: street lights upturned, pipes dug up and bent in the open, deep craters. In front of a mountain of rubble and plaster an old woman howls in despair. In Via Serra the flames reach the eaves, the hissing indicates the gas leaks that feed the flames. I walk uphill along the facades still standing in Via Assarotti, not knowing that they hide the void inside; only through some window can you see the skies. Holding my breath in anxiety and fear I run onto Via Montaldo . . .

The next day the atmosphere in the city is like a fair. Downtown is jammed: everyone is out, noses looking up. Genoa, that superb city, reduced to rubble in two hours with the same ease one knocks down a toy city of cardboard. Never before so many cars, and in so many styles; especially from the country, people have come *en masse* to enjoy the spectacle. In everyone a strange excitement: the cheerfulness of escapees.

May '44. In advance of allied landings, the German command throws us out of Spotorno. I find in the mountains just above here, in Barsana, a house in ruin, abandoned for years by the owners, who emigrated to America. The plant of Arthemesia in bloom in the walkway is all it takes to make me decide to settle down right there.

August. They come to tell us that in the night they bombed our house in Spotorno. Coming down to it in that torrid noon I hear for the first time pine cones pelting down.

vano. Pigiata contro me, una donna trema tutta; per farle animo l'afferro forte per un braccio: "Chi mi tocca?" strilla: il sesso è l'ultimo a morire.
Uscendo cessato l'allarme, la strada le strade lastricate di cocci di vetri. Verso piazza Deferrari, stendardi altissimi di fiamma; di là, il cielo illuminato a giorno dall'incendio del porto. Nel timore, superfluo, d'un servizio d'ordine che mi tagli la strada di casa, scorcio per via Foscolo; la romantica via delle coppie, sconvolta: lampioni divelti, condutture contorte allo scoperto, crateri. Davanti a un mucchio di calcinacci, una vecchia ulula. In via Serra, il fuoco morde dei cornicioni con sibilo di fiamma ossidrica. Rasento in salita le facciate rimaste in piedi di via Asarotti, ignorando che mascherano il vuoto; solo, per qualche finestra, il cielo. Col fiato sospeso m'affaccio a via Montaldo . . .
L'indomani, in città aria di fiera. Il centro, congestionato: tutti fuori a naso in su: la Superba ridotta in due ore come fosse di cartapesta. Mai viste tante macchine in giro e di tante fogge; specie dalla campagna la gente si è riversata in massa a godere lo spettacolo. In tutti una strana eccitazione: l'allegria degli scampati.

maggio '44. In previsione di sbarchi alleati, il comando tedesco ci caccia da Spotorno. Trovo nei monti qui sopra, a Borsàna, una casa in rovina, abbandonata da anni dai proprietari emigrati in America. Mi decide a fissarla la pianta di santolina che è in fiore sul ponticello d'accesso.

agosto. Ci vengono a dire che stanotte han bombardato la nostra abitazione a Spotorno. Scendendovi nel torrido mezzodì odo per la prima volta le pigne al sole scrosciare.

September. My sister arrives on leave, unexpected. I run around in what countryside is left to stuff myself with tiny black figs; perhaps hurt by my opinion of them, all seeds, they burn my throat; and so I pick the peach I have been eyeing for a long time. That's all the tree has, dying as it is of thirst.

October. In the dark of the room where Benedetta, lying on the couch that serves her as a bed, tries to sleep, I nurse the little wine that remains, when all of a sudden in that great silence of the countryside, two or three, hesitating but very clear tolls of bells break away from the tower just below Portio. Hard to imagine there is a service at this hour (it is midnight); could it be the partisans sending a warning? I wouldn't think so. Prone to excitement and incapable of keeping the great news to myself, I get closer to Benedetta and whisper:—You know, perhaps the war is over? They rang the bells!—Realizing that it was the euphoria of the wine making me indulge in the foolish hope, Benedetta pulls me closer to her like a baby:—Have another little glass—she tells me.

March '45. Horror in Spotorno (he had gone down to Voze with his mother to have his first pair of long pants fitted; happy in his new suit, he was showing off with his friends; stopped by the bravoes of San Marco he committed the rashness of running off. Now he is a rag in the street on that spot they point out to me, but where I will not be able to go and look). The sun is ablaze.

April. While in the hills the partisans continue to shoot an occasional round, the bulk of a German division in an orderly retreat marches on the Aurelia highway. Once, at the village. a soldier breaks away and crosses the town's main street, machine gun in hand, his eyes peeled to the windows in bold defiance.

6 May. Today at 2:41 Germany has capitulated. All afternoon pealing of bells. Parade, red flags up ahead, men greeting with closed fists. In the square young men, the look of executioners

settembre. Inaspettata, arriva in ferie mia sorella. Corro per queste fasce a fare incetta di ficuzzi neri; risentiti come sono, tutti seme, bruciano in gola; e spicco per l'occasione la pesca che tenevo d'occhio da tempo. Non ne ha che una, l'albero morto di sete, ma tutta la sua bontà l'ha concentrata in quell' una.

ottobre. Nel buio della stanza dove Benedetta, sul sofà che le serve da letto, sta prendendo sonno, io cerco di far durare il vinello che resta, quando si staccano dal campanile qui sotto di Portio, esitanti ma nitidi nel gran silenzio della campagna, due tre rintocchi. A una funzione a quest'ora (è quasi mezzanotte) non è da pensare; che possa essere un avvertimento ai partigiani, non mi viene in mente. Facile a accendermi e incapace di tenere per me la grande notizia:—Sai che forse è finita la guerra?—mi accosto a sussurrarle—Hanno suonato le campane!—Comprendendo che è stata l'euforia del vino a farmi accogliere la folle speranza, Benedetta mi attira a sé come un bambino:—Beviti un altro gottino—mi dice.

marzo '45. Orrore a Spotorno (era sceso da Voze con la madre per misurare i primi pantaloni lunghi; felice nel vestito nuovo, da uomo, si pavoneggiava coi compagni; fermati dai bravi della San Marco, lui ebbe la sventatezza di scappare. Ora è uno straccio per terra in un punto che mi indicano ma dove non *potrò* andare.) Sole sfolgorante.

aprile. Mentre dalle colline i partigiani sparacchiano, il grosso d'un reparto tedesco in ritirata sfila ordinato sull'Aurelia. Giunto all'abitato, un soldato se ne stacca e percorre la strada interna del paese, il mitra alla mano, la faccia alzata a sfida alle finestre.

6 maggio. Oggi alle ore 2,41 la Germania ha capitolato. Tutto il pomeriggio gran scampanare. Corteo preceduto da bandiera rossa, uomini che salutano col pugno chiuso. In piazza, gio-

about them, shave the heads of girls who have flirted with the Germans; one of them laughs impudently as if to say: sex is international.

*

The sea lily is in bloom on the beach; I go down to pick some; from the street someone yells that there are mines all along there. I knew it, but . . .

*

I return to Voze after so many years. It was at this very curve, I'd swear to it, that our father hid with us children in the brush, waiting to scare Uncle Pierino, who was left behind. To our great amusement our uncle, a man, but one who believed in brigands, took off at the scare and never even turned around to look.

*

I see again after many years the countryside around Siena. In this silence marked only by voices that spur the oxen along, it looks all cut up without margins in pieces of red soil and fields of cultivation; it seems more like a model farm exhibited under glass than a real farm. Nothing disturbs this harmony. To add some lightness to this model there are the olive trees that trimmed look more like ornaments, silver frills or filigree.

*

Many are upset by nature; most people don't even see it. I, instead, pour myself into it. It is the only constancy, the only fidelity I know in the uncertainty of all things.

*

So many things between us, known only to us: a bunch of field flowers so large we were unable to hold it in our arms: how many flowers we must have dropped along the way! So many things that even together we would not be able to remember them all; but that forgotten one, when it strikes again it's bound to fill me with light.

vinotti con piglio di giustizieri tosano le ragazze che hanno amoreggiato coi tedeschi; una che ride sfacciata par dire: *il sesso è internazionale.*

*

È fiorito sulla spiaggia il giglio del mare; scendo a coglierne; dalla strada un passante mi grida che lì tutto è minato. Lo sapevo, ma . . .

*

Torno dopo tanti anni a Voze. Fu a questa svolta, giurerei, che nostro padre si appostò con noi bambini nella macchia, in attesa che lo zio Pietrino, rimasto indietro, passasse. Con nostro grande divertimento, perché senza neppure volgersi allo schiamazzo, lo zio—un uomo! ai nostri occhi—credendo a briganti se la dette a gambe.

*

Rivedo dopo anni la campagna senese. In questo silenzio sottolineato da voci che incitano i bovi, ritagliata senza margini in appezzati di terra rossa e in coltivi, sembra più che vera una campagna-modello esposta sotto vetro. Nulla ne disturba l'armonia. La fan leggera gli olivi che, potati a questo modo, paiono a fior d'aria dei fregi, delle corbelie di filigrana d'argento.

*

Molti la natura li disturba; i più non la vedono. In lei io mi verso. È la sola costanza, la sola fedeltà che conosco nell'incertezza di tutto.

*

Tante cose tra noi, note a noi: un fascio di fiori di campo che non si arriva a abbracciare: quanti ne andran persi per via! Tante cose che in due non riusciremmo a ricordarle tutte, ma una dimenticata si affacci e mi riempie di luce.

*

Of my mother, out of focus in my memory, all in all a mere apparition. It must have been Easter because, brought to her, the first thing I spotted in the penumbra of the room was the little basket of sweets and colored eggs. I grabbed hold of it and that is when, at the end of a hand and with a voice that cuddled me, I raised my eyes and saw, bent over me, a lady in a long robe. She, then, was my mother; with her I could talk, tell her everything. Like a puppy I hung from her neck, and, fidgeting, I wimpered over some wrong suffered at the hands of Benedetta. My mother knew she was about to leave me and it was to the care of Benedetta that she was leaving me.
An apparition that would be a remorse forever if human attachments depended on nothing but senses. What ties us to another human being is habit; what rends us in our memory is an habitual gesture, a weakness uncovered, perhaps an imperfection. When habit fails to fuel that attachment, even the love of a mother is not really love.
Her portrait is that of a stranger; my affection toward her the mere affection one owes someone, and that is nothing; the regret of such realization the mere attempt to deceive oneself. And even her name . . . an eternity in comparison to our possessions! It's still around the house, it lasts like a reprimand, the cup in which she drank her *caffelatte* in the morning. More than in my heart, her name remains on that cup: written in gold among flowers and flourishes: Angelina.

*

When I am tempted to confirm with words something I was thinking, it's a sure sign that I am trying to give it some consistency: I'd like it to be so but? it is not.

*

A higher tone, a gesture to give emphasis to one's expression, that's all it takes to corrupt even the noblest sentiment. Avoid it with shame the way you do pretentiousness.

*

Di mia madre, sfocata nella memoria in tutto un'apparizione. Dovera essere una pasqua perché, introdotto da lei, la prima cosa che scorsi nella penombra in cui era la camera, fu il canestrino di pasta dolce con l'uovo colorato. Impossessatomene, a una mano e a una voce che mi vezzeggiavano alzai gli occhi e, china su di me, vidi una signora in lunga vestaglia. Era questa dunque la mamma; a lei dunque potevo dire. Bestiola, m'appesi a quel collo, smaniando piagnucolai d'un torto patito da Benedetta. Mia madre sapeva di andarsene e era a Benedetta che mi lasciava.

Un'apparizione che sarebbe un rimorso per sempre se gli attaccamenti umani nascessero da altro che i sensi. Che ci lega a una creatura, è la consuetudine; che strazia al suo ricordo, un gesto abituale, una scoperta debolezza, magari un'imperfezione fisica. Mancando l'alimento dei sensi, non è neppure l'amore per la madre.

Il suo ritratto è quello d'una sconosciuta; l'affetto per lei, il nulla d'un affetto dovuto; il rimpianto che sia così, un tentativo d'ingannare me stesso. E anche il suo nome . . . Eternità a nostro confronto degli oggetti! È ancora in casa, vi dura come un rimprovero, la tazza in cui predeva il caffelatte del mattino. Più che nel mio cuore, il suo nome resta su quel coccio: scritto in oro tra fiori e svolazzi: Angiolina.

*

Quando una cosa che penso mi viene di confermarla con la voce, è che tento di darle consistenza: vorrei che la cosa fosse e non è.

*

Basta abbisogni per esprimersi d'un tono più alto, d'un gesto, perché il sentimento più schietto si inquini di enfasi. Da vergognarsene come di una simulazione.

The verb used by the ancient Greeks to indicate "to make love" meant literally *to be young together*. What a clean way of seeing things: love made similar to the romping of frolicking puppies.

*

Life is like a remnant of cloth that the young see rightside, and the old from the reverse.

*

He who gives in to the sin of gluttony will often, to be held in esteem, raise the stern face of Cato.

*

Being on the edge of sleep is like being on a precipice; you don't know what will happen to you in the world of larvae into which you are descending. Implacability of the brain that churns even blankly; not even in sleep does it rest. You come out of these adventures shaken or injured; some adventures can contaminate the soul. And if of these you should retain memory when awake, you can look forward to remorse as well: inevitable, though, just as in the case of a guilt for which one is hardly responsible.

*

Of the two of us it seems curious that I should always appear the younger and richer. There must be some trifle of truth in this if the illusion is not blunted by the evidence.

*

Who would have ever guessed on the day that Uncle Nino taught us to blow bubbles that one of the two children was to continue to make soap bubbles his whole life.

*

In the December '32 volume of *Solaria*, in a piece entitled "Les quatres" by André Castagnou, I read: " . . . Il reste qu'à mes yeux la lyrique italienne offre seule après la grecque ces quelques bois sacrés, bosquets d'oliviers consumés de lumière." Of the four *Images*, I'll transcribe that of Montale and that of mine:

Per dire far l'amore i greci dicevano *esser giovani insieme*. Che modo di sentire pulito: l'amore come ruzzare di cuccioli.

*

La vita è una stoffa che i giovani vedono dal diritto, i vecchi dal rovescio.

*

Sul vizio cui cede della gola alza, a tenere in rispetto, un viso di catone.

*

Sull'orlo del sonno sei su un precipizio; non sai che ti accadrà nel mondo di larve in cui scivoli. Implacabilità del cervello che macina a vuoto, neppure nel sonno dà tregua. Uscirai da avventure turbato o contuso; ma da altre, sporcato nell'anima. E se di queste serberai da desto memoria, anche il rimorso ti aspetta: di una colpa che non hai.

*

Tra i due mi par sempre, curioso, d'esser io il più giovane e il più ricco. Avrà pure radice in un briciolo di vero, l'illusione, se a intaccarla non basta l'evidenza.

*

Chi avesse detto a zio Nino il giorno che ci insegnò il gioco che uno dei due bambini avrebbe seguitato tutta la vita a far bolle di sapone.

*

Nel numero di "Solaria" del dicembre '32, sotto il titolo *Les quatres*, a firma di André Castagnou: ". . . Il reste qu'à mes yeux la lyrique italienne offre seule après la grecque ces quelques bois sacrés, bosquets d'oliviers consumés de lumière". Delle quattro, trascrivo l'*image* di Montale e la mia:

"Des os de seiche les pouples des profondeurs et ce soleil d'apocalypse. Les cailloux du rivage hérissent un mur qui tourne, tourne, tourne. On en regrette les culs de bouteille des après-midi de Seine-et-Oise. Arabie Petrée, pourtant tu as bien tes charmes."

"Le matin brille aux cordages, aux vitres des amants, aux coqs de l'Eglise; aux palazzi de Byron, à l'ourlet des précipices, le matin brille. Une charette les bras au ciel, le coq chante. Moréas dort sur une voiture de maraîcher, le bidon du lait éveille Apollinaire. Sbarbaro mord une feuille d'hysope."

*

In my work as translator the only reward that can never fail is the delight I find in it; delight, perhaps because in translating I exhaust my last possibilities, as a writer of my own work: modest possibilities, to be sure, if the turn of phrase, a cadence, the choice of an adjective are all it takes to appease them.

*

They call seriousness *modesty, pride*. . . . Anything not to make it recognizable. It would disturb them.

*

What in the body humiliates, love redeems.

*

Suckers was perhaps the title that corresponded best to the content of this book made up of fragments which had been discarded at one time, and of third page articles I had not kept and for a long time considered irretrievable on account of my laziness: fragments and articles which, although favored by circumstances, see the light again on their own merit. Thus, something which recalls the return or survival of plants. Unfortunately, to one who has a delicate ear and no familiarity with the plant kingdom, *sucker* sounds unpleasant because of its affinity in sound to words that have in Italian a pejorative

"Des os de seiche, les poulpes des profondeurs et ce soleil d'Apocalypse. Les cailloux du rivage hérissent un mur qui tourne, tourne, tourne. On en regrette les culs de bouteille des après-midi de Seine-et-Oise. Arabie Petrée, pourtant tu as bien tes charmes."

"Le matin brille aux cordages, aux vitres des amants, aux coqs de l'Eglise; aux palazzi de Byron, à l'ourlet des précipices, le matin brille. Une charette les bras au ciel, le coq chante. Moréas dort sur un voiture de maraîcher, le bidon du lait éveille Apollinaire. Sbarbaro mord un feuille d'hysope."

*

Al lavoro di tradurre il compenso che non può mancare è il diletto che vi trovo; diletto, forse perché traducendo esaudisco le possibilità che mi restano di scrittore in proprio: modeste, se le appaga il giro dato a un periodo, una cadenza, la scelta d'un aggettivo.

*

Chiamano la serietà *modestia, superbia* . . . Comunque, pur di non riconoscerla. Li disturberebbe.

*

Quel che nel corpo umilia, l'amore lo redime.

*

Ributti era forse il titolo che rispondeva meglio al contenuto di questo libro, costituito di frammenti a suo tempo scartati e di articoli di terza pagina non conservati e da lunga data, per pigrizia, considerati irrecuperabili: frammenti e articoli che, sebbene favoriti da circostanze, per virtù propria si può dire rivedono la luce. Qualcosa quindi che richiama il ributto o rimessiticcio della pianta. Disgraziatamente, a chi ha orecchio delicato e nessuna dimestichezza invece col mondo vegetale, "ributto" suona ingrato per affinità di suono con parole di significato spregiativo. Fatto è che, a udirlo, l'amico poeta: No,

meaning. Fact is, my friend the poet, hearing that word, said: No, no, no! vibrating three fists in the air and taking precipitous distance as if to separate from mine his responsibility for that unhappy choice. Willy nilly, therefore, as I had done for the first book, for this one too, which could be my last, I renounce my title; and fall back on *Remnants*, synonym, in a way of *Shavings* (minus that good smell of lumber). Willy nilly, especially since not even *sucker* says exactly what I intended to say: the plant which, cut down or in any way broken off, manages just the same to give a flower, even if only off on the side, and no matter how modest. (Introduction to *Remnants*, 1959).

*

Today another lichen discovered: the world is not yet altogether finished.

*

The community, says Socrates, should maintain the nightingale with pinenuts. True; but would the nightingales keep on singing? And to force them to sing, would the community resort to blinding them?

*

Other things are aims, art is an end.

*

Don't create art, let it make itself.

*

Nov. 4. To remind children not to run, they always tell them of when they fell; but with nations, they never remind them of their defeats.

*

Only man labors to eat (and some animals forced by man to do the same); but since it is ours, we call this condemnation *Privilege, Nobility*.

no, no! insorse, vibrando tre pugni all'aria e distanziandomi precipitoso quasi a dividere dalla mia la sua responsabilità per la scelta infelice. Di buon grado perciò, come già per il mio primo libretto, per questo che potrebbe essere l'ultimo, rinuncio al mio titolo; e ripiego su "scampoli", sinonimo in certo modo di "trucioli" (con in meno il buon odore di falegnameria). Di buon grado, tanto più che neanche "ributto" dice esattamente ciò che intendevo: la pianta che falciata o comunque stroncata riesce lo stesso a dare il suo fiore, s'anche di lato e meschino. (Premessa a *Scampoli*, '59).

*

Anche oggi un lichene nuovo: il mondo non è finito di fare.

*

I suoi usignoli, dice Socrate, la comunità dovrebbe mantenerli a pinòli. Vero; ma canterebbero ancora? e per farli cantare, la comunità non li accecherebbe?

*

Le altre sono vie, l'arte è una meta.

*

Non fare arte, lasciala farsi.

*

IV novembre. Ai bambini perché non corrano ricordano le cadute; ai popoli, mai le sconfitte.

*

Solo l'uomo lavora per mangiare (e qualche animale, costretto dall'uomo); ma perché è nostra, chiamiamo la condanna *privilegio, nobiltà*.

*

In a cage a tiger chaces its tail; in the absence of company it doubles itself.

*

Poetry, another lonely vice.

*

La tigre in gabbia rincorre la propria coda; in mancanza di compagnia, si sdoppia.

*

Poesia, altro vizio solitario.

Appendix

Eugenio Montale, *Gli ossi di seppia,*
Poesie per Camillo Sbarbaro

Caffè a Rapallo

I

Christmas in the silvery
tepidarium, disguised by the steam
of smoking cups, veiled
tremor of lights beyond the closed
crystals, profiles of women
in grey, amidst flashes of gems
and swishing of silks . . .
They have come
to these your native shores,
the new sirens! and here you are
dearly missed, Camillo, historian
of cupidity and horrors.

There is great clamor in the street.

The indescribable music
of play trumpets
and children's cymbals
made of tin has just gone past:
The music of innocence is gone.

A world of gnomes went with it,
the dinning of play mules and wheel barrows,
between the groaning of rams

made of paper-mache and the shining
of swords covered with tin cans.

The generals went by with their cocked hats
made of cardboard,
brandishing their spears made of nougat;
then came the enlisted men
with candles and lamps,
and boxes jingling
with a sound more vapid,
bright stream that enchants
the dubitant soul:
(enraptured I would listen).

The whole army went by with the din
of a galloping herd
stirred by the recent thunder.
They were absorbed by the pasture
that for us is no longer greening.

Epigramma

II

Sbarbaro, mercurial child, folds multicolored papers
and turns them into ships and thrusts them to the slow
moving slush of a brook; watch them take off.
Be watchful over him, you there, who pass by:
with your cane gather the delicate flotilla,
don't let it get lost; gently guide it to a cove made of rocks.

Scripta humanistica

Published Volumes

1. Everett W. Hesse, *The "Comedia" and Points of View*. $24.50.
2. Marta Ana Diz, *Patronio y Lucanor: la lectura inteligente "en el tiempo que es turbio."* Prólogo de John Esten Keller. $26.00.
3. James F. Jones, Jr., *The Story of a Fair Greek of Yesteryear*. A Translation from the French of Antoine-François Prévost's *L'Histoire d'une Grecque moderne*. With Introduction and Selected Bibliography. $30.00.
4. Colette H. Winn, *Jean de Sponde: Les sonnets de la mort ou La poétique de l'accoutumance*. Préface par Frédéric Deloffre. $22.50.
5. Jack Weiner, *En busca de la justicia social: estudio sobre el teatro español del Siglo de oro*. $24.50.
6. Paul A. Gaeng, *Collapse and Reorganization of the Latin Nominal Flection as Reflected in Epigraphic Sources*. Written with the assistance of Jeffrey T. Chamberlin. $24.00.
7. Edna Aizenberg, *The Aleph Weaver: Biblical, Kabbalistic, and Judaic Elements in Borges*. $25.00.
8. Michael G. Paulson and Tamara Alvarez-Detrell, *Cervantes, Hardy, and "La fuerza de la sangre."* $25.50.
9. Rouben C. Cholakian, *Deflection / Reflection in the Lyric Poetry of Charles d'Orléans*. $25.00.

10. Kent Ljungquist, *The Grand and the Fair: Poe's Landscape Aesthetics and Pictorial Techniques*. $27.50.
11. D. W. McPheeters, *Estudios humanísticos sobre la "Celestina."* $24.50.
12. Vittorio Felaco, *The Poetry and Selected Prose of Camillo Sbarbaro*. Edited and Translated by Vittorio Felaco. With a Preface by Franco Fido. $28.50.
13. María del C. Candau de Cevallos, *Historia de la lengua española*. $33.00.
14. *Renaissance and Golden Age Studies in Honor of D. W. McPheeters*. Ed. Bruno M. Damiani. $25.00.

Forthcoming

* Carlo Di Maio, *Antifeminism in Selected Works of Enrique Jardiel Poncela*. $20.50.
* Philip J. Spartano, *Giacomo Zanella: Poet, Essayist, and Critic of the "Risorgimento."* Preface by Roberto Severino. $24.00.
* Juan de Mena, *Coplas de los siete pecados mortales: Second and Third Continuations*. Ed. Gladys Rivera. $25.50.
* Barbara Mujica, *Spanish Pastoral Characters*. $25.00.
* Susana Hernández Araico, *La ironía en tragedias de Calderón*. $25.00.
* *Estudios literarios en honor de Gustavo Correa*. Eds. Manuel Durán, Charles Faulhaber, Richard Kinkade, T. A. Perry. $25.00.
* Francisco Delicado, *Portrait of Lozana: The Exuberant Andalusian Woman*. Translation, introduction and notes by Bruno M. Damiani. $33.00.
* Salvatore Calomino, *From Verse to Prose: The Barlaam and Josaphat Legend in Fifteenth-Century Germany*. $28.00.
* Darlene Lorenz-González, *A Phonemic Description of the Andalusian Dialect Spoken in Almogía, Málaga, Spain*. $25.00.
* Maricel Presilla, *The Politics of Death in the "Cantigas de*

Santa María." Preface by John E. Keller. Introduction by Norman F. Cantor. $27.50.

* Gloria Gálvez Lira, María Luisa Bombal, *Realidad y fantasía*. $25.00.

www.ingramcontent.com/pod-product-compliance
Lightning Source LLC
Chambersburg PA
CBHW020942310726
48980CB00001B/21

9780916379193